The Economics of
the Construction Industry

CONSTRUCTION TECHNOLOGY AND MANAGEMENT

A series published in association with the Chartered Institute of Building.

This series will, when complete, cover every important aspect of construction. It will be of particular relevance to the needs of students taking the CIOB Member Examinations, Parts 1 and 2, but will also be suitable for degree courses, other professional examinations, and practitioners in building, architecture, surveying and related fields.

Project Evaluation and Development
Alexander Rougvie

Practical Building Law
Margaret Wilkie and Richard Howells

Building Technology (3 volumes)
Ian Chandler
   Vol. 1 Site Organisation and Method
   Vol. 2 Performance
   Vol. 3 Design, Production and Maintenance

Management of Building Organisations
Richard Fellows, David Langford and Robert Newcombe

The Economics of the Construction Industry
Geoffrey Briscoe

The Economics of
the Construction Industry

Geoffrey Briscoe

Mitchell · *London*

in association with the Chartered Institute of Building

To Faye and Guy

© Geoffrey Briscoe 1988
First published 1988

Typeset by Deltatype, Ellesmere Port, South Wirral
and printed in Great Britain by Biddles Ltd, Guildford and Kings Lynn

Published by The Mitchell Publishing Company Limited
4 Fitzhardinge Street, London W1H 0AH
A subsidiary of B. T. Batsford Limited

A CIP catalogue record for this book is available from the
British Library

ISBN 0 7134 5038 X

Contents

List of Figures

Preface

This textbook aims in the first instance to meet the needs of students taking Economics and Building Economics and Finance examinations in the CIOB Member Examinations, Parts 1 and 2. in addition, it is likely to prove valuable to students on HTC building courses, where the TEC unit Economics of the Industry is studied. The text will be valuable to all who study economics for professional body examinations associated with the construction industry. These might include those of the Royal Institute of Chartered Surveyors (RICS), the Society of Architectural and Associated Technicians (SAAT), and the Incorporated Association of Architects and Surveyors (IAAS).

In addition to students studying specifically for professional body examinations, the text is also aimed at students taking economics as part of either a University or CNAA degree course in building studies, quantity surveying and estate management. This book should prove useful to all who seek an introductory analysis to the economics of the UK construction industry. While several texts have been written on specific areas of construction activity, most notably housing, few have been written for the sector as a whole. This textbook seeks to fill this gap.

Acknowledgements

The author is grateful to Her Majesty's Stationery Office for general permission to reproduce selected statistics from various HMSO publications, especially *Housing and Construction Statistics*.

Thanks are also extended to Marilyn Riley and Joan Burr who helped in the production of the final draft and to Gerry Horne who refined the diagrams. The text benefited from discussion with colleagues in the Civil Engineering and Building Department at Coventry Polytechnic.

Part One

Basic Economic Analysis

1 The Construction Sector in the UK Economic System

1. Construction and the economy

In any economy construction is a key activity. It influences the final flow of goods and services produced in the economy—the gross national product—and in turn is influenced by the size of that gross national product. It is therefore valuable to analyse the contribution which construction makes to the total output of the UK economy.

Measured in terms of gross output, where the value of materials used in the construction process is also included, construction in 1974 accounted for 18.3% of all census of production industrial output. By 1984 this proportion had fallen to only 12.6%. When allowance is made for materials and supplies purchased from other industries, the construction sector's share in net output was about 7% during the early 1970s. By the mid-1980s this proportion had reduced to 6%. It is clear from these statistics, therefore, that the construction sector in the United Kingdom remains a very important industry, despite a decline in its fortunes in recent years.

Construction output trends

In Table 1.1 the trend in construction output over a recent 15-year period is detailed. This data refers to Great Britain rather than the United Kingdom. Overall activity has clearly declined from the peak value which was reached in 1973. Pronounced cycles in construction output are apparent, and these are further discussed on pp. 9–10.

Construction output derives from a number of distinct types of work, the trends in which are also shown in Table 1.1. The recent decline in new work in the public sector is manifest in the downward trend in new housing and other work in this sector, which incorporates civil engineering and the construction of all public buildings. Since the early 1970s, a decline has also occurred in the two categories of new private sector work: new housing and

1.1   Selected output statistics for the GB construction sector

Year	GB total output	Public new housing	Private new housing	Public other new work	Private industrial and commercial new work	All new work	All repair and maintenance
						£ Million at 1980 prices	
1972	25,938	2,580	4,594	5,883	5,768	18,825	7,113
1973	26,100	2,512	4,793	5,741	5,597	18,643	7,457
1974	23,391	2,439	3,455	4,989	5,245	16,128	7,263
1975	22,054	2,689	3,114	4,672	4,964	15,439	6,615
1976	21,701	2,970	3,318	4,641	4,554	15,473	6,228
1977	21,617	2,702	3,142	4,425	4,906	15,175	6,442
1978	23,109	2,539	3,558	4,238	5,323	15,658	7,451
1979	23,260	2,180	3,283	3,905	5,394	14,689	8,570
1980	22,052	1,711	2,585	3,524	5,236	13,055	8,997
1981	19,947	1,124	2,351	3,343	4,940	11,758	8,189
1982	20,260	940	2,701	3,493	5,057	12,190	8,069
1983	21,101	1,001	3,238	3,556	4,893	12,688	8,413
1984	21,821	910	3,118	3,599	5,501	13,128	8,693
1985	22,072	751	2,968	3,396	6,067	13,182	8,889
1986	22,615	665	3,272	3,374	6,221	13,533	9,082

Source: Housing and Construction Statistics, Department of Environment (DOE)

industrial and commercial new work. Generally, the reduction in private sector new work has been less pronounced than that experienced by the public sector. In contrast to the reduced activity levels in new output, the volume of repair and maintenance output has increased over recent years. Whereas in 1972 repair and maintenance constituted only 27% of all construction output, by 1986 this proportion had risen to 40%. Within the overall trend of construction output, differential trends are apparent for specific categories of work.

Construction employment trends

It is not only in terms of output that construction makes a significant impact on the UK economy, for the industry also exerts an associated influence on national employment. Throughout the 1970s the construction sector was responsible for about 6.8% of jobs in the economy. Since 1980 this proportion has fallen but construction remains a major provider of employment opportunities. In particular, almost one-fifth of all self-employed workers are active in the construction industry.

1.2 *Selected employment statistics for the GB construction sector (000s)*

Year annual averages	GB total all manpower	Self-employed	Employees in employment			
			Contractors		Public authorities	
			Operatives	APTC	Operatives	APTC
1972	1,794	377[1]	846	214	246	111
1973	1,911	442[1]	886	227	243	113
1974	1,857	425[1]	859	237	228	108
1975	1,747	363[1]	806	234	232	112
1976	1,677	327[2]	774	231	232	113
1977	1,597	291[1]	743	229	224	110
1978	1,616	318[2]	737	231	221	109
1979	1,668	344[1]	763	232	217	112
1980	1,691	367[2]	767	235	212	110
1981	1,606	389[1]	678	230	205	104
1982	1,524	400[2]	619	223	187	95
1983	1,494	409[1]	600	214	183	88
1984	1,519	464[1]	585	214	172	84
1985	1,491	464[1]	556	213	169	84
1986	1,458	474[2]	530	212	160	82

[1] Estimated by Department of Employment (DE)
[2] Estimated by interpolation/extrapolation
Source: Housing and Construction Statistics, DOE

Details of recent trends in construction manpower are given in Table 1.2. It can be clearly seen how, as output has fallen over the period since 1973, there has been an associated reduction in the numbers of workers employed in construction. Once again some cyclical variation about this downward trend is apparent. The reduction in construction jobs has contributed significantly to the increasing levels of unemployment experienced in the UK economy. Many construction workers have specific skill-training and when the demand for these skills disappears, such workers cannot easily switch to jobs outside the construction sector. Statistics published for 1980 indicated that some 13.7% of all unemployed workers in Great Britain had last worked in the construction sector and so might be regarded as possessing construction skills.

The data in Table 1.2 indicates that the decline in the industry's manpower has been mainly a decline in the number of operatives, both skilled and unskilled manual workers. Since the early 1970s there has been a pronounced reduction in the demand for most grades of operative. Far fewer bricklayers, carpenters, painters, plumbers and electricians are currently employed than a decade ago. Both contracting firms and public authority employers (mainly the direct labour organisations of local authorities) have shed operative jobs as demand for construction output has declined. Employment of non-manual or administrative, professional, technical and clerical (APTC) workers has not suffered in the same way. During the late 1970s there was some growth in non-manual construction employment and, although there has been a small subsequent decline, the proportion of non-manual to manual jobs has been steadily increasing. As the number of direct employees has shown an overall reduction, so there has been a steady increase, since 1977, in the numbers in self-employment. This trend is very significant, as the self-employed worker continues to replace the direct employee.

Construction in the economy

The construction sector is greatly dependent on changes in the UK economy, and particularly on those which are the direct result of government policy. Construction output is a response to the demand for buildings, and this is a derived demand for other products and services. Variations in the gross national product will, in this way, influence the demand for construction work and the associated level of employment. However, the construction sector itself will also determine the demand for products from other parts of the economy, especially the material supplies sector. Changes in the level of construction activity lead to further changes in supplying industries and services and these feed back into the overall level of national output.

2. Construction and other sectors

The output of the construction sector is a response to the demand for new investment, for replacement of existing buildings and also for intermediate input into other industries. In Table 1.3 a breakdown of the demand for UK construction output in 1985 is provided. Final demand by end-users accounts for about 73% of total demand. The majority of this final demand is for new buildings, dwellings and work required by both the private and public sectors of the economy. The construction sector is responsible for supplying roughly half of all the gross fixed investment in the UK. Construction output is therefore especially sensitive to changes which affect the level of investment demand in the economy.

1.3   Analysis of demand for and supply of construction output in 1985 (percentages of total supply)

	%
New investment demand	54.2
Private sector replacement demand	12.6
Public sector replacement demand	5.8
Stockbuilding	0.1
All final demand	72.7
Intermediate demand	26.8
All home demand	99.5
Export demand	0.1
Total demand	99.6
Import supply	0.4
Total supply	100.0

Source: Institute for Employment Research, University of Warwick. (Analysis of commodity demands and supplies)

More than one-quarter of construction output is required as an intermediate demand to enable other firms to produce a final output. Full details of the relationship between construction and other industries are to be found in input-output tables of the UK economy. Most industries purchase some construction output in order to produce their final products and services. The biggest component of such intermediate demand arises from construction firms buying output from each other. Sub-contracting is probably more pronounced in construction than in any other sector and input-output statistics provide some measure of this interdependence.

While construction provides products and services to other industries, it also purchases a very significant proportion of its material and service inputs from these other sectors of the economy. Table 1.4 presents a breakdown of the inputs purchased by the construction sector in 1985. More than 30% of all inputs arise from within the construction industry itself. Nevertheless, the industry remains critically dependent on material supplies from elsewhere. Not surprisingly, construction is the major consumer of brick and concrete products, as well as timber and metal products. Key inputs are required from the engineering industries, the materials distribution sector, the transport industries and particularly from the financial and professional services sector. Over time, the construction sector has tended to buy in more and more goods and services, as a proportion of gross output value. In this way the construction sector has become a key customer for many

1.4   Analysis of purchased inputs for construction sector in 1985. Sources of all purchased inputs and percentages of total

Supplying industry	%
Mined and quarry products	3.4
Chemicals	3.5
Iron and steel	4.7
Other metal products	5.2
Mechanical engineering	6.9
Electrical engineering	2.7
Bricks and concrete products	15.0
Timber and furniture	7.7
Road transport	3.0
Distribution (merchants)	4.9
Financial and professional services	3.2
Other manufacturing and service industries	8.1
Total from outside construction	68.3
Total from within construction	31.7
All purchases	100.0

Source: Institute for Employment Research, University of Warwick.

other industries in the economy. When final demand for construction output declines the impact is felt in many other dependent sectors.

Input-output analysis indicates that the construction sector is involved in import and export activity to only a relatively small degree. Certainly the very nature of most construction output renders it unsuitable for direct movement between countries. However, many large construction firms derive valuable revenue and profit flows from overseas construction ventures, although such activity is not recorded as part of UK output. Perhaps of greater importance are the materials used in domestic construction, several of which have been imported by the supplying industries. In particular a very high proportion of the timber and wood products used in construction are imported. Construction is therefore affected by changes in international trade, by sterling exchange rates and by balance of payments policies.

3. Fluctuations in the construction sector

An examination of Table 1.1 reveals how construction output fluctuates markedly from year to year and how quite rapid and extreme changes are possible. Between 1973 and 1974 construction output fell by more than 10%, whereas between 1977 and 1978 it rose by almost 7%. Booms and slumps are commonplace in all sectors of construction activity. In recent years some of the more pronounced fluctuations have occurred in the demand for housing, especially in the private sector. New private industrial and commercial work also tends to vary cyclically, although the peaks and troughs in this output cycle do not generally coincide with those experienced in other categories of work. Usually, demand for public sector new work has tended to be more stable than that for private sector work, although the output trend has been consistently downwards. Even repair and maintenance output, the main growth sector in recent years, has been subject to cyclical variations. Fluctuations in repair and maintenance activity, however, are not usually quite as significant as those experienced in new work markets.

The origins of these fluctuations in demand derive from changes in the UK economy and the government's management of it. Barnard[1] has explained how the whole problem of 'stop-go' and the closely linked relationship of the industry to the overall rate of national economic growth is a problem which is shared by almost all West European countries. Moreover, Hillebrandt[2] asserts that the role of government influence, together with the link between investment and demand, means that demand tends to fluctuate particularly according to the state of the economy and the social and economic policies of the government, with consequent effects on construction. The management of the UK economy and the implications of this for the construction sector are fully discussed in Chapter 2.

Cyclical changes in demand produce some difficult problems for building firms and their workforces. One obvious consequence of fluctuations in construction output is the need to adjust manning levels in line with the available workload at various points in the cycle. The employment statistics in Table 1.2 show how employed manpower has also varied cyclically about the trend. As output and orders begin to increase, so firms gradually take on more manpower, but when output declines these workers are laid off. The variation in numbers employed is not as great as the variation in output. Firms often use overtime and short-time working as an initial response to variations in demand and in this way delay making adjustments to the numbers in employment. Increasingly, many building firms when confronted with the problem of highly cyclical demand choose to sub-contract labour rather than hire direct employees. The casual employment of operatives for the duration of a single contract is the common practice adopted by firms confronting highly variable market demand.

Large variations in output lead to fluctuations in turnover and inevitably, because profit margins are frequently very low, the profitability of firms is somewhat unstable. While the relatively few large firms in the construction sector usually manage to stabilise turnover, even in a recessionary period, they are not typical of the sector as a whole. The multitude of small firms which dominate the industry often experience strong variations in both turnover and profitability. Bankruptcy and liquidation statistics for the construction industry indicate the large number of firms which fail to survive each year. Over the period 1970–80 each year witnessed, on average, some 1890 liquidations and bankruptcies among building firms. These numbers tended to increase in the years following a pronounced downturn in the output cycle.

4. Unique aspects of construction

It is clear that construction is an integral sector of the UK economy. As such it makes an important contribution to, and at the same time is heavily influenced by, changes in the economy. While there are many economic characteristics which the construction industry experiences in common with other sectors, there remain a number of features which set it apart. Such features can be conveniently discussed under the broad headings of *demand* and *supply*.

Demand for construction products and services

Much of the demand for buildings and dwellings is for a highly distinctive product made to the unique requirements of the client. The majority of structures are individually designed and the builder offers a bespoke service to the customer. Little by way of continuous production is possible and the marked lack of standardisation in the resulting product renders a strict comparison of output very difficult. Variations in quality are very important and no simple economic analysis of demand is possible. In a few areas, most notably in that of speculative housing, some continuity of production is possible, but even here builders rarely produce a large number of identical housing units on the same site. The nature of the building product is quite distinct from the manufacturing product, for which standardisation and long production runs are commonplace.

Behind the demand for construction output lies a number of very diverse clients. Perhaps the most marked difference in these is between the public and private sector clients. The former category includes central government departments, local authorities, housing associations and various other public corporations. The private sector consists of private households on the one hand and firms and corporations on the other. This latter group is itself diverse, with manufacturing organisations generating a demand for factories and warehouses, and commercial organisations demanding offices and shops. There is an obvious and important distinction to be drawn between the demand for dwellings and that for non-housing work. The clients in each case are very different and the factors determining their demands are quite separate. A further distinction can be made between those clients requiring new construction work and those requiring repair and maintenance services. The importance of these differences will be made apparent in Chapter 4.

It is not only the nature of the product and the diversity of the customers which renders construction demand somewhat unique, but also the manner in which demand is put to the supplier of the product—the building contractor. While manufacturing firms often deal with their customers through a chain of wholesalers and retailers, the building firm usually receives the demand for its services after several intermediary agents have intervened to shape and mould the original client's requirements. Foremost amongst such intermediary agents are the design team, most commonly led by the architect, acting on behalf of the client to interpret his requirements in a form which can be built. Financial agents are also likely to figure prominently in making the demand effective. Most construction work involves large-scale capital investment and hence the client's ability to finance a venture is a crucial component of demand. Even with the purchase of speculative housing, the role of the bank or building society cannot normally be ignored. A further category of agent who influences construction demand includes the local authority planner and the building control inspectorate. Such agents serve to modify the physical characteristics of buildings and in this way may also come to change their final value. This process of intermediate agents shaping the nature of the client's demand has no ready parallel in the manufacturing sector.

The final product of the construction sector is not only expensive and complex but also bulky and heavy, and usually has to be assembled on the site where it is required. Typically, in manufacturing industries, the product is assembled in a central factory and is then distributed for sale in a number of separate geographical markets. For the most part, buildings are immoveable objects and it is the producer, the building contractor, who moves to the point of demand rather than vice versa. This means that the *location* of demand is critically important in the construction sector. During the late 1970s many large UK civil engineering firms systematically searched for demand in overseas markets, as demand for their services fell significantly at home.

As a result of pronounced fluctuations in the demand for construction output the forecasting of future trends is rendered particularly difficult. Few firms find forecasting an easy exercise but most find some degree of prediction essential, as a basis for corporate decision-making. In an industry such as construction, where demand can change rapidly and by quite large amounts, forward planning is usually quite difficult. The failure of a building firm to anticipate significant changes in markets, however, will almost certainly affect its profitability—and perhaps even its survival. Larger firms continue to grow by switching resources between the different categories of construction demand and by diversifying into new markets, as traditional areas of business decline. All firms need to plan ahead but the costs of not doing so in construction markets can be particularly high.

Supply of construction output

Construction output is highly diverse and many of the services required to achieve such output have become highly specialised. The industry is dominated by a large number of relatively small firms, many of which tend to specialise in a given skill. Consequently, a relatively high proportion of a main contractor's workload is sub-contracted out. While sub-contracting is a common feature of many industries, the scale on which it is used in the construction sector is unusual. The production of a building is typically dependent upon the combined inputs of several firms, with the main contractor fulfilling the role of managing co-ordinator. In such a situation good communications are at a premium and efficient production in the construction industry hinges much more on the working relationships between several contributory agents and firms than it does in other sectors.

The main justification for sub-contracting so much work is that specialist firms tend to be the most productive. However, despite this practice, productivity growth in the UK construction industry has proved difficult to realise. The very nature of much construction work renders it hard to achieve high output for each man-hour of input. The unique character of most construction activities means that gains from standardisation and repetition of tasks often prove elusive. Construction, relative to other industries, has come to be regarded as a low productivity sector and in consequence the unit cost of the industry's output is comparatively high.

Building firms not only buy in a high proportion of their labour requirements, but they also purchase from other industries most of their material and plant requirements. (Some statistics relating to these purchases were given on pp. 7–9.) The building contractor has very little control over these material markets, which tend to be dominated by much larger suppliers. Frequently, the small builder must acquire the materials on the terms and conditions imposed by manufacturing firms who exercise a very strong hold on the total market supply. This is certainly the case with the key building materials of brick, cement, ready-mixed concrete, steel and plastic products. A few larger construction firms have diversified to control the sources of supply of some of their key materials, but such behaviour is not typical; construction output still remains peculiarly dependent on the conditions prevailing in other sectors of the economy. This point has been made in a recent report for the Building and Civil Engineering EDC[3].

While the larger building firms are in a position to supply all types of construction output, in practice they usually concentrate on producing only the largest of new structures. Much of the larger firms' workload is concerned with civil engineering and with industrial and commerical building. Most large firms are also very active in speculative house building; some may also specialise in public sector housing provision. They are generally not so active in the repair and maintenance markets which are dominated by the smaller firms, who are not equipped to carry out the bigger contracts. The resulting division of output concentrates most new work in the hands of larger firms who seek to realise the economies of larger-scale buildings, while most repair and maintenance work is taken on by smaller firms who use their specialisation to advantage. In this way it sometimes appears that construction output is supplied by two distinct groups of firms: the large contractors and the small builders.

The high number of small construction companies inevitably means that quite a lot of these firms lead a precarious financial existence, especially when construction demand begins to decline. Cash flow is critical to all small firms, but especially to those in the construction sector. The need to maintain liquidity is crucial and the bankruptcy statistics referred to in the previous section provide ample evidence of the failure, each year, of a significant proportion of these firms. The role of credit and loans in providing working capital for the building firm is critical in ensuring the continuity of construction output.

5. *Statistics of construction*

In this chapter, use has been made of published statistics to illustrate the importance of the construction sector and its linkages with the rest of the UK economy. The construction industry is rich in potential sources for such statistics; Fleming[4] has provided a comprehensive guide to the available sources of data and his review extends to some 650 pages. In this section it is only possible to provide a very simple guide to the most obvious sources of statistical information. Anyone seeking fuller and more detailed information is referred to Fleming. A listing of the more important statistical sources is provided at the end of this chapter, however.

Output statistics

The main source for production statistics is *Housing and Construction Statistics*, published by the Department of the Environment (DOE). Each year the DOE publishes a comprehensive volume giving data for the most recent ten-year period; it also produces quarterly updates (in two separate parts) of the more important key series. Output data is analysed by type of work done, by the sector carrying out the work and, most recently, by the region of the country in which the work originates. Output statistics are given in terms of both current and constant prices, and also as a set of index numbers. Often, data for the most recent periods is subject to revision and therefore the latest available set of statistics should always be used, on the assumption that these are the most accurate. From time to time the base year used in the calculation of the constant price and index number series is changed—usually every five years. Such a change can make for continuity problems, although sufficient information is published to enable the user to form a linkage between the respective series valued at different base year prices. The output series valued in constant prices is far more useful than that given in current prices, as the effects of price inflation are eliminated and changes in real output over time can be examined.

Output statistics for the construction sector are also published by other government departments. In particular, the Central Statistical Office (CSO), through its monthly publications, *Economic Trends* and *Monthly Digest of Statistics* and its annual publication, *United Kingdom National Accounts (Blue Book)*, details the index numbers of industrial production for the construction sector. Most of these series are for the United Kingdom rather than Great Britain; in other respects too they differ from those produced by the DOE, most significantly in the coverage of their output enquiry. Consequently the two valuations of output attributable to construction do not tally.

The Construction Industry Training Board also generates estimates of construction production—these are published as part of *Housing and Construction Statistics*—but they use their own register of private contractors and once again their definition of the construction industry does not match those used by either the CSO or the DOE. Such differences are not important as long as the source of discrepancy is understood and no attempt is made to use the various statistics interchangeably.

Another important source of construction output data is that provided in the annual census carried out by the Department of Trade and Industry (DTI). The details of this census are published by the Business Statistics Office (BSO) as *Business Monitor: PA 500*, providing information on work done, net output, selected cost items, direct employment and capital expenditure. For larger construction firms, employing more than 20 workers, output is analysed according to the principal activities identified in the *1980 Standard Industrial Classification*. The output information generated in the census is broadly consistent with that published by the DOE, as the census uses the DOE register of construction firms.

Order statistics

Apart from output data, important information is regularly published on new orders obtained by private contractors. (This can be found in *Housing and Construction Statistics*.) The published information is usually more detailed than that available for output, and the main categories of both public and private sector clients, from whom the orders originate, are identified. Order information is also regularly analysed according to region of origin and range of value of contract. However, this information is generally incompatible with any of the published output data. Orders only relate to *new* work and the statistics therefore exclude the very important area of repair and maintenance. Moreover, the orders included are only those received by private contractors and do not include new work given to the direct labour organisations of the local authorities. Some orders may well be cancelled, while in other cases the eventual valuation of output resulting from an order will be very different from the original order value. Probably the most significant problem associated with using this order data as a forward indicator of output is the difficulty of identifying when exactly an obtained order will be carried into production. Attempts to predict output changes on the basis of received orders have therefore proved very hazardous.

Housing statistics

Detailed statistics dealing with the construction of housing are regularly published. Once again the most important of these are to be found in *Housing and Construction Statistics*. Details of starts, completions and works-in-progress are analysed according to the originating sector (public versus private) and the region and area of location. Statistics for completed housing units are represented according to size, number of bedrooms and type—housing or flats—by region and by sector. Much fuller information is published on local authority and new town housing tenders. Details on the existing stock of dwellings by region and tenure are reported annually. No comparable information is published for other types of construction work.

Other production statistics

An indirect source of information on construction production is afforded by published statistics on capital expenditure. The *United Kingdom National Accounts Blue Book* annually estimates new capital formations in dwellings and buildings and works, analysed by industry classifications. More detailed information on capital expenditure on construction work is obtainable from census-of-production sources and this information is published in a series of *Business Monitors* for individual trades.

There are some important differences between construction expenditure data and output data, such that changes in one set of statistics are not necessarily mirrored in the other set. (Fleming[4] has provided a full account of these differences.) The register of firms responsible for construction output will not necessarily include every company doing construction work; some categories of construction expenditure, including professional fees and general interest charges, will not be recorded in contractors' output returns; often, expenditure statistics will not coincide in timing with the execution of work and, similarly, valuations of work done may not be the same for the client as for the contractor. Classifications of construction expenditure distinguishing between capital and current items and between plant and buildings will also make a difference to the recorded series. Investment expenditure statistics provide very useful information on clients of the construction industry, but they are not a particularly good guide to output changes within the construction sector.

Manpower statistics

After production information, labour statistics constitute the next most important set of published data. Probably the most comprehensive manpower statistics for the whole construction sector are those regularly published by the Department of Employment (DE) in the *DE Gazette*. Monthly statistics are reported, relating to employment in the construction industry, and an annual census is taken. The DE are also the only source of information on the number of self-employed workers in the construction sector. Recent estimates of self-employment are based on labour-force surveys carried out every year, but such estimates are subject to a very wide margin of error and are liable to require extensive revision. The series given as part of Table 1.2 may well be significantly revised in future years as new information on the self-employed comes to light. The *DE Gazette* is also a source of data relating to unemployment and vacancies in the construction industry; however, since 1981 the publication of unemployment statistics for individual occupations has been discontinued. More generally, the DE is the source of statistics on hours worked, wage rates and general labour costs in the construction sector; most of this data is published in either the *DE Gazette* or the *New Earnings Survey*.

A second important source of manpower statistics is the series produced by the DOE and published in *Housing and Construction Statistics*. The DOE use a wider definition of the construction industry than that employed by the DE. In addition to including all employees within the standard industrial classification of the construction industry, they also include construction workers in building and civil engineering establishments run by authorities whose major activity is classified as being within some other sector; this includes the bodies working within local and central government. Consequently the DE and DOE series are not strictly comparable. The DOE statistics for employees in work are especially useful as they break down the data into classes, distinguishing between manual and non-manual employees and between those employed by private contractors and those by public authorities. These series are based on quarterly returns from private contractors and half-yearly returns from the public sector.

A third valuable source of data on manpower trends in construction is that provided by the Construction Industry Training Board (CITB). Most of their key statistics are regularly published in *Housing and Construction Statistics*, alongside the DOE labour data. The CITB register of construction workers is narrower than that used by either the DE or the DOE. (It is a by-product of the administration of the levy-grant system of training, in which the CITB imposes a pay-roll levy on private sector construction firms to collect revenue, which it then disburses to those firms which provide training.) This CITB data is produced twice each year, in April and October; employees in work are distinguished by occupation. Currently, the CITB generates employment statistics for some 44 individual occupations. Separate series are provided for trainees; these are categorised as employed workers whose employers have undertaken to provide them with training in a specific skill for a specified period of not less than 12 months.

The CITB manpower data, while more detailed than that produced by the two main government agencies, is not as comprehensive in its coverage. It excludes all construction workers employed by the public authorities. In addition it only covers employers who are 'in-scope', or affiliated, to the CITB and thereby a large number of very small firms and self-employed workers are also excluded. Over recent years the number of separate occupational categories has been increased; this means that discontinuities are frequent in the series. Nevertheless, the CITB statistics remain a unique source of information on occupational trends in the construction sector.

Other statistics

Beyond production and manpower statistics, data on many other aspects of construction is readily available from a wide variety of sources; Fleming remains the most comprehensive guide to such information. *Housing and Construction Statistics* publishes data on most aspects of housing finance and also on the production of construction materials. Use will be made of this in later chapters of this book.

Questions

1. Assess the importance of the construction sector to the UK economy in terms of production and employment.
2. Describe how the construction sector and other industries are interdependent in terms of input and output.
3. How might an input-output analysis be useful in predicting the demand for future construction work?
4. Analyse the data presented in Table 1.1 in the form of a graph, illustrating the cyclical nature of construction activity in both the new work and the repair and maintenance markets.
5. Compare the fluctuations in construction manpower (Table 1.2) with those in construction ouput (Table 1.1) and comment on your findings.
6. Discuss the main characteristcs of construction demand which differentiate it from manufacturing demand.
7. Identify the most important ways in which building firms differ from manufacturing firms.
8. Distinguish the main sources of statistics relating to production output. Why cannot these statistics be used interchangeably?
9. What are the differences between output statistics, order statistics and expenditure statistics as measures of construction production?
10. List the problems we can expect to encounter when attempting to compile a chronological series of data on:
    (a) self-employment in construction
    (b) employment by occupation

Statistical sources referred to in chapter 1

Central Statistical Office

1. *United Kingdom National Accounts: CSO Blue Book* (formerly *National Income and Expenditure*). Published annually
2. *Economic Trends*. Published monthly
3. *Monthly Digest of Statistics*
4. *Guide to Official Statistics*. Published annually
5. *The Standard Industrial Classification* (revised 1980)

Department of Employment
  6. *DE Gazette*. Published monthly

Department of the Environment
  7. *Housing and Construction Statistics*. Published quarterly and
     annually

Department of Trade and Industry
  8. *Business Monitor PA 1004: Input-Output Tables for the United
     Kingdom*. Published occasionally
  9. *British Business* (formerly *Trade and Industry*). Published
     weekly
 10. *Business Monitor PA 500: Report on the Census of Production:
     Construction*. Published annually

All of the above are published by HMSO.

Further reading

ANDREWS, P. W. S. and BRUNNER, E., *Studies in Pricing*, Chapter 5,
    Macmillan, 1975
BECKERMAN, W., *An Introduction to National Income Analysis*, Chapter 6,
    Weidenfeld and Nicolson, 1980
DOLAN, D. F., *The British Construction Industry*, Macmillan, 1979
HILLEBRANDT, P. M., *Analysis of the British Construction Industry*,
    Chapter 1, Macmillan, 1984
TURIN, D. A., *Aspects of the Economics of the Construction Industry*,
    Chapters 1 and 2, George Godwin, 1975

2 Management of the UK Economy and the Implications for the Construction Industry

1. Composition of the gross national product

Effective management of any economy begins with the measurement of the amount of activity occurring in that economy and an understanding of the main components which constitute such activity. The gross national product (GNP) is a measure of the total value of goods and services produced in an economy for a given time period, most usually a year. GNP can be measured in a number of different ways, but each has a common basis in the national accounts statistics. It is usual to approach the measurement of GNP and its key components by reference to the *circular flow of income model*.

Circular flow of income in the simple economy

The circular flow of income in a simple economy, consisting only of firms and households, is represented in Fig. 2.1. Real output and factors of production flow in one direction, while income and financial expenditures flow in the other. Households provide firms with essential labour, land and capital factors and in return they receive payment in the form of wages, rent, interest and profit respectively. Firms combine these factors to produce a marketable output of goods and services. Part of this output is purchased by other firms, with one company producing capital goods (e.g. factory buildings) for the use of another firm. This type of capital output constitutes an input into the firm producing goods and services for the consumer market. The output which is sold to the household sector is paid for out of the incomes received from the selling of the factors of production. In this way the income cycle is completed.

Fig. 2.1 suggests that there are three ways of measuring the amount of economic activity in the circular flow of this economy. Measurement can be taken of either income, expenditure or the output of goods and services. Each represents a different point in

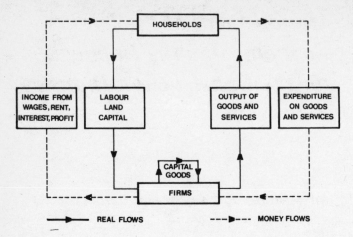

Fig. 2.1 *Circular flow in a simple economy*

the cycle at which measurement can be made and in theory it should not matter which measure is used, as all the measures are exactly equivalent, each corresponding to the GNP of the system. Hence once economic activity has already occurred, it must be true that:

National Income = National Expenditure = National Output

Income is measured by adding together the receipts from wages, rents, profits (dividends) and interest payments. In practice, the divisions of income are much more complex. Most income information is collated by the Inland Revenue. Only those incomes received for work done or services carried out count towards the total of national income. Incomes which represent simple transfers from one group of people to another, without any corresponding production, are not counted. Transfer payments, such as social security benefits and grants, are not added into the total of national income.

Expenditure is measured by adding together all the final sales to households with the value of goods which are not sold in the given time period, but which are either taken into stock or purchased by other firms as capital goods. Expenditure in the simple economy model consists of spending by consumers and investment spending by firms. In this simple model no distinction is made between investments and savings; these are in effect treated as the same thing. If households do not spend all their income on consumption, but instead save a proportion of it, these savings are used to meet the investment expenditure of the firm sector. Once investment has been made it must be matched by the supply of savings. This identity between savings and investment only holds true for the simple model.

In practice, expenditure data is collated from a wide number of different sources by several government departments, especially the Customs and Excise Department. Inevitably, the final total of national expenditure shows some divergence from that of national income, although, in theory, the two measures should remain equivalent.

Output is measured by valuing all goods and services produced in the economy, including goods which go into stock and work-in-progress. The method of summing the output of different firms is made difficult by the existence of intermediate output, whereby one firm purchases the output of another firm for use as a material input in its own production process. Construction firms use the outputs from several building material manufacturers in order to create new buildings and works. The measure of output used in this case is net or value-added output. This is gross or total output with the value of intermediate output deducted, to avoid double counting. The main source of output data is the Census of Production and the principal collating agency is the Central Statistical Office. In practice, totals of national output are constrained by statisticians at the CSO to be consistent with the national income statistics.

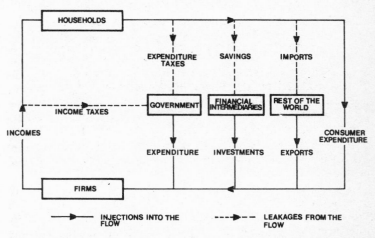

Fig. 2.2 *Circular flow including government, financial intermediaries and the rest of the world*

Circular flow in the full economy

In reality, the simple economy is rendered very much more complex by the existence of a government sector, a financial sector and the rest of the world, with whom international trade is carried out. While the inclusion of these sectors complicates the nature of the circular flow of income model, it does not disturb the basic concept. In Fig. 2.2 the circular flow for an open economy with a government and financial sector is represented. This diagram shows how leakages from the basic flow (shown by broken lines) and injections into it (shown by continuous lines) occur. The measurement of GNP requires that once economic activity has already happened, the sum total of leakages must exactly equal the sum total of injections. This is a basic principle of national income accounting and it ensures that the three measurement approaches to GNP are consistent.

The three main types of leakage from the circular flow are due to savings, government taxation and imports, whereas the injections are attributable to investment, government expenditure and exports. Out of received income households often save a significant proportion and such savings are withdrawn from the circular flow and put into banks or into the control of other financial intermediaries. Government similarly withdraws spending from the income flow by taxing both incomes and the goods and services on which expenditure is made. Although subsidies may be given to re-inject some spending power, the net effect of government taxation is to reduce the flow of income in the economic system. Imports involve the spending of domestic incomes on foreign goods and services, and in this way income leaks from the UK system. Offsetting these leakages are injections into the system. Financial intermediaries channel savings they receive into investment expenditures and this increases the spending flow. Government spends the revenue it receives from taxation in a wide variety of ways involving both current and capital expenditure programmes. This too adds to the circular flow. Finally exports from the UK to other countries in the world bring income into the economy and so consitute an injection into the flow.

Within the full model of the economy, it is not necessary for savings to exactly equate with investment. Often, more will be saved by households than is demanded for investment expenditure by firms. Similarly, government revenue will rarely, if ever, exactly match government spending. Most commonly, spending exceeds revenue and the government draws on savings in the financial sector to accommodate its borrowing requirements. Exports are unlikely ever to be in perfect balance with imports. A deficit or surplus in the balance of exports and imports will be offset by balances in the savings/investment and government revenue/spending accounts. National income accounting requires total leakages to be identical to total injections so that:

Table 2.1 Gross National Product at current market prices, UK, 1985

Expenditure measurement

	£m	% TFE
Consumers' expenditure	213,208	47.4
Government consumption	74,012	16.4
Gross fixed investment	60,118	13.4
Investment in stocks	528	0.1
Exports	102,304	22.7
Total final expenditure (TFE)	450,170	100.0
Less imports	−98,603	
Gross Domestic Product (GDP)	351,567	
Net property, income from abroad	3,400	
Gross National Product (GNP)	354,967	
Less net expenditure taxes	−49,102	
GNP at factor cost	305,865	

Income measurement

	£m	% TDI
Income from employment	195,350	63.3
Income from self-employment	29,859	9.7
Company gross profits	52,977	17.2
Public sector gross profits	7,370	2.4
Income from rents	20,541	6.6
Imputed charge for consumption of capital	2,681	0.8
Total domestic income (TDI)	308,778	100.0
Less stock appreciation	−3,037	
Gross Domestic Product	305,741	
Less residual error	−3,276	
GDP at factor cost (expenditure base)	302,465	
Net property income from abroad	3,400	
GNP at factor cost	305,865	

Output measurement

	£m	% Total
Agriculture, forestry and fishing	5,485	1.7
Energy and water supply	34,335	10.6
Manufacturing	75,800	23.5
Construction	18,551	5.8
Distribution and transport	53,297	16.5
Banking and business services	42,473	13.2
All other services[1]	92,683	28.7
Total output	322,624	100.0
Less adjustment for interest payments	−16,883	
GDP at factor cost (income base)	305,741	
Net property income from abroad	3,400	
Less residual error	−3,276	
GNP at factor cost	305,865	

Source: United Kingdom National Accounts: CSO Blue Book, HMSO, 1986
[1] 'Other services' includes communications, education, health, local and central government. Also included in this residual category is output arising from the ownership of dwellings.

Savings + Government Revenue + Imports = Investment + Government Expenditure + Exports

UK national income accounts

It is easy to state the basic principles for measuring GNP but it is more instructive to examine the applications of national income accounting. For this purpose use is made of UK National Accounts as they appear in the *CSO Blue Book*. Table 2.1 has been adapted from various tabulations in the 1986 edition of the *Blue Book*. The three measurement approaches for the full economy are set out in Table 2.1, which also reveals useful details about the composition of the UK's GNP.

The expenditure approach to GNP is the most commonly used measure, as it is expenditure components which are varied in the management of aggregate demand (see pp. 32–5). Expenditure is undertaken by four distinct sectors: consumers, government, firms (investment) and the rest of the world (exports). Of these sectors, consumer expenditure is by far the most important, even allowing for the fact that the purchase of housing is treated as an investment expenditure and is classified with the gross fixed investment of firms. When the value of imports is deducted from the total final expenditure, the gross domestic product (GDP) for the UK is determined. The move from GDP to GNP involves making a small adjustment, in recognition of the fact that the term 'national' refers only to UK nationals. Property income received from abroad by UK nationals is added to the domestic total and property income generated in the UK, but when paid to foreign nationals, it is deducted. Since the adjustment is very small, the terms GDP and GNP are often used interchangeably.

Expenditure is valued at current market prices and as such these prices will in some cases contain elements of expenditure taxes and in others they will reflect subsidies. If the expenditure measure of GNP is to be rendered consistent with the income and output measures this net expenditure tax component will need to be taken into account. The income and output measures do not contain any expenditure tax or subsidy element. The deduction of net expenditure or indirect taxes is known as the factor cost adjustment and when applied it yields GNP at factor cost, as opposed to market prices.

The income approach to GNP distinguishes income earned from direct employment, income from self-employment, income from profits and income from rents. Income from direct employment is by far the most important of these categories. Profits made in the private company sector are very much higher than those arising in the government and nationalised industry sector. In order to render total domestic income consistent with GNP at factor cost, measured on the expenditure side, a number of adjustments are necessary. The need to allow for net property income from abroad is self-evident. Stock appreciation occurs when the value of stocks increases through higher prices. Such appreciation is counted into company profits and hence into total domestic income but it has no counterpart in the expenditure approach. Consistency requires that this element of stock appreciation is eliminated from the income estimate. The final adjustment is the residual error which ensures complete agreement with the expenditure measure. The error component is a simple recognition of the realities of attempting to get accurate estimation from millions of individual income returns. It is inevitable that errors and omissions will arise, and this residual error figure simply reflects the size of the discrepancy between income measures and expenditure measures in the real world.

The output measurement of GNP distinguishes between the value-added contributions made by different industrial sectors of the UK economy. In Table 2.1 only a few broad sectors are separately identified. In practice, net output can be analysed by individual industries and their principal sub-divisions. The UK economy in the 1980s derives most of its output from the widely defined services sector and manufacturing now contributes less than one-quarter of all national output. In recent years, the energy and water supply sector of the economy has become much more important, while construction has declined slightly. When the output measure is adjusted to eliminate double counting arising from the interest receipts of financial firms, the resulting total domestic output is rendered consistent with the corresponding income measure.

Anyone who is concerned to carry a study of the national accounts to a finer level of detail should be familiar with the work of Copeman[1]. Before use is made of the GNP statistics, the reader is recommended to study the notes contained in the *United Kingdom National Accounts: CSO Blue Book*. This prime source of statistics provides full definitions of all the terms used in Table 2.1.

2. Central Objectives and Demand Management

Key objectives

Gross national product provides a measure of a country's economic performance. It is a prime objective of any economy to generate growth in the GNP over time. Economic growth means systematic increases in the real GNP per head of population. This is the long-term objective for any economy, since unless the capacity to produce goods and services is expanding, no increases in the overall standard of living will be possible.

In the shorter term it is often the case that a country will not be producing goods and services to its full potential. Where its achieved GNP is significantly lower than the maximum possible GNP, this indicates that some resources are being under-utilised. Most seriously, unemployment will arise, such that some members of the working population who are actively seeking jobs are unable to find them. Usually high unemployment is associated with low rates of growth of GNP, but unemployment can also exist in an economy where the GNP is increasing. Where the growth in output is concentrated on industrial sectors which use relatively little labour in the production process, unemployment can be quite marked, despite an increasing level of GNP. In the short term the composition of the GNP is just as important as its overall level.

While growth in real GNP ensures an increase in potential economic welfare, the distribution of this welfare amongst the country's residents is significantly affected by changes in the prices ruling in the country. This general increase in prices is known as inflation and in recent years it has become a major objective of governments everywhere to try to keep prices as stable as possible. Changes in GNP are usually accompanied by price changes and such changes serve to redistribute incomes in a rather haphazard fashion. Economic growth, which is accompanied by marked increases in employment opportunities, will often also give rise to inflation. Economic growth and fuller employment are sought-after objectives, but price inflation most certainly is not.

As the GNP of an economy changes, so the relationship between exports and imports is likely to alter. When a country's exports exceed its imports, such that a balance of payments surplus is said to result, governments will be content that gold and currency reserves are accumulating. However, when imports exceed exports, such that a balance of payments deficit arises, the same gold and currency is drained away and governments will need to take action to remedy this situation. Even where economies are growing, the balance between exports and imports can be wrong, so that payment deficits persist. When inflation is more rapid in an economy than in that of its trading partners this will serve to favour imports over exports and so lead to balance of payments problems.

It is now widely agreed by economists (for example, see Burningham[2]) that governments everywhere pursue four main macro-economic objectives:

(1) Economic growth
(2) Full employment or very low levels of unemployment
(3) Price stability or low rates of inflation
(4) Avoidance of a deficit in the balance of payments

Sometimes other objectives are considered as important. A desire for a more equitable distribution of income is a long-term objective for many governments but it is rarely actively pursued. In recent years the need to constrain and limit the public sector borrowing requirement has appeared as a macroeconomic objective, but, in practice, restraint in government borrowing is more a strategy for realising other objectives than an objective in itself.

Economic growth

An indication of the recent success or otherwise of the UK government's pursuit of the four central objectives can be gained from published statistics. Fig. 2.3 shows the annual percentage growth rate for GDP over recent years. It is immediately clear that the government has not succeeded in maintaining a stable high rate of economic growth. Cyclical patterns are discernible in this annual growth rate and in both 1980 and 1981 small declines in GDP were recorded, although significant growth occurred between 1982 and 1985.

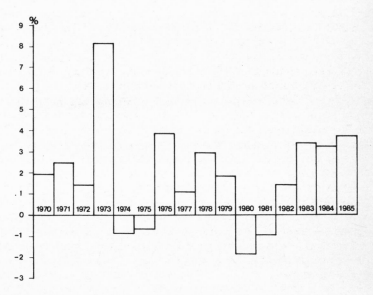

Fig. 2.3 *Annual percentage growth in UK gross domestic product* (UK National Accounts: *CSO Blue Book, HMSO 1986*)

In Table 2.2, the average annual growth rate over the years 1973–85 has been estimated and the UK rate is compared to that achieved by other leading industrial countries. It can be seen how the United Kingdom has been less successful in generating economic growth than its main world trading partners. When allowance is made for growth in the population, and when a modified measure of economic growth (GDP per capita) is estimated, the UK is seen to be comparable with the USA, but still lags behind other countries. In particular, the UK growth rate is less than half of that which has been achieved in Japan in recent years. In terms of absolute value, the UK's GDP per capita in 1986 was found to be significantly less than that of the USA and, to a lesser extent, Germany and Japan.

2.2   Economic growth rates

Country	Average annual growth rates 1973–85 at constant prices		1986 Absolute GDP per capita £ per capita
	GDP%	GDP per capita %	
United Kingdom	1.4	1.2	6,500
France	2.1	1.8	6,700
Germany	1.8	2.0	7,400
Japan	3.8	3.3	7,000
USA	2.2	1.2	9,800

Source: CSO/OECD Economic Indicators

Low unemployment

Table 2.3 presents data showing unemployment rates in the UK. The post-war period up until the late 1960s proved a very successful time for the achievement of the full employment objective. During the 1930s extremely high rates of unemployment had been experienced. The unemployment rate for most years in the period 1944 until 1970 was between one and two per cent. Such low rates were regarded as an inevitable friction in the economy as workers moved between jobs. By most definitions a state of full employment existed in the UK. The trend away from full employment began in the 1970s and as Table 2.3 indicates, the unemployment level in 1985 was broadly comparable with that experienced in the 1920s, before the government became concerned with achieving full employment.

2.3 Unemployment in the UK

Year	Average annual unemployment rate (%)
1926	12.5
1932	22.1
1950	1.3
1960	1.7
1965	1.5
1970	2.6
1975	4.2
1980	6.8
1985	11.8

Source: *DE Gazette*

Low inflation

During the post-war period when full employment and, to a lesser extent, economic growth were both achieved, the economy also experienced a small amount of price inflation. However this inflation was of a comparatively low order prior to 1970 and, as such, it was deemed acceptable and not markedly inconsistent with the price stability objective. Table 2.4 details two measures of inflation; the differences in the two series before 1970 and afterwards are quite apparent. The indices given for retail prices imply an average annual inflation rate of only 4% for the period 1960–70, but a rate of 14% for the period 1970–80. It can be seen how average earnings increased even more rapidly after 1970. Clearly, in the most recent period, the price stability objective was not being met and it is perhaps not surprising to find that since 1980 more attention has been paid to achieving this objective than any other.

2.4 Indices of inflation in the UK (1970 = 100)

Year	General index of all retail prices	Average earnings index of all employees
1950	45.2	32.1
1960	67.2	54.1
1965	79.9	72.2
1970	100.0	100.0
1975	184.4	227.6
1980	366.6	452.4
1985	518.2	697.3

Source: *DE Gazette*

Balance of payments equilibrium

Table 2.5 provides summary details of the UK balance of payments
for selected years between 1950 and 1985. While the critical balance
is the net total of the current and capital transactions combined (for
it is this total which has to be financed out of reserves), most concern
attaches to the current account balance. This account measures the
net result of trade in both visible goods and invisible services, and
the major objective is to avoid deficits in this balance. The data for
benchmark years shows how prior to 1980, when exports of North
Sea oil became important in generating a surplus, the current
account had a tendency to move into deficit. (A fuller description of
balance of payments policy follows; see pp. 48–54.)

2.5   UK balance of payments (£ million, current prices)

Year	Current account balance	Net capital transactions	Official financing[1]
1950	297	−59	−437
1960	−272	−187	190
1965	−30	−316	353
1970	823	682	−1,420
1975	−1,523	154	1,465
1980	3,629	−1,270	−1,372
1985	3,602	−5,508	−1,788

Source: *UK Balance of Payments: CSO Pink Book*
[1] Official financing is the final balance to be met after allowing for any
balancing errors. In 1985 these balancing items were especially large. In this column,
a positive entry indicates a balance of payments deficit, negative a surplus.

Demand management

The main approach used by the UK government in the post-war
period to realise its four central macroeconomic objectives has been
demand management. Only in the 1980s has the government
slackened its attempt to produce full employment through the
management of aggregate demand. For almost 30 years in the
period since 1944, demand management was used to keep unemployment at acceptably low levels; while checking the tendency
of the balance of payments to move into deficit, at the same time it
generated modest economic growth. It was only in the 1970s that
the rate of inflation became unacceptably high; at this point the
government began to look beyond demand management for the
means to realise its objectives.

Demand management has developed from the work of Lord

Keynes, who in the 1930s was particularly concerned by the very high levels of unemployment in the UK. Keynes demonstrated how, if aggregate expenditure in an economy was not sufficient to stimulate high enough levels of aggregate supply, significant unemployment would persist and there would be no automatic tendency for the economy to move back towards full employment.

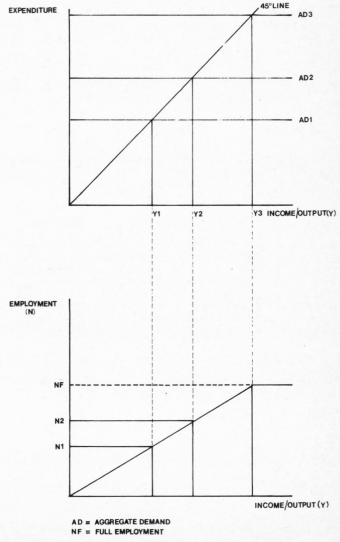

AD = AGGREGATE DEMAND
NF = FULL EMPLOYMENT

Fig. 2.4 *Demand management and the level of employment*

The basic Keynesian concept can be demonstrated with the aid of a '45° diagram', using the analysis developed on pp. 20–7.

The top diagram in Fig. 2.4 shows how different levels of aggregate demand, composed of consumer and government expenditure, investment, and exports net of imports, determine different levels of national income. A low planned level of aggregate demand (AD1) produces a low level of income (Y1), but when aggregate demand is increased to AD2 this produces a correspondingly higher level of income (Y2). In this representation, the 45° line from the origin shows all points at which total income equates to total expenditure. If it is assumed that manufacturing firms always plan for output levels to exactly balance total expenditure, then this 45° line can be regarded as an aggregate supply schedule which is fixed for shorter time periods.

Corresponding to the equilibrium level of income, set by the intersection of aggregate demand and the 45° line, there is an associated level of employment. The bottom diagram in Fig. 2.4 shows the relationship between national income (output) and employment. It is assumed that employment will increase as income increases, until the point where full employment is reached. At this stage further increases in income, brought about by planned increases in aggregate demand, will have no impact on employment, as all those who want to work are already employed. The two diagrams together show how a low level of aggregate demand (AD1), produces low income (Y1), which in turn leads to a low level of employment (N1). The gap between N1 and NF, the full employment level, provides a measure of the extent of unemployment. In order to produce full employment, aggregate demand has to be managed up to level (AD3). How might this be achieved?

A government can increase aggregate demand by either increasing planned injections into the economy or reducing the planned level of leakages. If increases occur in consumer expenditure, in government expenditure net of taxation, in investment spending and in exports net of imports, the circular flow of income is boosted and aggregate demand will be seen to have increased. A government, therefore, through its fiscal, monetary and balance of payments policies, is able to change the planned components of aggregate demand. The decision by households of how much to spend on consumer goods depends on the amount of income they receive and on the attractiveness of saving relative to consumption. Through changes in taxation on the one hand and interest rates on the other, the government can produce changes in aggregate consumption. Changes in the government's own budget can be made, directly altering both government expenditure and its taxation receipts. The level of investment spending is less easily influenced by government policy changes than are other components of aggregate demand. Planned investment remains sensitive to the supply of money in the economy and the level of interest rates. Both are variables which the government attempts to control. The level of exports and imports depends to a large extent upon decisions made in other countries, but a government can exert some influence on the balance of payments through its policies—and in particular through its policy for the exchange rate. A government's control over the various components of aggregate demand is far from perfect, but it is to some degree able to bring about changes in planned expenditure levels.

Demand management has normally been used to try and realise the objective of full employment. Whenever aggregate demand is increased, inflationary pressures are created. Prior to the 1970s such inflation was not especially serious and a small increase in general prices, often accompanied by an associated increase in imports, was considered an acceptable price to pay for full employment. In recent years, attempts to expand aggregate demand have tended to produce very high, unacceptable levels of inflation. In consequence the UK government in the 1980s is concerned with restraining aggregate demand, in order to check high inflation.

3. Fiscal policy

The most direct method of managing the components of aggregate demand is through fiscal policy, a government's use of taxation revenue and state expenditure. Both central and local government collect taxes, and both engage in current and capital spending. The construction sector is very significantly affected by fiscal policy. Changes in fiscal policy, designed to realise one or more of the main economic objectives, usually have marked implications for the level of construction demand.

Direct taxation

Table 2.6 presents a general government budget in which the sources of revenue and the applications of expenditure are shown. The main source of government revenue is taxation, and income tax is by far the most important form of this. Income tax is a critical determinant of personal disposable income and it is received income which determines the ability of individual households to spend money on housing and associated construction work. In recent years, the UK government has attempted to switch some of the tax burden away from income tax towards expenditure taxation.

A reduction in the effective rate of income tax not only gives householders greater potential spending power, but also has an effect on the willingness of the individual to work. When workers are able to take home a higher proportion of their gross earnings, they are likely to be more willing to give up their leisure time in exchange for working hours. It is generally recognised that self-employment provides greater opportunities, mainly through the generous allowances that can be claimed against tax, to retain a higher percentage of total earnings than is possible for employees, who pay income tax on the Pay-As-You-Earn (PAYE) basis. This is an important factor in the decision of many construction operatives to opt for self-employment.

2.6   *The general government budget for 1985 (£000 million)*

	£ billion		£ billion
Income tax	35.5	Current spending on military defence	17.9
Corporation tax	9.1	On the National Health Service	16.7
North Sea oil tax	7.4	On other government goods and services	16.4
L.A. rates	13.6	Current subsidies	7.7
National Insurance (including surcharges)	24.1	Grants to local authorities	20.7
VAT	21.0	Social security benefits	37.0
Excise duties (alcohol, tobacco, oil)	14.7	Other personal sector grants	9.1
All other expenditure taxes	7.5	Net current grants paid abroad	3.4
All taxes and National Insurances	132.9	All current expenditure	128.9
Rents and profit	5.4	Debt interest	17.5
Interest and dividends	6.3	Direct fixed capital investment	6.6
Capital taxes and other capital receipts	2.2	Investment in stocks	0.5
		Capital grants to other sectors	3.5
Total revenue	146.8	Total expenditure	157.0
Borrowing required	10.9	Balancing item	0.7
Revenue balance	157.7	Expenditure balance	157.7

Source: *UK National Accounts: CSO Blue Book*, HMSO, 1986

Annual budgeting adjustments are often made to the basis for paying income tax, as the government engages in fine modifications to the components of aggregate demand. Changes are made either in the allowances which income earners receive before they start to pay tax, or in the basic rate at which this tax is paid. It is customary for the government to raise personal allowances annually, and hence raise the starting point for the payment of income tax, as inflation raises incomes and increases liability for income tax. Interest paid by home-owners on mortgages up to a maximum loan of £30,000 can be offset as an allowance against income tax. This is a very important concession for the house purchaser and it constitutes a very significant effective subsidy, stimulating the demand for private housing.

Corporation tax is levied on the profits of firms and although the basic rate of this tax is set higher than that of income tax, the yield to the government from corporation tax is comparatively small. This low yield arises from the volatile nature of company profits and also from the fact that firms can claim a large number of allowances to offset against tax when they undertake investments. These capital allowances have been especially important for firms undertaking industrial and commercial building work. In 1986 several of these capital allowances were removed by the UK government and firms were compensated by a reduction in the basic rate at which corporation tax is paid. The expected result of this change is that the government will collect more revenue from corporation tax, but firms may have less incentive to invest in new buildings.

In recent years, government taxation has been significantly boosted by revenues from North Sea oil operations. Table 2.6 indicates how by 1985 the combined income taxes derived from North Sea oil accounted for more than 5% of all government revenue. Without this comparatively new source of income the burden of taxation would fall more heavily on consumers.

Local authority rates

Revenue from local authority rates is a direct tax on property and, together with grant aid from central government and revenue from rents and charges for various local services, it constitutes a prime source of local authority income. Rates are essentially a local tax paid as a contribution to local services. The rateable value of a property is assessed and the actual number of pence in the pound rates, which are levied against the rateable value, are fixed annually by individual local authorities. In recent years, rates in many areas have been increasing more rapidly than inflation and so the real cost of maintaining property has risen. Rates fall unevenly upon different classes of taxpayer. Rates for business users are higher than those for householders, but while the businessman can offset rates against direct tax, the domestic ratepayer has no such relief. Relatively high rates are a disincentive to new building work as well as changes to a property which may increase its rateable value— meaning higher annual rates bills. On the other hand, it must be remembered that local authorities use some of the income from rates for spending on construction activity in the public sector.

National insurance charges

National insurance and health contributions now constitute the second most important source of government revenue, after income tax. At each annual budget, national insurance contributions are increased at least in line with inflation, and during the early 1980s a surcharge was added to these contributions, enhancing further the yield from this tax. For the most part, national insurance charges are levied as a percentage of gross income and the effect is similar to income tax. The surcharge in national insurance fell on employers and was widely viewed as a tax on jobs. In the construction sector, the existence of this surcharge provided further incentive for workers to become self-employed.

Expenditure (indirect) taxation

Of the expenditure taxes, Value-Added Tax (VAT) has come to have the most significance for the construction industry. VAT is an *ad valorem* tax, which means that it is levied as a percentage of the value of a product or service; as such, the revenue from this tax rises in line with inflation. Since the introduction of VAT in 1973 it has been applied to an increasingly wider range of goods and services. At present, VAT is not applied to new building work or to house sales, but in 1984 VAT was extended to cover alterations to existing buildings, dwellings and civil engineering works. In this way the cost of improvement work carried out by contractors has been increased and the advantage enjoyed by registered building firms over firms and individuals operating in the 'black' economy and the do-it-yourself market has been eroded.

While VAT is the main expenditure tax used to raise revenue, duties on alcohol, tobacco and hydrocarbon oils (i.e. petrol) are a very important and long-standing source of income for the UK government. In addition, taxes on betting, car sales and imported goods yield significant amounts of revenues; motor vehicle duties and, more recently, a levy on gas sales are also important. The stamp duty levied on house sales is of special significance to the construction industry; in recent years, the rate at which this duty has been levied has been reduced, so that a uniform rate of only 1% is charged on all house purchases in excess of £30,000.

Other sources of revenue

Besides taxes and national insurance, the government derives revenue from rents, profits, interest and dividends. Local government derives revenue from the renting of council houses and the operation of local services for which a charge is made. The government remains a large shareholder in a number of public companies and dividend income is obtained on these shares. Equally, the government makes loans to public corporations and a few private companies, on which interest accrues. Taxes on capital have been in existence in the UK for longer than taxes on income, but, as Table 2.6 indicates, such taxes do not constitute a major source of revenue. Capital gains and capital transfer taxes are the principal types of tax on capital.

Current expenditure

Government expenditure is a very important component of aggregate demand and it is annually subject to many fine adjustments, some of which have implications for the construction sector. The main division in expenditure is between current and capital spending; the latter has a special significance for the construction sector. Table 2.6 shows how in 1985 current expenditure composed 82% of total spending. In the 1980s current expenditure has shown a persistent tendency to increase at the expense of capital expenditure and this has led to reductions in public sector construction work.

Most current expenditure is absorbed in paying the wages and salaries of those who work in the public sector, and in paying grants and benefits to pensioners, the unemployed, students and all who qualify for state assistance. Table 2.6 indicates some of the main categories of current government spending. Within these categories some part of the expenditure produces demand for construction work. Within the current expenditure total given for military defence, most new construction work is incorporated. Equally, some of the current expenditure of the Health Service and also of the local authorities consists of spending on the repair and maintenance of buildings and dwellings. Within that component of current expenditure which is given over to subsidies, part of this spending goes towards the subsidisation of housing. In this way the government, by effectively reducing the cost of housing, is encouraging demand.

As unemployment has increased in the UK in recent years, social security benefit payments have taken an increasing share of total expenditure. In 1973 such payments formed only 18% of total expenditure, but by 1985 this figure had increased to almost 24%. Government attempts to limit current expenditure by reducing jobs in the public sector often only succeed in switching expenditure out of one category into another (the social security category) when the displaced persons fail to find new employment. The UK government usually finds it far easier to reduce capital spending programmes than to trim current expenditure.

A large and significant category of expenditure is the interest which government must pay on its accumulated debts. As a result of persistently spending more than it receives in revenues, the UK government has to borrow from the private sector, both at home and abroad. The debt so incurred must be serviced each year in the form of interest payments on the outstanding loans. This debt interest goes on growing over time, as each year the government spends more than it receives in revenue, incurring a budget deficit and creating the need for a public sector borrowing requirement (PSBR). Table 2.6 indicates how in 1985 this PSBR stood at some £10.9 billion. When government attempts to reduce the size of the PSBR, it can either increase revenue, reduce current expenditure or cut back on capital spending. In practice, while all three approaches are used, reductions in capital spending often prove the easiest option to implement.

Capital expenditure

There are two main categories of capital expenditure. First, the government undertakes direct investment in the provision of public housing (through the local authorities), roads, hospitals, schools, higher education establishments, military buildings, other local and central government buildings, and factory buildings for the nationalised industries; general infrastructure provision also involves direct expenditure. Secondly, the government makes capital grants to the private sector to enable investment to take place; these grants are made to private sector firms (often as part of regional aid incentives) as well as to housing associations and to householders, for improvements to dwellings. A large part of such capital spending is directed towards buildings and works, although expenditure on plant, machinery and vehicles is also incorporated within this. Changes in both the level and composition of these capital expenditures are therefore highly significant for the construction industry.

When the government sells off a publicly-owned capital asset, such as British Telecom (shares floated in 1984) or British Gas (1986), the proceeds from the sale are used to reduce the level of capital expenditure. In the 1980s, revenue from the sale of public corporations has become very significant and such capital receipts are important in financing new state expenditure. Without these sales, the government would need to borrow more in order to close the gap arising from total expenditure exceeding revenue.

The government multiplier

If the government decides to increase its expenditure without increasing its revenue, it is clear that GNP will be increased (see pp. 23–6). It is perhaps not quite so obvious that a net increase in such expenditure will cause a 'multiplier impact' on the level of national output. The effect of an increase in government spending of £100 million is to raise national output by much more than the initial £100 million injection. Such a result will also occur from other injections into the circular flow, such as an increase in private sector investment or a higher level of exports. Equally, if withdrawals from the circular flow are increased, through higher levels of net taxation, savings or imports, then negative multiplier impacts are exerted on national output.

The concept of the multiplier arises from the observation that one person's expenditure constitutes another person's income. If the government were to initiate and invest in the building of a new motorway then the initial payments would be made to the design engineers, the contractors and the materials suppliers. The employees of each of the firms involved in the project would then spend a high proportion of the income they receive and in this way they would enhance the income of a second group in the economy—the landlords, retailers and hoteliers. In turn this second group would also spend a significant proportion of their extra income on various goods and services. Hence the value of the initial investment is multiplied by successive rounds of spending and the growth in national income is only checked by leakages out of the economic system. In practice the value of the multiplier is reduced by government taxation, by spending on imported goods and by savings. A much fuller appreciation of the workings of the multiplier can be obtained from Brooman[3].

When the government is seeking to increase aggregate demand it might choose to do so by either increasing expenditure or reducing taxation—or by a combination of both. However, the multiplier impact associated with an increase in net expenditure of a given value tends to be greater than the impact derived from a decrease in income tax of equivalent magnitude. This difference occurs because not all of the increase in income resulting from reduced taxation will be spent. Some of it will be saved and so the value of the income tax multiplier will be lower than that of the government expenditure multiplier. Such a difference means that the government can simultaneously increase expenditure and taxation by the same amount, so that its budget position remains balanced—and yet the overall result is an increase in national income. This balanced budget multiplier provides a justification for government increases in taxation on the one hand and the use of the proceeds to increase expenditure on the other. The result for the economy is an expansion of the gross national product.

4. Monetary policy

The second main method for manipulating aggregate demand is through monetary policy, a government's use of interest rates and credit availability, together with its control of the money supply. In the post-war period up to 1970, monetary policy was considered to be much less important than fiscal policy and was generally used to assist the balance of payments rather than to influence the domestic components of demand. Since 1970 the role of monetary policy has been brought into prominence and it is now widely regarded as essential for the regulation of output, employment and especially prices. The impact of monetary policy on the construction sector is considerable, as interest rates are important determinants of the willingness and ability to undertake investment in buildings and dwellings. Most construction work is financed by loan capital and where monetary policy tightens the availability of loans and raises the cost of borrowing, demand for construction is likely to be significantly reduced.

Measurement of the money stock

Monetary policy in the UK has undergone several significant changes since its re-establishment as a major policy in 1971. The major objective of the government's approach to money in the economy is the control of its supply. Various definitions of money may be used and some of the more popular definitions are presented in Table 2.7. The government, acting through its monetary agent, the Bank of England, attempts to regulate the annual rate of growth in one or other of the various monetary aggregates. Traditionally, attention has concentrated on 'Sterling M3'; this involves regulating not only the flow of notes and coins in circulation but, of much greater significance, the growth in both the private and the public sector's bank deposits. In recent years such regulation has proved very difficult and the government has switched its attention to simpler aggregates, such as 'MO'.

2.7   *Money stock in the UK, as at December 1986*

Measure	Components	Value (£million)
MO	Mainly coins and currency in circulation plus currency at Bank of England	£15,956
M1	Notes and coins in circulation plus private sector sterling current deposits of UK residents in UK banks	£75,194
Sterling M3	M1 components plus all other private and public sector sterling deposits in UK banks	£151,680
Total M3	Sterling M3 components plus all deposits held with UK Banks by UK residents in non-sterling currency	£180,267
M2	Coins and currency in circulation plus sterling 'retail' deposits held by the private sector in UK banks, building societies and National Savings Bank ordinary accounts	£169,411
PSL2	Sterling M3 components plus other liquid deposits held by the private sector in UK building societies and the National Savings Bank	£276,035

Source: *Financial Statistics*, CSO (monthly)

Control of bank deposits

By far the largest component of money supply is formed by deposits in bank accounts. Banks are able to expand the money supply by accepting deposits from customers and then using such deposits to make loans to new clients. When these new clients spend their loans, much of this money is returned to the banking system in the form of new deposits and the process is able to continue, unless the newly loaned funds leak outside the banking system. In order to control the money supply, the government must be able to either regulate the deposits of the banking sector or to limit the loans made by the banks. In practice a wide range of measures are adopted to achieve this objective.

In the period 1974–80, the UK government attempted to control bank deposits by placing ceilings on the banks' interest-bearing deposits. This scheme was known as the Supplementary Special Deposits Scheme or, more popularly, 'The Corset', the scheme

being a device to squeeze a fat lady. If banks exceeded the
stipulated growth quota they were obliged to lodge excess deposits
with the Bank of England as an interest-free deposit. Such a
measure was relatively successful in the short term but it was soon
found that such ceilings were easily evaded. In theory, it is also
possible for the government to cause banks to pay a significantly
lower rate of interest on deposits than that offered by other financial
institutions such as building societies. The effect of this approach
would be to cause depositors to reduce their bank deposits and
lodge their money elsewhere. In this way the 'M3' measure of
money would be reduced but not the wider measures such as 'PSL2'
(see Table 2.7). In practice, the government does not employ this
method of regulation.

Control of bank lending

Perhaps the most obvious approach to controlling the money supply
is for the government to restrict bank loans to the private sector. In
practice it is much easier to regulate loans than to limit deposits. In
the period 1952–71 the main method of monetary control was the
setting of selective ceilings on bank lending. This measure was
reinforced by restrictions on credit in the form of hire purchase
finance. Usually, limits are placed on the minimum percentage
deposit required when buying a durable good on hire purchase, and
a maximum payback period is also stipulated. Faced with such
ceilings, banks usually discriminate in favour of preferred
customers; inevitably these are the larger firms and the wealthier
individuals. Small firms, in particular, such as are commonplace in
the construction sector, may often be squeezed out of the queue for
loans. Higher-risk customers are more likely to go away empty-
handed, despite their apparent willingness to incur higher interest
costs as the price to be paid for obtaining the loan. Firms and
individuals who fail to get loan finance at the banks are forced to
look outside the banking sector, where the cost of borrowing is
inevitably much higher. In more recent years, although some hire
purchase restraints remain, quantity restrictions on bank loans have
been abandoned, because they are thought to be unfair to smaller
customers and, at the end of the day, an ineffective method of
limiting money supply growth.

Changes in interest rates

Far more popular as a means of limiting bank lending to the private
sector has been the use of interest rates to discourage private
demand for loans, by putting a higher price on borrowing. In the

period 1971–3 variations in interest rates were adopted as the prime control on the money supply. The government introduced the Minimum Lending Rate (MLR)—the fixed price at which the Bank of England was prepared to lend to the banking system, by way of the money market. Changes in this Minimum Lending Rate meant changes in interest rates in the banking sector, charged to loan customers. Control of the money supply by interest rate variations alone was not deemed a success, and in 1981 the government appeared to abandon MLR as an indicator to the banking sector of the appropriate level of interest rates. Nevertheless, the government, through the Bank of England, remains actively involved in the setting of bank interest rates and informal guidance is given to the banking system on the need for changes. Where circumstances arise such that the banks fail to respond to informal promptings, the government will intervene to force market interest rates to new levels.

The construction sector is especially sensitive to changes in the general level of interest rates. All sorts of construction work is financed by loan capital and an increase in the price of borrowing is likely to lead to delays in commissioning new work or to a reduction in sales of speculative buildings and dwellings. High bank interest rates usually result, although often with some delay, in higher mortgage rates, and this rapidly chokes off some of the demand for private dwellings.

Higher rates will also affect the property developer and the industrial client, who is especially sensitive to changes in interest rates. Public clients will not be anxious to take out loans at fixed interest rates when the general level of such rates is relatively high.

Use of PSBR to control money supply

Banks not only lend to private sector customers, but also to the public sector. Whenever government fiscal expenditure exceeds revenue, a public sector borrowing requirement (PSBR) is created; when this overspending is funded by bank borrowing, the money supply will be increased. Gowland[4] has pointed out that since 1974 variations in the PSBR have become a major weapon of monetary policy in the UK and that the major concern about PSBR has been over its monetary rather than its fiscal effects. In an attempt to restrict the growth of the money supply, the government has imposed cash limits on the PSBR. As discussed earlier (see pp. 39–40), such a restraint tends to have particularly severe implications for the construction industry, because of its effect on public sector investment in buildings and works.

Open-market operations

A government is able to reduce its borrowings from the banking sector, and hence the growth in the money supply, when it is able to borrow from private individuals. The most obvious ways in which the UK government borrows directly from the private sector are through national savings, through sales of gilt-edged securities (longer-term government bonds) and through sales of local authority bonds. Since 1974 the government has vigorously promoted the open-market sales of government bonds. The offer price of these bonds is set sufficiently low so as to render them a very competitive investment. If private individuals draw on their bank accounts in order to purchase the bonds (or national savings certificates), bank deposits will be reduced and hence the money supply will be checked. However, if private investors choose to take out bank loans with which to purchase government securities, these open-market sales will not be effective in controlling the growth of the money supply. Where bank deposits are squeezed as a result of open-market sales, banks may be forced to restrict loans to the private sector. In this way, government borrowing is said to 'crowd-out' private sector borrowing. Banks will often seek to protect their deposits, in the face of open-market sales, by raising interest rates. Clearly such open-market sales have a damaging effect on the private borrower, through restricted bank lending, higher interest rates, or a combination of both.

Monetary policy and the balance of payments

Whenever a bank increases its net sterling loans to foreign customers, or when sterling is supplied to acquire foreign assets, the money supply is increased. If the country is running a balance of payments deficit this will initially help to control the money supply, because deposits from UK residents will be transferred into foreign bank accounts and so the capacity of UK banks to make loans is restricted. However, in order to rectify this deficit, UK interest rates will be raised (see pp. 51–4) and new deposits will be attracted. If, in addition to this, the monetary authorities choose to defend the exchange rate by supplying sterling, this will serve to increase the money supply. When a country is experiencing a significant surplus on its balance of payments its money supply will be increasing and so it becomes very difficult to control this component of monetary growth.

Other monetary controls

It is clear from the above that there are several methods for controlling the money supply and the application of these various techniques carries implications for the construction industry. In addition to the methods described, other control techniques are available. It is possible for the Bank of England to apply a strict reserve-base system to the banking sector. In such a system, banks are required to maintain a minimum proportion of their assets in the form of reserve or liquid assets. A loose form of this control was used over the period 1971–81, but the Bank of England never made it a binding restraint. It is sometimes claimed that money supply can be regulated by the government not printing bank notes. However, as Table 2.7 shows, currency in circulation is only a very small part of the total money supply and a shortage of bank notes, while causing considerable inconvenience, can be easily overcome by the use of bank deposits.

The impact of monetary policy

Monetary policy has become more important in recent years because of its claimed effectiveness in regulating price inflation. In the early 1980s many officials in both government and the civil service held 'monetarist' views about the economy. Strictly speaking, a monetarist is someone who believes that a 1% change in the money supply will always lead to an equivalent 1% change in nominal income in the medium term. If real income does not change, then the whole of the increase in nominal income will be reflected in a 1% increase in prices. While in practice this relationship, because of definitional and timing problems, has been hard to prove, there is undoubtedly a significant link between the amount of money in the economy and the general level of prices. Monetary policy remains very difficult to implement with any degree of precision and in the mid-1980s the UK government appeared to have recognised this limitation. Apart from the various definitions of money and the problem of deciding which aggregate ought to be controlled, there remains the issue of an adequate definition of the banking sector. The banking sector on which monetary policy is currently concentrated was redefined in the 1979 Banking Act; a description of this sector can be found in Gibson[5].

Firms in the construction sector are particularly sensitive to changes in monetary variables—especially to rises in interest rates. Apart from the impact on customer demand, higher interest rates cause profitability and liquidity problems for many building firms. Many companies may attempt to pass on higher interest charges in the form of higher prices; this may serve to reduce demand still further. Faced with declining orders, firms may be tempted to cut tender prices to compete more effectively and this will result in lower profitability. For those firms which are heavily dependent on loan finance the extra interest costs may damage cash-flow and lead to liquidity problems. Customers are likely to be slower in paying their bills and merchants may press for more rapid payment as the cost of borrowing money rises. Many small firms faced with this situation go into liquidation every year.

5. Balance of payments policy

Almost all fiscal and monetary changes will to some extent affect the UK balance of payments. However, there also exists a set of policies which is specifically concerned with directing trade flows. The most obvious of these policies is the management of the exchange rate, but policies on import tariffs, export subsidies and capital movements through exchange controls are also important for the balance of payments. The construction sector is a significant importer of raw materials, particularly timber. Equally, UK construction firms who carry out projects overseas are exporting their services. Changes in the balance of payments policy will have direct implications for the construction industry. In addition, policy changes which are made in the first instance to influence external trade and capital movements may also lead to adjustments in the domestic economy and so produce an indirect impact on the derived demand for construction output.

UK balance of payments

The balance of payments is a summary statement of the value of all economic transactions between residents of a country and those of the rest of the world. The UK's balance of payments for 1985 is summarised in Table 2.8. All items which create a sterling receipt into the UK are positively recorded, while those which produce a payment out of the UK are recorded negatively. There are several types of balances shown within the summary statement, although the overall balance corresponds to the balance for official financing, since if this balance is negative, this deficit will have to be financed by the government. In general, balance of payments policy aims to avoid incurring significant and persistent deficits on the balance for official financing.

Table 2.8 indicates the nature of the main components which make up the overall balance. The current account consists of a balance of visible items, the difference between the export and import of goods, and a balance of invisible items, the difference between the export and import of services and financial items. In

2.8   Analysis of UK balance of payments for 1985

	(£ million)	
Current Account		
Visible Items: Net Balances		
Food, beverages and tobacco	−3,592	
Basic materials	−2,634	
Mineral fuels and oils	6,625	
Semi-manufactured goods	185	
Finished manufactured goods	−3,102	
Unclassified items	507	
Total visibles		−2,111
Invisible Items: Net Balances		
Services	5,812	
Interest, profits and dividends	3,400	
Transfers	−3,499	
Total invisibles		5,713
Current account balance		3,602
Capital Account		
Net investments	−15,092	
Net bank transactions	6,358	
Net government and other transactions	3,196	
Total investment and other capital transactions		−5,538
Balancing items (unallocated)		3,694
Balance for official financing		1,758
(+ represents an addition to official reserves)		

Source: UK Balance of Payments: CSO Pink Book, HMSO, 1986

the post-war period up to 1976 the UK experienced recurring high deficits on the balance of visible trade, but since 1976 the revenue earned from North Sea oil and gas production has produced some reduction in the size of this problem. The UK is a consistent net importer of foodstuffs and basic raw materials; until recently it also tended to be a net importer of oils and other mineral fuels. Traditionally, the UK has paid for such imports by exporting manufacturing goods—in which it enjoyed a comparative advantage. However, in recent years, this advantage has been progressively eroded and, as can be seen, in 1985 the UK was a net importer of manufactured goods. Only the large exports of North Sea oil and gas prevent the visible trade account from showing a very high deficit.

The UK has for many years enjoyed a positive balance on its trade in invisibles and before the advent of North Sea oil this surplus was critical for overall balance. In particular, the UK has strong net earnings from its financial services, tourism and income received in investments made abroad by UK residents. In the future the surplus on invisible trade is likely to grow, as in the UK comparative trade advantages accrue more in service industries than in manufacturing products. The 1985 surplus on invisibles more than compensates for the deficit on visible trade.

The balance of payments statistics are concerned with all transactions made between UK residents and those of the rest of the world, so many transactions do not involve payments for goods and services. Capital transactions involve the movement of funds between countries for a variety of both short- and long-term purposes. When such capital flows into the UK it is positively recorded and, although a capital import, it adds to the balance of payments. Equally, when UK residents invest capital in other countries, this constitutes a capital export and is negatively recorded. The UK residents receive income in the form of interest and dividends upon these investments and this income later adds to the invisible trade balance; the act of investing the capital sum overseas leads to a deficit entry on the capital account balance.

Balances on the capital account are a very volatile component of the overall balance of payments. Capital flows in response to the relative rates of interest that can be earned in the UK compared to those in other countries—after allowing for the effects of risk and taxation. The capital account for 1985 indicates how on balance more capital left the UK than was received. In particular, UK residents made longer-term capital investments abroad and although some shorter-term money, in the form of bank deposits, flowed into the UK, the net effect was a significantly large deficit on the capital balance. Changes in interest rates can cause very rapid fluctuations in international capital flows, but as already explained (pp. 44–5), such changes carry profound implications for control of the money supply—and so for the management of the domestic economy. Changes in exchange rates are another important determinant of short-term capital flows.

When the balances on the two current accounts are taken together with the capital account balance, and when allowance is made for the balancing item (a statistical item to compensate for all measurement errors and omissions in the accounts), the balance for official financing is determined. In 1985 there was an overall surplus, after taking account of the large positive balancing item. This surplus enabled the authorities to increase the UK's existing reserves of gold and currency. Where any loans from the International Monetary Fund (IMF) remain outstanding, the surplus may be used to pay off these earlier debts.

Policies for correcting the balance of payments

While it is perfectly reasonable for a country which finds itself with a balance of payments deficit in any one year to either draw on its reserves or to increase its official borrowing, it cannot expect to sustain this position over a long period of time. Reserves are finite and if continuously depleted they will run out. Other countries, who provide the loan funds for the official borrowing, will not want to go on financing a deficit without any prospect of the borrower being able to pay back the loans. The debtor nation must take steps to rectify the balance of payments deficit. Although in recent years the UK has managed to avoid being in overall deficit, its balance on visible trade remains unhealthy, and sudden changes in capital flows can rapidly change a surplus into a deficit situation.

Changes in the exchange rate

The most obvious policy for keeping external payments in balance is to change the rate at which the country's currency is traded with the currencies of other countries. Since 1972 the sterling exchange rate has floated against the other major world currencies. In theory, a freely floating exchange rate will work automatically to correct balance of payments disequilibria in the long run. If the UK has a trade deficit this implies that UK residents have spent more on imports than residents of other countries have spent on UK exports. There will therefore be an excess supply of sterling, relative to its demand, provided to pay for the higher imports. This excess supply will exert a downward pressure on the exchange rate, causing the value of the pound to fall in terms of other currencies. The lowering of the exchange rate will lower the international price of UK exports and raise the international price of UK imports. In theory, the balance of payments should move towards equilibrium as exports increase and imports decrease, following the law of demand (see next chapter).

In practice, the pound has not been allowed to float entirely without government intervention. It is open to governments to enter the currency markets and to use the national reserves to support a currency where its exchange value is felt to be depreciating too rapidly. In this instance, the country's central bank will actively enter the market as a buyer of the currency and will artificially increase the demand for it, thus stemming the fall in its exchange rate. In February 1985, when the pound was falling rapidly against the dollar, the Bank of England carried out such a supporting exercise. Unfortunately a floating exchange rate allows currency speculators to enter the market, buying or selling large quantities of a currency in anticipation of future gains. Such activity does not derive from balance of trade considerations and it can cause exchange rates to change very rapidly, meaning that the rates may well overshoot the values required to establish equilibrium in the balance of payments.

The main advantage of a floating exchange rate, as opposed to the fixed rates which existed between 1945 and 1972, is that it permits domestic economic policies to be pursued with more independence. As Metcalfe[6] has pointed out, an economy with a floating exchange rate tends to behave in the same manner as a closed economy, so that such an economy is far more sensitive to the repercussions of monetary and fiscal policy, meaning that domestic demand management needs to be conducted with much greater caution.

Use of interest rates

When a country's exchange rate is depreciating, a loss in real purchasing power occurs as the price of imports increases. Governments may often adopt other policy measures to prevent this erosion of the exchange rate. The most commonly adopted policy measure is the use of interest rates to improve the balance of payments and so defend the exchange rate. When interest rates in a country are high relative to those prevailing in other countries, short-term capital can be expected to flow into that country to earn the best return. The use of the Minimum Lending Rate to raise interest rates in the UK in January 1985 was carried out primarily to prevent further depreciation of the pound/dollar exchange rate. As Table 2.8 illustrates, an inflow of capital into the UK improves the balance of payments and so removes some of the pressure on the exchange rate. An alternative option to using interest rates in this way is to place exchange control limitations on the outward movement of capital. Throughout the post-war period until 1979 such exchange controls were actively employed in the UK in one form or another, but in 1979 all such limitations were relaxed. The result has been a large net outflow of investment capital in each year since controls were removed.

Use of import controls

It is sometimes argued that a country faced with balance of payments difficulties should introduce a system of import controls and export subsidies to rectify the deficit. There are many variant forms of import control which a country could, in theory, apply. These range from straightforward customs tariffs to physical quotas, currency controls on importers and administrative delays on imports which serve to discourage the foreign seller. For an open economy, such as that of the UK, the objections to such an approach are obvious: other countries could be expected to retaliate in kind against UK exports. Membership of the European Economic Community expressly forbids the use of tariffs between member countries and so the import control option is only available to the UK against countries outside the EEC. More generally, the use of tariffs is a discouragement to international trade, which can be shown to be beneficial to all countries.

Demand deflation

When fiscal and monetary policy are used to deflate domestic demand, such measures will usually be beneficial in the approach towards balance of payments equilibrium. In the UK a relatively high proportion of consumer spending is directed towards imported goods, so that policies which restrict consumer spending will also serve to limit imports. Equally, where monetary control works to limit the rate of inflation, UK goods are likely to become more competitive in price with their imported counterparts and some substitution of home-produced goods for imports might be expected. When UK producers are faced with reduced demand for their products at home, as a result of deflationary demand management, there will be an incentive to pursue more actively the export markets which could take up the consequent surplus production capacity. Conversely, attempts to inflate aggregate demand to eliminate unemployment may well cause imports to increase more rapidly than exports.

Impact on construction firms

Any construction company actively carrying out work overseas will be significantly affected by changes in the balance of payments when such changes lead to movements in the exchange rate. Most overseas contracts will be negotiated in currencies other than sterling, so that a depreciation in the sterling exchange rate means that such firms will earn more than they originally anticipated. However, movements in the exchange rate can also go the other way, as occurred when sterling appreciated against most other currencies in the early 1980s. In this situation, construction firms will earn less than expected and their international competitiveness will be seriously threatened.

Within the UK, construction firms who import a high proportion of their material requirements are particularly sensitive to exchange rate variations. Given the high proportion of timber which is imported, housebuilders concentrating on timber-frame construction were confronted with rapidly escalating costs as the sterling exchange rate depreciated over the period 1983–5. Equally, much plant used by contractors is also imported and the cost of buying and renting such plant rises when the exchange rate moves downwards.

When domestic interest rates are manipulated for the specific purpose of correcting the balance of payments, the impact on construction firms will be very significant. This impact has been described above (see pp. 47–8). Where exchange controls are actively applied, construction firms attempting to carry out overseas projects may be adversely affected.

6. Conflicts in policy objectives

Present-day governments have little difficulty in declaring their central policy objectives. As this chapter has made clear, there is a wide concensus of opinion that economic growth, full employment, price stability and equilibrium in the balance of payments are the main aims of macroeconomic management. One problem which arises is that attempts to pursue one or other of these objectives with full commitment often entails sacrificing one or more of the remaining objectives. In recent times, the most obvious conflict has arisen between full employment and the control of inflation. The pursuit of fuller employment also sometimes leads to conflicts with objectives in the areas of economic growth and balance of payments. The attempt to resolve these conflicts and to devise a set of policies which enable all the central objectives to be simultaneously realised has inevitably given rise to various radically different proposals. It has led many authors to conclude that macroeconomics in the 1980s is in a state of disarray (see for example Chrystal[7]). The disagreements focus not on the macroeconomic goals themselves, but rather on deep divisions in opinion about how the economy actually works.

Policy prior to 1970

During the period from 1930 until 1970 the conflicts between policy objectives in the UK were not apparent. The unemployment of the early 1930s occurred in an economy characterised by predominantly stable and even falling prices. The use of demand management to raise aggregate demand and so reduce unemployment did not result in significant increases in prices or wages. Rising employment levels provided a spur to investment, which produced economic growth. Under the system of fixed exchange rates which prevailed until 1972, periodic balance of payments deficits arose and, unless the government chose to devalue the exchange rate, some temporary reduction in aggregate demand was necessary to meet the balance of payments objectives. In consequence, the post-war period up until 1970 experienced a succession of 'stop-go' cycles and economic growth in the UK was not as high as that achieved in other developed western nations. However, until 1970, full employment was generally maintained, price increases were regarded as acceptable, persistent deficits on the balance of payments were avoided and some economic growth was achieved. The demand management techniques described earlier (pp. 32–5) predominated, and formed the generally accepted strategy for realising the central macroeconomic objectives.

Policy changes in the 1970s

In the 1970s, relationships at the macroeconomic scale underwent a significant change and almost all countries began to suffer from high rates of inflation. Not only did price inflation become a serious problem, but it was often associated with high rates of unemployment. High inflation in the UK led to balance of payments problems in the early 1970s and in the second part of the decade economic growth was seriously affected. The suitability of demand management for dealing with this situation was called into question.

Demand management, as practised in the 1960s, recognised the inflationary consequences of attempts to manage the economy at close to its full employment limits. The nature of the trade-off between unemployment and inflation is conveniently summarised in the Phillips curve (named after its originator), shown in Fig. 2.5. This diagram, based on actual observations of the relationship between unemployment and wage inflation, indicates how when unemployment is relatively high—usually taken as 5% or more in the 1960s—there will be zero inflation. When attempts are made to reduce unemployment from this relatively high level the result will be an increase in inflation, although the rate of this will only become severe as full employment is approached. There is nothing in the basic Phillips curve model which suggests that both high inflation and high unemployment can occur simultaneously. In the 1970s, when high inflation began to manifest itself in many economies, governments set about reducing aggregate demand to allow higher levels of unemployment to check the inflationary pressures. By 1980 it was obvious that only very high levels of unemployment would be sufficient to slow the growth of inflation. The Phillips curve model no longer seemed valid. Moreover, the technique of demand management no longer appeared appropriate to dealing with this new situation.

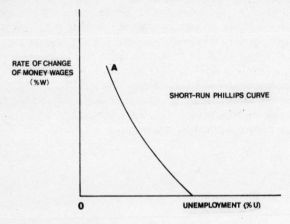

Fig. 2.5 *The basic Phillips curve*

Policy conflicts in the 1980s

Inflation had become the predominant concern of governments by the early 1980s. Many of the cost influences on the general level of prices, such as the increasing cost of oil and other key imported materials, lay beyond the power of the UK government to constrain. However, it was widely believed that even where significant unemployment already existed, too high a level of aggregate demand in the economy could contribute to inflation. Demand management was to be used, not as originally intended, to maintain high levels of aggregate demand, but rather to constrain existing demand. In particular, cash limits on the public sector borrowing requirement were used to achieve this end.

If the Phillips curve is amended to allow for the impact of inflationary expectations on those in work, an insight can be gained into how high unemployment and high inflation can co-exist. In Fig. 2.6, two short-run curves are shown. The original curve, labelled A, is that associated with zero expected inflation. If unemployment is maintained at the level U*, wages will remain perfectly stable, but if government increases demand to achieve a lower level of unemployment, such as U1, wages will increase to level W1. In the next time-period those bargaining for higher wages will note the recent increase and will build this inflationary component into their wage demand. In this way, inflationary expectations cause the short-run Phillips curve to shift to a higher position, such as that of curve B. On this higher curve, wages have now increased to level W2, while unemployment remains at U1. This trade-off of higher inflation for more jobs might be acceptable if the position was stable. However, once all prices in the economy are raised in line with the wage increases, the increase in aggregate demand will be absorbed entirely in price changes, and unemployment is likely to return to its original level, U*. The short-run Phillips curve only offers a temporary trade-off between inflation and unemployment. Once inflationary expectations have been realised, unemployment drifts upwards again. It can be seen how the long-run Phillips curve, which traces out points of stable inflation, is a vertical line corresponding to the original level of unemployment, U*.

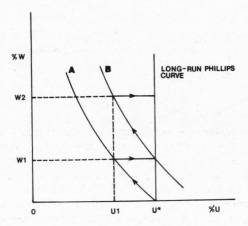

Fig. 2.6 *Phillips curves with inflation expectations*

This level of unemployment, which is compatible with long-run price stability, has been termed the 'natural' rate of unemployment. Any attempt to manage demand to push unemployment below this natural rate will provoke inflation and so bring the two central policy objectives into conflict. While no one can say with any certainty exactly what level of unemployment corresponds to this 'natural' rate, the critical rate is thought to be much higher in the

1980s than it was even a decade earlier. So, in the interests of maintaining more stable prices, present-day governments do not vigorously pursue the full employment objective, nor do they utilise the demand management concept to its full extent.

In the 1980s the UK government has sought to control inflation not only by restricting aggregate demand, but also by carefully controlling the growth of the money supply. This has meant that public sector capital expenditure has been much reduced in real terms; thus contractors' output in this sector has fallen significantly. At the same time, the restrictive monetary policy has led to a régime of much higher interest rates than was previously experienced and this has caused additional difficulties for building firms. A return to higher levels of aggregate demand and a more expansionist monetary policy would clearly be beneficial to the construction sector, but, given the present orthodoxy of macroeconomic policy, such a turnaround is unlikely.

To try to induce higher levels of economic growth in a period when aggregate demand is so constrained, a government concentrates on expanding the supply side of the economy, providing incentives to workers to supply their labour skills and on firms to improve their productivity, thus supplying the market more efficiently. In practice, the government uses tax incentives to increase aggregate supply in this way. Fiscal policy focuses on reductions in income and corporation tax and lower national insurance contributions. These measures, which aid supply, are considered more desirable than expenditure increases which stimulate demand. In practice, private sector firms are expected to be the beneficiaries of such an approach. Contractors might expect an increase in the demand for private industrial and commercial buildings to offset reductions in the demand for public sector work.

Questions

1. Describe the circular flow of income in a simple economy and outline three methods for measuring the gross national product of such an economy.
2. Outline the nature of leakages and injections which occur in the circular flow of income in an open economy with a government sector.
3. Discuss your understanding of the following terms:
   (a) gross national product at factor cost
   (b) value-added output
   (c) gross domestic product at market prices.

4. Explain the central macroeconomic objectives of any present-day economy.
5. Use the statistics in Tables 2.2, 2.3, 2.4 and 2.5 to assess how far recent UK governments have been successful in realising the central objectives.
6. Explain what you understand by the term 'demand management' and analyse the impact of aggregate demand on levels of employment in an economy.
7. Discuss the main ways in which changes in taxation policy affect the demand for construction work.
8. Explain your understanding of the Public Sector Borrowing Requirement and in so doing comment on its relevance to demand for new construction work arising from the public sector.
9. Why will an increase in government expenditure, net of revenue, exert a multiplier impact on the national economy?
10. How does an increase in the general level of interest rates in the economy affect construction firms?
11. Discuss some of the problems the Bank of England faces in trying to accurately control the growth of the money supply in the UK economy.
12. Outline the main techniques that have been used in recent years for controlling the money supply.
13. Describe the composition of the UK balance of payments and establish the significance of oil export revenues to the balance of trade in the 1980s.
14. Identify those policies which are most commonly used to correct any balance of payments deficit and briefly explain the consequences of each for the construction sector.
15. Explain the nature of the conflict between the full employment objective and the objective of stable prices.
16. Why have governments in the 1980s not attempted to push the UK economy back towards full employment?

Further Reading

ALDCROFT, D. H., *Full Employment: The Elusive Goal*, Wheatsheaf Books, 1984
ALLEN, R. G. D., *Introduction to National Accounts Statistics*, Macmillan 1980
BEGG, D., FISCHER, S. and DORNBUSCH, R., *Economics*, Part 4, McGraw-Hill, 1987
BLACK, J., *The Economics of Modern Britain*, Basil Blackwell, 1985
BROOMAN, F. S., *Macroeconomics*, Allen and Unwin, 1981

BURNINGHAM, D., *Understanding Economics*, Part 2, Hodder and Stoughton, 1984

CROWSON, P. C. F., *Economics for Managers*, Chapter 5, Macmillan, 1985

GOWLAND, D., *Controlling the Money Supply*, Croom-Helm, 1984

GREENAWAY, D. and SHAW, G. K., *Macroeconomics: Theory and Policy in the UK*, Part 3, Martin Robertson, 1983

JACKSON, D., *Introduction to Economics: Theory and Data*, Chapter 2, Macmillan, 1982

LIPSEY, R. G., *An Introduction to Positive Economics*, Part 10, Weidenfeld and Nicolson, 1983

PREST, A. R. and COPPOCK, D. J. *The UK Economy*, Chapters 1, 2 and 3, Weidenfeld and Nicolson, 1986

ROWAN, D. C., *Output, Inflation and Growth*, Part VI, Macmillan, 1983

STANLAKE, G. F., *Macroeconomics: An Introduction*, Longman, 1984

3 Basic Economics of the Construction Firm: Supply and Demand Analysis

1. Types of firm and their organisation

Construction output is produced by two main types of organisation: the private contracting firm and the direct labour organisations of the public authorities. The private sector is the dominant producer, with the DLOs typically contributing only about 10–15% of the total output. In terms of employment, the DLOs are rather more important and as Table 1.2 (p. 5) indicates, the public sector accounts for almost a quarter of all construction employees in employment.

The structure of private contracting firms

The contracting industry is highly fragmented and the dominant firm is the very small unit. While all types of firm are well represented in the industry, in terms of numbers alone the small firm predominates. Table 3.1 shows how in 1985 over 40% of all construction firms employed only one employee. If the conventional definition of a small firm (one employing less than 25 employees) is adopted, then 97% of the construction sector consists of small firms. The statistics produced by the Department of the Environment suggest, at first sight, that the numerical importance of the small firm is increasing over time. However, this apparent trend is largely attributable to an extension of the DOE survey specifically to incorporate more small firms in recent years. Indeed, as Hillebrandt[1] has claimed, it is difficult to make any satisfactory statement about the change over time of the number of firms and their size distribution in the industry because of discontinuities in the data series.

While small firms dominate the construction sector in terms of numbers, they are not so important in terms of either the amount of work done or in the amount of employment they create. Table 3.1 indicates how small firms employing less than 25 employees carried

3.1   *Structure of private contracting firms in Great Britain, October 1985*

Size of Firm No. of employees	Number of Firms		Work Done[1]		Total Employment	
	No.	% Total	£m	% Total	000	% Total
1	72,896	43.4	382.8	6.4	67.8	7.2
2–3	54,405	32.4	564.7	9.5	120.5	12.8
4–7	24,171	14.4	584.5	9.8	108.3	11.5
8–13	7,164	4.3	405.2	6.8	71.8	7.6
14–24	4,582	2.7	522.4	8.7	82.2	8.7
Less than 25	163,218	97.2	2459.6	41.2	450.6	47.8
25–114	3,849	2.3	1204.8	20.2	178.0	18.9
115–1,199	719	0.4	1530.4	25.6	203.9	21.7
1,200 and over	39	0.1	779.4	13.0	108.6	11.6
All firms	167,825	100.0	5974.2	100.0	941.1	100.0

Note: 1. Based on the value of work done in the third quarter of the year
Source: *Housing and Construction Statistics*

out 41% of all the construction work done in the survey period, and accounted for 48% of industry employment. In contrast, large firms (those employing over 115 employees) although only constituting 0.5% of the total numbers of firms, carried out 39% of the work done in the survey period and employed 34% of the workforce. In particular, the very large firms (those employing over 1200 employees) were few in number but crucial in terms of amount of work done and numbers employed. Differences in the nature of the work done by small and large firms are discussed in Chapter 5.

Sole trader firms

The most numerous type of firm found in the construction sector is the sole proprietor business. In this traditional form of enterprise a single person provides the capital, takes all the management decisions and, most significantly, incurs all the risks. The proprietor of such a firm has a direct personal interest in the business and as such the firm's fortunes closely correspond with those of the owner. The organisational structure of such a firm is simple and it is usually flexible enough to respond very rapidly to changing market conditions. Often the proprietor will be a self-employed craftsman and the firm may have no other employees. Equally, as market demand dictates, the proprietor may engage a small number of employees on either a permanent or temporary basis. By definition, sole proprietor businesses remain small, never employing more than a handful of employees.

Sole proprietor firms do not have limited liability; thus the owner is personally liable for the debts of the firm and in the event of the firm becoming insolvent, the owner stands to lose much of his personal wealth. A further problem with such a firm is its restricted financial basis. The only finance available to the firm is that which the proprietor provides, either from his own resources or from personal borrowing. Inevitably, many sole proprietor firms in the construction sector experience liquidity crises and the rate of insolvency is quite high. However, as one small firm disappears, so another rises to take its place. Construction is an easy sector to enter, and self-employed craftsmen find it relatively simple to set up sole proprietor firms with very little capital.

Partnerships

A logical development for the sole proprietor business is the partnership, whereby between two and 20 persons can combine together for trading purposes. As the sole proprietor firm seeks to grow, there is an urgent need for more capital and this need can be most readily met by introducing partners into the business. As well as increasing capital, partners can bring new management skills to the firm and thereby permit a greater degree of specialisation of function. Often, partners may be family members, or else they may simply be acquiring a financial interest in the business, sharing in the profits as a reward for supplying extra capital. In the latter case, the partner who does not participate in the active running of the firm is known as a 'sleeping partner'. Many examples of partnerships are to be found in the construction sector. Partnership is a common form of business organisation in professions such as architecture, surveying and engineering.

Most partnerships remain unlimited in law and, as in the case of the sole proprietor business, this means that each partner is fully liable for the debts of the firm. This is a serious constraint on a firm seeking to grow and taking risks in pursuit of greater profit. Often partnerships get into difficulties when the partners disagree or when one or other of the partners chooses to leave the business. Frequently, partnerships are dissolved upon the death of one of the partners. Inevitably, both partnerships and sole proprietor firms tend to be relatively unstable types of organisation.

Limited liability companies

Small firms seeking to grow commonly form themselves into private limited companies. Such a company consists of an association of people who contribute towards the joint stock capital of the company; their personal liability for the debts of the company is limited to the amount of this original contribution. The owners of the company are separate in law from the company itself, which engages in business, owns assets, incurs debts and enters into contracts entirely in its own right. Usually, a private limited company—as distinct from a public limited company—is a small firm with ownership restricted to a limited group of people, often members of one family. A private limited company cannot ask the general public to subscribe for its shares and because of this restraint, ownership remains restricted. Private limited companies are very popular in the UK—there are about 600,000 trading at present. The construction sector contains many private limited companies and some of these firms have become very large, with annual turnovers reckoned in millions of pounds.

Without the benefits of limited liability, it would be difficult to induce owners to contribute capital on the scale needed by most medium- and larger-sized firms. A succession of Companies Acts, dating back to 1844, have established the principle that it is no longer necessary to participate in a business in order to take a financial interest and have it safeguarded. Moreover, the limited liability company, with its transferable shares, facilitates the permanent use of capital for the firm and so ensures a greater degree of continuity. Where an owner in a limited liability firm dies, his rights to ownership can be sold without any withdrawal of capital from the firm. Limited liability does not insure against insolvency, but it facilitates the input of larger amounts of equity for the permanent use of the company.

The owners of the limited liability company are the shareholders who provide the capital for the firm; in a smaller private company these same owners will often be the managers too. However, where ownership has become extended, as will certainly be the case with a public limited company, ownership may become divorced from management. Directors are appointed by the shareholder-owners to manage on their behalf. Where owners are not completely in control of company policy a divergence of interests may well arise. This lack of control is the price which must be paid for a more stable form of business organisation.

Public limited companies

When a limited liability company can offer its shares for sale to members of the general public and so raise capital on a very wide basis, it achieves the status of a public limited company and will have the abbreviation 'Plc' after its name. Public companies are usually much larger firms than their private counterparts and, although there are only approximately some 15,000 such public companies in the UK, in terms of work done and numbers employed, they constitute the most important type of firm. Certainly the largest companies in the construction sector are all public limited companies, enjoying a share price quotation on the Stock Exchange. Ownership of these firms is widely spread although increasingly the majority of shares tend to be held by large institutions such as insurance companies and pension funds.

In Table 3.2 a listing of the 20 largest contracting firms in the UK in 1985/6 is provided. The criteria used for measuring size is annual turnover. It can be seen how George Wimpey, the largest firm, is more than eight times the size of Henry Boot and Son, the twentieth largest firm in the country. If the amount of capital employed were to be used as the criteria of size, Wimpey is at least 20 times bigger than Henry Boot. Compared to all the other thousands of firms in the private sector of the construction industry, these top 20 firms are

3.2 *The 20 largest construction firms in the UK (based on company reports for 1985/6)*

Firm	Turnover (£m)	Pre-tax profit (£m)	Capital employed (£m)
1 George Wimpey	1551	74	713
2 Tarmac	1536	149	655
3 Trafalgar House	1224[1]	78	—
4 Balfour Beatty	988[2]	27	—
5 Costain Group	805	74	388
6 John Laing	783	36	140
7 AMEC	751	26	118
8 Taylor Woodrow	739	55	507
9 Bovis	608[3]	50	—
10 Barratt Developments	538	32	327
11 C. H. Beazer (Holdings)	517[4]	39	251
12 John Mowlem	414	17	85
13 Alfred McAlpine	393	23	116
14 F. J. C. Lilley	357	13	98
15 Newarthill	274	18	211
16 London and Northern Group (Evered Holdings)	264	21	149
17 Y. J. Lovell (Holdings)	238	13	63
18 Norwest Holst Group	222	9	44
19 Higgs and Hill	192	9	52
20 Henry Boot and Sons	183	−6	33

Notes:
[1] Firm has interests outside construction; only construction results considered here.
[2] Part of BICC Group; results apply only to Balfour Beatty.
[3] Part of P & O Group; results apply only to Bovis.
[4] Combined results for C. H. Beazer and French Kier Holdings.
Source: The Times 1000, Times Books, 1986

very big indeed. In the context of all firms in the UK, however, these construction 'giants' are seen to be of quite modest size: even George Wimpey fails to qualify for a place in the ranking of the top 50 firms in the UK.

Large public limited companies tend to have relatively complex organisational structures. Most of these companies have established separate operating divisions, which reflect the wide diversity of their interests. Typically, the larger contractors have separate divisions for civil engineering, housing, property, overseas work and materials and plant supply. Usually, the largest public limited companies operate across all national regions and frequently they own associated companies in foreign countries. They grow not only by increasing turnover in established markets, but also through acquisition and mergers with other companies. The AMEC company, which in Table 3.2 appears as the seventh largest construction company, was created out of the merger in 1982 of two smaller firms—Fairclough and William Press. The construction interests of the third-ranked Trafalgar House have been developed through a series of takeovers of well-known construction firms, such as Cementation, and Trollope and Colls. The growth of Tarmac has been very rapid in the last twenty years and much of this growth is attributable to a programme of active acquisition of smaller firms.

The capital structure of a joint-stock company makes it easy for one company to acquire ownership of another. Often the capital of one company is used to purchase the capital of another, and only a very small amount of cash will be used to complete the transaction. Sometimes companies gain control of other firms by acquiring ownership of relatively small amounts of share capital. Larger public companies take over smaller private companies in this way. Large size is no guarantee against a possible takeover. In 1985 the comparatively small firm of C. H. Beazer successfully completed the takeover of the much larger and better known firm of French Kier, a company which enjoyed a top 20 ranking in its own right. Where large firms are struggling to make profits they are quite likely to attract the attentions of potential predators from other sectors of the economy. The sixteenth-ranked firm, London and Northern Group, was recently absorbed by a company in the engineering industry.

Consortia of firms

For very large contracts, especially those involving complex civil engineering work, it is common to find a number of contractors grouping together in a consortium to fulfil the contract. The Channel Tunnel scheme provides an obvious example of a project where the work involved—and the associated risks—are too great for any one individual firm. Frequently, consortia are to be found on high-value overseas projects and it is quite common for UK contractors to share the contract with leading foreign companies. The building of the Thames Barrier involved overseas companies combining with major UK construction firms. Sometimes the consortium arrangement may result in one firm taking the central role of managing contractor, whilst the other firms concentrate on specialist parts of the job. This type of consortium was used in the construction of Terminal 4 at Heathrow Airport.

Direct labour organisations (DLOs)

Public ownership in the construction industry is concentrated on the direct labour organisations run by various types of local authority. Langford[2] has provided a detailed history of the development of DLOs and their contribution to construction output. The first DLO was set up by the London County Council in 1892. It was not until the inter-war period that DLOs became widely established. Immediately after the Second World War DLOs were very active in both new building and repair and maintenance activity. It is recorded how the DLO sector built some 175,000 new dwellings in 1948. Since the 1950s the role of the DLOs has been more restricted, such that today DLO work concentrates primarily on repair and maintenance. Direct labour organisations tend to be favoured by Labour administrations, who support a public interest in construction production. Direct labour organisations are not so favourably regarded by Conservative administrations who favour the private firm sector and relegate the publicly owned DLOs to a minor role.

The current structure of DLOs in Great Britain is shown in Table 3.3. Most local authorities maintain a direct works division; a significant number of these divisions are comparatively large units employing over 250 operatives. Direct labour organisations also employ non-manual staff, but these are not usually counted for the purposes of analysing the structure of this sector. It can be seen how all types of local authority, from the very large down to the very small, maintain DLOs. In recent years, the number of local authorities operating DLOs has declined only slightly.

In comparison to the private sector firm, some important differences can be observed in the DLO operation. The DLO work-load is dominated by repair and maintenance activity; only the larger DLO units engage in new build, and then on only a modest scale. The DLO has traditionally maintained a repairs service for local authority housing, a sector of the construction

3.3   Structure of direct labour organisations in Great Britain, October 1985

By size of authority

Size of authority by number of employed operatives	Number	Work done[1] (£m)	Operatives employed[2] (000s)
1–30	76	8.3	1.7
31–99	177	50.2	11.1
100–249	137	96.9	20.9
250 and over	139	403.8	87.7
Total	529	559.2	121.4

By type of authority	Number	Work done	Operatives employed
Greater London Council	1	4.7	1.0
Metropolitan Counties	6	12.0	2.5
Non-Metropolitan Counties	47	105.4	17.9
London Boroughs	32	57.7	12.2
Metropolitan Districts	36	126.3	31.4
Non-Metropolitan Districts	331	163.7	36.9
Scottish Regional Councils	9	46.9	8.6
Scottish Island Area Councils	3	2.2	0.4
Scottish District Councils	49	37.3	9.8
All New Towns	15	3.0	0.8
Total	529	559.2	121.4

Notes:
[1] Based on the value of work done in the third quarter of the year.
[2] DLOs also employ non-manual staff but they are not included here.
Source: Housing and Construction Statistics

market which historically has not proved attractive or profitable to the private contractor. Prior to 1980, DLOs were not required to make any form of profit, but the Local Government, Planning and Land Act of 1980 created a new legal framework for DLO operations, such that DLOs must now achieve a specified rate of return on capital employed. DLOs are not free to compete for private sector work and, unlike private contractors, they cannot cross-subsidise one job against another. Any DLO which does not achieve the specified rate of return on capital in three consecutive years may be closed down by central government. Increasingly, local authorities are required to put out to general tender all work above prescribed minimum values and in this way the DLO is obliged to compete with private contractors for work which previously it would have been awarded on the basis of negotiation.

Direct labour organisations aim to offer secure and continuous employment to their workforce. This is in marked contrast to the casual employment which predominates in many private sector firms. Similarly, the DLOs insist on high standards of safety—and, likewise, on relatively high levels of training. The DLOs have evolved working rules agreements which are distinct from those found elsewhere in the industry. DLOs do not adjust their workforces in the same way as private firms and in consequence this has led to charges of over-staffing and low productivity; this point is examined in more detail in Chapter 12. For the most part the DLOs concentrate on different types of construction work to that carried out by most large private contractors and so productivity comparisons are difficult to draw. To sum up, DLOs are quite different in their organisation from the private firms in the construction sector.

2. Supply costs

The central objective of firms is usually taken to be the maximisation of profit. Whilst firms are often held to pursue a variety of objectives, such as increasing sales turnover, ensuring corporate growth and achieving a high return on capital, most of these objectives will be satisfied when the firm is maximising its profits. In the short term some profit opportunities may have to be sacrificed to facilitate sales growth, but the main rationale for higher sales must be profit maximisation over the longer run. Certainly, contracting firms are conscious of the need to make high profits. Most builders try to avoid 'leaving money on the table' in their dealings with clients and they price their products and services in accordance with what they believe the market will bear. The assumption of profit maximisation lies at the heart of the economic theory of the firm—the subject of the remainder of this chapter.

Profit is the difference between the revenue obtained from selling output and the cost incurred in producing and distributing it. Any understanding of profit maximisation must begin with a study of the forces of demand and supply as experienced by the firm. In this section the nature of the firm's supply costs are explained, while in the following section the nature of demand is examined. In the final section the concepts of supply and demand are brought together to provide the theory of the firm. The application of this general economic theory to the case of the construction firm is discussed on pp. 94–7.

The firm's short-run costs

A firm produces goods and services by combining the various factors of production—labour, capital plant, materials, land and

3.4   The firm's short-run costs of production

(1) Quantity produced	(2) Fixed costs (£)	(3) Total variable costs (£)	(4) Total costs (£)	(5) Average cost per unit (£)	(6) Marginal cost (£)
0	50	—	—	—	—
1	50	20	70	70	—
2	50	70	120	60	50
3	50	106	156	52	36
4	50	130	180	45	24
5	50	150	200	40	20
6	50	166	216	36	16
7	50	181	231	33	15
8	50	206	256	32	25
9	50	247	297	33	41
10	50	310	360	36	63
11	50	390	440	40	80
12	50	490	540	45	100

Explanatory notes
Column (4): Total costs = Fixed costs + Total variable costs
Column (5): Average cost = Total costs ÷ Quantity produced
Column (6): Marginal cost = Successive differences in total costs

technology. In order to acquire these essential inputs the firm must first make payments to the various factors. As we have already seen (pp. 21–7) firms pay factor incomes, consisting of wages and salaries, interest and profit, and rents. These payments constitute the supply costs of the firm and, in the first instance, the amount of output which a firm plans to supply to the market will be governed by the supply costs. An example is given in Table 3.4.

At any given point in time a firm operates in a short-run situation, such that the firm has some fixed levels of plant and some established production technology. The firm cannot readily change these fixed factors in the short run and so the firm is of given size, with limitations on its ability to vary output. Manufacturing firms are more constrained by such fixities that construction firms, who tend to hire or sub-contract their additional input needs. Over a longer time-span a firm can vary its size by changing its capital plant, introducing new technology or acquiring other firms through mergers and takeovers. However, in the short run the firm has to operate with fixities in certain key areas. Land, buildings and technology are the most obvious fixed factors, but the firm may also be limited in its ability to increase the input from various classes of skilled labour. Construction firms frequently experience short-run problems in recruiting specific types of craftsmen, and sometimes in obtaining managers of the required quality.

Where factor inputs are variable, it will often be the case in the short run that increased quantities of such inputs can only be obtained by paying higher unit costs. If a firm wishes to increase the input in man-hours of its workforce, the most obvious way of achieving this in the short run is to pay the existing employees to work overtime. In this way, each hour of overtime working will normally cost the firm more than each hour of normal-time working, although the output produced through each man-hour of labour will remain the same. Thus a firm's supply costs in the short run tend to be characterised by fixities and increasing factor prices where the firm seeks to significantly increase its usage of particular inputs beyond a normal level.

Fixed costs

In the short term it is usual to distinguish between a firm's fixed costs of production—those which remain the same with respect to output—and its variable costs of production—those which change as output increases. In Fig. 3.1 the fixed and variable components of a firm's total costs are shown. Most firms incur fixed costs in the form of rental payments for buildings, plant and utilities, which have to be paid regardless of the intensity of usage. Equally, the costs of some managerial and administrative staff can, in the short term, he regarded as fixed since their salaries will be paid whether the firm is producing very little or a lot of output. Over time, such staff costs may well be capable of variation, but presently they constitute a fixed cost which does not change with variations in production levels. Generally, as a firm increases in size, the proportion of fixed cost in the total cost of production tends to increase as head office cost overheads become more significant.

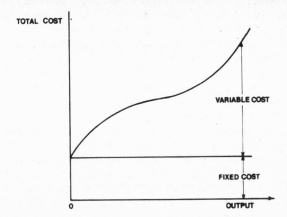

Fig. 3.1 *A firm's total costs of production*

Small firms, such as those which dominate the construction industry, tend to have only a low proportion of fixed costs, so that almost all their production costs vary with output.

Short-run variable costs

The main categories of variable cost incurred by a firm are its purchases of materials and its employment of labour. While such costs vary with the level of output it is not usual for these costs to vary linearly in strict proportion to the change in output. In Fig. 3.1 the variable cost graph is represented not as a straight line, but as a curvilinear function of the level of output. Specifically, as output increases from very low levels towards its middle range, total variable costs do not increase at the same rate as output increases. When output grows from the middle range towards much higher values (see the right-hand half of Fig. 3.1) total variable costs are seen to increase more rapidly than output has increased. The nature of this relationship between the firm's variable costs and its level of output can be more readily appreciated when the firm's short-run average cost curve is drawn. Fig. 3.2 shows how when a firm's total costs are divided by the corresponding level of output, the resulting average cost curve turns out to be U-shaped. So, unit costs fall as output increases from low to middle-range values, but thereafter unit costs begin to rise again as a firm moves towards higher output levels. A number of different factors are responsible for the U-shaped average cost curve.

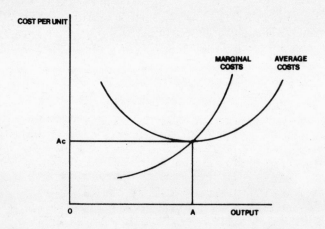

Fig. 3.2 *A firm's short-run average and marginal costs of production*

Continuously falling average fixed costs

When output increases, average fixed cost must fall, and as output continues to grow, so the basis over which fixed costs can be spread increases. Large firms can afford high fixed costs because they are able to spread such costs over a high volume of work. Once a large building firm has invested in its own plant depot or, perhaps, set up a material-testing laboratory, it has incurred fixed costs. If the firm is only able to win a few contracts and thus produce relatively low levels of output, the average fixed cost per unit of output will be very high. When more contracts are gained and the overall output level expanded, the average fixed costs of the depot or laboratory will fall. The higher the output achieved, the smaller will be the fixed cost component in the average total cost. Moreover, the type of investments which give rise to a firm's fixed costs will often lead to lower variable costs. Hence, the firm with its own plant depot would expect to have lower variable costs associated with its use of plant than the firm which was obliged to fulfil its plant needs by hiring or leasing externally.

Large-scale economies

At very small output levels, the unit cost of both materials and labour tends to be relatively high; when output begins to expand, however, unit costs are frequently found to fall. In the case of materials, 'minimum order' rules may well apply and delivery costs will be significant where only small quantities are being purchased. Generally speaking, small volumes of materials are bought through merchants rather than directly from the manufacturers. There will also be costs associated with the ordering and requisition of the materials. The small-scale purchaser of materials is unlikely to enjoy the best credit terms and so this factor too serves to keep the unit costs relatively high.

When output expands, economies of scale associated with larger purchases of materials can be realised. Discounts and rebates are usually available for larger orders. The transport costs on larger orders also tends to be lower per unit, as do administrative costs. Perhaps most significantly, the firm engaged in large-scale material purchasing will find it worthwhile to create a specialist buying department who can ensure the most favourable terms for obtaining supplies. An organisation which consumes large quantities of materials has much greater bargaining strength than one which is only a smaller consumer. For all these reasons the unit cost of materials is likely to fall as the volume of a firm's output increases.

Where a firm is employing labour directly, but its scale of output is such that it cannot keep this workforce fully employed, the unit labour cost will be necessarily high. Usually employees will have to be guaranteed payment for a normal working week, but if, because of low output, the workers cannot be continuously employed, the average cost per unit will be relatively higher. Frequently, even when output is low, specialist skilled craftsmen will need to be used and the costs of recruiting and possibly training such workmen will have to be borne—regardless of the amount of work they are required to do. Low output may mean that the workforce has to be frequently switched between tasks; in this case 'switching time' must be paid for, even though no output is being produced. In the construction sector, larger firms who are confronted with low demand tend to resort to sub-contracting in preference to inter-mittent hiring and firing. The sub-contractors in turn rely upon self-employed workers to meet their short-term labour needs. While these solutions serve to hold down the firms average labour costs when output is low, only higher levels of output offer the potential for significant reductions in unit costs.

As output increases, so the firm is better able to keep its workforce fully employed and to ensure that more paid-for hours are actually spent in producing output. The firm is able to employ specialist craftsmen, either directly or through sub-contracting, ensuring that there will be enough work for them to do. There is more room for repetitive tasks with higher output and there is likely to be less switching between jobs, so there is less unproductive learning time involved. In manufacturing situations, the skilled operative is kept fully employed performing a single, repeated task and in this way output per man-hour is raised—and unit labour costs fall.

It is not only in the case of material and labour costs that higher output produces economies of scale. Often the costs of operating plant do not increase in proportion to the increase in output, so that overall the unit cost of production can be expected to fall as output expands. Frequently, the major cost component of plant is of the fixed cost type, for example, hiring a crane. Thereafter, the more intensively an item of plant is utilised to generate output, so the average cost of this plant falls. The same scale economy applies to office machinery—especially to computers and data processing machines. Indeed, where manage-ment resources in total are a fixed or at least a semi-fixed cost, the greater the volume of output that can be generated, the lower the average management cost per unit of output.

As output expands, firms often find that their costs per unit of output decline. The terms on which funds can be borrowed tend to be more favourable to the large-scale borrower. The lending of money in this respect is very similar to the bulk supply of materials. The financial institutions favour lending to larger firms with big order-books, because they are considered more credit-worthy.

Economies of scale apply just as much to finance as to materials, labour, plant and management.

Eventually diminishing returns

Falling average fixed costs and economies of scale can together account for the fall in unit costs as a firm expands from low to medium-range output values. The explanation for why unit costs eventually begin to increase at very high output levels lies with the so-called 'law of diminishing returns'. This law asserts that as more and more units of a single factor of production are added, while the input of other factors remains fixed, the rate of increase of output will fall. As a firm initially expands output from very low levels it should be possible to increase all inputs in proportion, but eventually shortages of one or other key factor of production will go on adding labour man-hours to fixed amounts of capital plant. Output will increase, but the ratio of the marginal change in output to the marginal change in labour which brings it about will fall. Given that the firm pays its workforce the same wage rates, the extra units of output will cost the firm more to produce. In this way, the unit cost of output must start to increase once the firm encounters significant shortages in its factor inputs.

At higher output levels, firms often find they are having to pay more for their basic units of input because scarcity has raised the unit cost. Most obviously, if operatives work overtime or if bonus payments must be made to obtain extra man-hours of input, the labour cost per unit of output is increased. Usually, overtime is paid at time-and-a-half. Where firms elect to buy in extra labour, probably for only a short period of time, the unit cost of such labour is likely to exceed the standard basic wage rate. Costs may also start to rise as very large volumes of materials are introduced on site. Wastage rates increase and the firm may have to pay for a security firm to guard the materials against theft. Again, the materials may need to be stored under cover. Most significantly, higher interest costs may be incurred where larger stocks of materials are maintained. If the higher volume of materials cannot all be obtained locally, more distant sources of supply will have to be utilised and this will also raise the unit cost.

In order to try to overcome the problem of diminishing returns in the short run, construction firms will often seek to supplement their existing plant by hiring additional machines and equipment. Such hiring will inevitably be more expensive than if the plant was owned or leased on a longer-term basis. In the same way, some firms will attempt to hire management staff to overcome shortages, but invariably they will need to pay significantly higher rates for this type of short-term employee. Frequently sub-contractors will be brought in to offset the shortage problem. Again, the cost per unit of output will be increased.

The short-run marginal cost curve

Where a U-shaped average cost curve exists there is an associated 'marginal cost curve'. The relationship between the average and the marginal cost curve is illustrated in Fig. 3.2. By definition, wherever the average cost curve is falling, the marginal cost curve must always lie below it, and wherever average cost is rising, marginal cost must always lie above average cost. Average cost will always be equal to marginal cost when average cost is flat or has a zero slope. In practice this means that marginal cost cuts average cost at its lowest point, where the slope of the average cost curve is zero. A fuller appreciation of these relationships can be gained from Table 3.4 (p. 70), where some representative cost data is presented. Between output quantities 1 to 8 average cost is falling, and the marginal cost— which is the extra cost incurred in producing one more unit—is also falling so that its values lie below those of average cost. At an output of 8 units, average cost is at a minimum and around this value average cost must equate with marginal cost. For higher output units beyond 8, average cost starts to rise and marginal cost also rises with its values exceeding those of average cost. The marginal cost curve is critically important to the firm's profit-maximising decisions; its relevance is discussed below (pp. 90–7).

The firm's long-run supply costs

In the short run a firm has to operate with fixed amounts of key input factors, but in the long-run it is assumed that there are no fixed factors, and thus a firm can freely vary the amounts of all the factors it uses. In practice, firms are always in a short-run situation, but it can be assumed that they plan in the long run. The consequence of eliminating fixities in the productive inputs is that the onset of diminishing returns and increasing factor prices can be delayed—perhaps indefinitely. A typical relationship between a firm's short-run and long-run costs of production is shown in Fig. 3.3. It is clear that long-run average costs lie below short-run average costs and, whereas at high levels of ouput, short-run average costs begin to increase, long-run average costs continue to fall. Usually, long-run average cost will attain a minimum level and, in theory, this minimum level will persist as output continues to increase. Within the range of attainable output there is no reason to suppose that long-run average costs will eventually increase. Hence, the long run

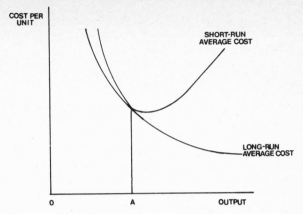

Fig. 3.3 *Short-run and long-run costs of production*

is a theoretic concept identifying a minimum level of average cost which is capable of being sustained in the face of further increases in output.

While in practice the long run can never be observed, some notion of how a firm's costs of production behave over time can be gained from observing the short-run cost curves of firms of different sizes, all operating within the same industry. A typical represent-ation of the short-run cost curves for firms of different sizes is given in Fig. 3.4. The smallest firm has a short-run average cost curve designated SRAC I, and, if it produces at lowest unit cost, it will produce output OX. If this firm attempts to produce beyond OX, its unit costs will rise, as it experiences diminishing returns resulting from fixed plant and equipment. In order to reduce unit costs this firm will need to grow and increase in plant size. Another firm in the same industry operates on cost curve SRAC II (which, it should be noted, overlaps SRAC I) but its minimum cost point realises an output of OY. If this firm produces at or near output OY, it will have significantly lower unit costs than the first firm ($OY_c < OX_c$). A third, much larger firm is also represented; this firm operates on cost curve SRAC III. In order to achieve minimum costs this firm, with its larger investment in plant, must operate at output OZ, the highest output of the three firms. However, the diagram indicates that $OZ_c > OY_c$, so that despite its larger size this third firm cannot produce unit output as cheaply as the second firm. In such a situation it is clear that diseconomies of a very large scale are starting to apply.

When a locus is drawn through the minimum short-run average cost points of firms, arranged in increasing order of size, an 'industry envelope cost curve' is produced (see Fig. 3.4). Such a schedule is valuable to firms in the industry as it indicates the

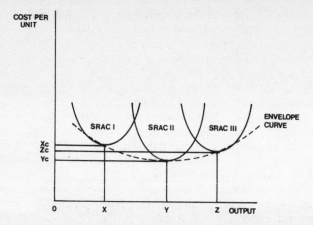

Fig. 3.4 *Industry envelope curve of short-run costs for firms of different size*

optimum size for achieving lowest unit costs. The exact shape of the envelope is likely to vary between industries and, while all industries will have an envelope which falls as the scale of output increases, it is not certain whether the envelope schedule will necessarily begin to rise at very high levels of output. In many manufacturing industries the lowest unit costs are enjoyed by the very largest firms and little evidence of significant diseconomies of very large scale are apparent.

In practice, it is rarely possible to observe directly the minimum cost points for firms in the industry. It is certainly impossible in the construction industry. However, the census of production for the construction industry, referred to in Chapter 1, does compare net output per employee statistics, averaged across classes of firms grouped according to size. Such data for 1984 indicates how the very largest firms (those employing more than 5000 employees) were on average 40% more productive than the smallest firms (employing between 1 and 19 employees). While output per head does not accurately mirror unit cost of ouput, it does imply that larger construction firms are likely to have significantly lower unit costs than their smaller counterparts.

3. Demand conditions

Analysis of a firm's supply costs provides only a part of the answer to what is the most profitable output level. In the absence of any information on the demand conditions confronting the firm—and hence any knowledge of the revenue the firm can expect to earn from output sales—the firm cannot make a sound decision on the optimum level of production. A firm produces goods and services to satisfy consumer demand. In an extreme situation, which could arise, there could be no effective consumer demand for the product; in this event, it would matter little what the unit cost of production was, as sustained losses would rapidly cause production to be abandoned. More realistically, product demand might be such that consumers are not willing to pay a market price which is greater than, or at worst equal to, the minimum cost of production. As Fig. 3.2 above illustrates, this means that only if the firm charges a price less than OA_c will it be able to sell any of its output. Clearly, unless the firm can either lower its short-run production costs or somehow raise demand for its product at existing price levels, continuing production is pointless. Where demand exists at price levels above OA_c (the minimum cost level) it does not necessarily follow that it will be in the firm's best interests to always produce OA units of output to achieve least cost production. Knowledge of the conditions of demand which a firm is likely to experience is just as important to the production decision, as is information on the supply costs.

The revenue a firm receives from selling its output derives from the volume of goods or services it is able to sell at the going market price. In the first instance, demand for the firm's product is determined by the nature of the market demand for this particular product. Market demand is the total demand of all individual consumers who constitute a product's market (i.e. the total amount of the product which consumers plan to purchase at different market prices). However, unless the firm has a monopoly or is the sole supplier of a product it will have to share this demand with other firms seeking to supply the same market. So, the second determinant of demand for a firm's product is the amount of competition which the firm experiences in supplying the market. Such competition is extremely variable, ranging from a large number of competitors all of similar size, through to very few or, in the limiting case, no effective competitors at all.

Market demand determinants

A market is the sum total of individual consumers, and market demand is the aggregate of the consumers' individual demand curves. An individual's demand curve for any given product shows the relationship between the price of that product and the amount which the individual plans to buy at that price. In Fig. 3.5, D_1 illustrates the typical downward-sloping demand curve. At a high price consumers plan to buy relatively little of the product, whereas when the price falls, consumers revise their buying intentions upwards. By plotting price on the vertical axis it can be noticed that even though it is the independent variable which determines the quantity of product demanded, a downward-sloping demand schedule is produced. Any normal good or service conforms to this law of downward-sloping demand. Very few products contradict this law, such that when their price is reduced consumers demand less, not more, of the product. The explanation for such a result lies with the nature of the product and its relationship to the consumers' incomes. For example, some products, such as plastic baths, may be considered inferior substitutes for better quality alternatives such as porcelain baths. When consumers' incomes rise, it is likely that they will seek to switch to the better quality product, so that even if the price of the inferior good falls, less rather than more plastic baths will be bought. Alternatively, where incomes are falling, consumers may buy more inferior goods, even when their price is rising. A fuller analysis of 'non-normal goods' is given in Burningham[3].

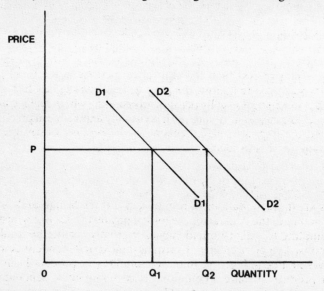

Fig. 3.5 *Consumer demand curves*

In drawing the demand curve it is assumed that factors other than the product's own price which may influence the amount of the product which consumers plan to purchase are held constant. Consumer demand is determined not only by the product's own price, but also by consumers' incomes and by the price of other products. In Fig. 3.5, if a consumer's income were to increase, the position of the original demand curve D_1 would shift outwards to position D_2. At existing price levels, consumers would be able to buy more of the product after their incomes have increased. Equally, the same result might be brought about if either the price of some alternative which competes with the existing product (and so is a substitute for it) were to increase, or the price of a good which is associated with the existing product (and so is a complement to it) were to decrease. The demand for bricks might shift in this way, if either the price of concrete blocks were to increase relative to the price of bricks, or the price of cement used in mortar were to fall. Clearly, the product's own price cannot be assessed in isolation from changes in the price of other products. Relative movements in product price help determine consumer demand.

Attempts to establish market demand curves for different products are confused by continuous changes in both consumer incomes and price relativities. For most products their absolute price never falls: it is only seen to rise over time. However, this price, relative to prices in general (as measured by the retail price index), will often rise and fall, such that real price changes frequently occur. Typically, there are times when the average price of new houses is increasing more rapidly than prices in general, so that the real cost of new houses to potential buyers increases. Equally, at other times, increases in the price of new houses may be less than the equivalent increase in the retail price index, so that in real terms the price of new housing has decreased. Such price changes usually occur in an economy where real income is subject to continuous change, so it is virtually impossible in practice to isolate the impact of a real change in the product's own price on demand for that product.

Price elasticity of demand

Despite these limitations, it is important for the firm to understand the nature of the demand curve for the product or service which it is attempting to sell. Demand can vary greatly, or hardly at all, in response to a price change. Consider the two independent demand curves plotted in Fig. 3.6. Initially, both D1 (for product 1) and D2 (for product 2) share a common price and quantity demanded at OP_A and OQ_A respectively. The manufacturers of each product lower the price to OP_B in an attempt to stimulate sales. Fig. 3.6 shows how demand for product 1 is relatively insensitive to the price reduction and the quantity demanded increases by an amount Q_AQ_{B1}. In contrast, demand for product 2 is relatively sensitive to this change in price and its quantity demanded increases by Q_AQ_{B2}, where $Q_AQ_{B2} > Q_AQ_{B1}$. A useful measure of the sensitivity of demand to a change in a product's price is the *price elasticity of demand*. This is defined as follows:

Price elasticity of demand measures the proportionate change in quantity demanded as a ratio of the proportionate change in price which has brought about the demand change.

More simply, it may be written:

$$\text{Price elasticity of demand} = \epsilon_p = \frac{\Delta Q}{\Delta P} \times \frac{P}{Q}$$

where Δ stands for the discrete change in the variable and P and Q refer to the original values.

It is particularly useful to distinguish between cases where $\epsilon_p < 1$ and $\epsilon_p > 1$. For the purposes of this distinction, the negative sign, which is always obtained for the price elasticity of normal goods, is ignored. When price elasticity is less than unity, demand is said to be 'price inelastic'. This case corresponds to demand curve D_1 in Fig. 3.6. Where price elasticity is greater than unity, demand is said to be 'price elastic' and this case is the same as demand curve D_2 in Fig. 3.6.

The demand for some products is intrinsically price inelastic, whereas for others the demand is price elastic. Products which are essential goods, such as basic housing and raw materials, are typically price inelastic. Products for which there are no ready substitutes and on which consumers typically spend a significant proportion of their incomes are usually taken to be price inelastic. When the price of such goods rises, consumers may trim back their

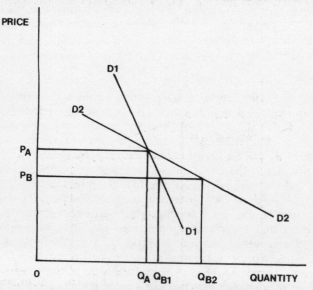

Fig. 3.6 *Demand curves exhibiting different price elasticities*

demand but, because of the essential nature of such products, the percentage reduction in demand will be much less than the percentage increases in price which brought about the change in demand. When the price of common bricks rises, the housebuilder has little option but to pay the higher prices, as no easy substitute exists in the short term.

Other products, which are deemed to be luxury items, are usually price elastic. For most consumers, building products such as shower units and double glazing are luxuries. They are not essentials, but for those consumers with higher incomes, they are desirable products. When the price of these products is increased it is quite likely that the quantity demanded will fall by proportionately more than the price increases. In practice, rising consumer incomes often make it difficult to observe the pure price reaction in isolation. Nevertheless, the manufacturers of these luxury housing items are very price sensitive and this is a tacit recognition of higher price elasticity.

While demand for a product may on the whole be price inelastic, such as in the case of the demand for bricks, the demand facing the individual firm selling a particular brand of the product, such as fletton bricks, may be much more price elastic. Unless the firm is aware of the price elasticity for its products and services, it may, in deciding on price changes, bring about a situation where it loses rather than gains revenue. Fig. 3.7 illustrates this situation for a

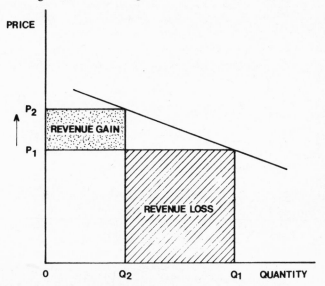

Fig. 3.7 *Price elastic demand*

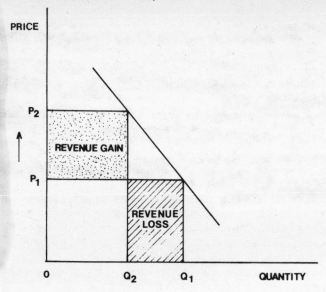

Fig. 3.8 *Price inelastic demand*

product with price elastic demand. When price is increased from OP_1 to OP_2, quantity demanded falls back from OQ_1 to OQ_2. The result of this price change is a net loss in revenue, as the lower volume of sales outweighs the increased revenue per unit resulting from the price increase. Where demand is deemed to be price elastic, a reduction in price is the most appropriate strategy for increasing product revenue.

In contrast, Fig. 3.8 shows the result of increasing the price of a product for which demand is price inelastic. Here, as price increases, the gain in revenue more than compensates for the loss in sales volume. Where demand is thought to be price inelastic, an increase in price is the preferred strategy for increasing revenues.

Unfortunately, a product's price elasticity is not usually constant over the range of possible prices, nor is it likely to remain constant over time. Where the demand curve is approximated by a linear schedule, as price falls and demand increases, so demand becomes less price elastic. This point can be illustrated by reference to the data in Table 3.5. When price or average revenue per unit decreases from £93 to £87, the price elasticity associated with this change in price is $(-)$ 15.5. When price decreases from £33 to £27, although in absolute terms the size of the price decrease is the same, the associated price elasticity is now $(-)$ 0.5. The demand schedule in Table 3.5 manifests a change from high price elasticity at high prices to price inelasticity at lower prices.

3.5   A firm's demand schedule

(1) Quantity sold	(2) Total revenue (£)	(3) Average revenue per unit (£)	(4) Marginal revenue (£)
1	93	93	—
2	174	87	81
3	243	81	69
4	300	75	57
5	345	69	45
6	378	63	33
7	399	57	21
8	408	51	9
9	405	45	−3
10	390	39	−15
11	363	33	−27
12	324	27	−39

Explanatory notes
Column (3): Average revenue = Total revenue ÷ Quantity sold
Column (4): Marginal Revenue = Successive differences in total revenue

Often, in the short term, the demand for many products will be intrinsically price inelastic as there are insufficient substitutes available. This is the case with most basic raw materials and foodstuffs. Over the longer run however, substitutes may be developed and, as competition increases, so demand becomes more price elastic. Structural steel has come to experience competition from reinforced concrete, and timber-framing has presented a challenge to traditional house-building materials.

Competition in the market

When the demand curves of all individuals who constitute the product's market are aggregated, a resulting market demand curve is established. The form of the market demand curve closely resembles that for the individual and it will follow the law of downward-sloping demand. When the size of the market population increases, the quantities sold will also increase, but the fundamental relationship between price and demand will remain.

The demand conditions facing the individual firm will only correspond to those of the market where the firm is the sole supplier of that market, such that no competitor is present. Most commonly, the firm will face significant competition but the degree of this competition may vary a lot. Often where a firm is selling the same product in several different geographic markets, it may face varying amounts of competition. The firm supplying ready-mixed concrete may be one of several such producers in an urban area such as

London, but the same firm may have a virtual monopoly of supply in a rural area such as the Scottish Highlands. The nature of market competition will determine the exact form of the individual firm's revenue schedules.

Economists usually distinguish between two main types of competition: *perfect competition*, which is rarely encountered in practice and so represents a limiting theoretic case, and *imperfect competition*, which is a generic classification for many different types of market, all of which experience some measure of imperfection. In practice, virtually all firms operate in imperfect markets, although sometimes the degree of imperfection is relatively slight. Most small building firms operate in highly competitive markets and in many ways their situation approaches that of perfect competition. Larger building firms, in comparison, tend to operate in a less fiercely competitive environment. Where such firms have developed a high degree of specialisation, such as in motorway construction or tunnelling, there are likely to be relatively few competitors and these markets may be regarded as extremely imperfect. Material supply firms frequently operate in markets which are highly monopolistic and it is usual for supply in such markets to be concentrated in the hands of a few large firms. Examples of this form of oligopoly can be found in the production of cement, brick, glass and especially plasterboard.

Perfectly competitive markets

For perfect competition to exist there must be a large number of firms all producing a similar product. Each firm and indeed each buyer in the market must be sufficiently small, relative to the overall size of the market, to avoid exerting any influence on the market price. Firms must be free to enter and exit the market for the product and no barriers should exist for a firm wanting to set up production in this industry. In most of these respects, the building industry has a market of perfect competition; at least, this is the case in that part of the industry dominated by small firms. However, strictly speaking, perfect competition also requires both perfect knowledge on the part of supplying firms and buyers and perfect mobility on the part of consumers, so that they can take advantage of any perceived price differentials which may arise. On these conditions of perfect knowledge and mobility the building industry falls short of the perfectly competitive ideal. Its customers are generally geographically immobile and the costs involved in searching prevent buyers seeking out the prices of large numbers of building firms.

The key idea of perfect competition is that firms operating in such a market are unable, by their own actions, to influence the market price. Firms in this market are passive price-takers and at any one time only a single market price can rule. Fig. 3.9 shows how the firm's demand curve derives from the conditions of market demand and supply. Market supply can be plotted by aggregating the marginal cost schedules of individual firms above the point of intersection with average cost. This shows how, as market price rises, firms will be willing to supply more and more of their product to the market. Where market demand and supply intersect, a single price is determined, known as the 'equilibrium market price'. Only at such a price are the forces of demand and supply exactly in balance. The initial equilibrium market price in Fig. 3.9 is price OP_1.

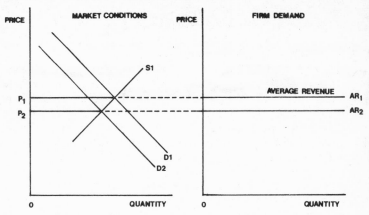

Fig. 3.9 *The firm's demand schedule in perfect competition*

The market determines the equilibrium price OP_1 and this price is received by the perfectly competitive firm and becomes its average revenue or demand curve. In effect, only one price, OP_1, can rule and regardless of the amount the firm attempts to sell it will always obtain the same amount of revenue for each unit. In perfect competition, a firm's average and marginal revenues coincide. If the individual firm attempts to sell its product at a price above the ruling market price, customers will stop buying from this firm and will take their business to a cheaper competitor. Equally, if the firm attempts to cut its price to below that of the rest of the market, it will only be able to sell at a loss. (See the next section for a full explanation of this point.) Either way, if the firm does not accept the perfect competition price, it will soon go out of business.

When changes occur in the market, a new price will be set for the firm. In Fig. 3.9 a fall in market demand from D_1 to D_2 is introduced. Such a fall could result from an overall reduction in the real incomes of consumers, stemming from a general increase in income tax. When market demand shifts down, a new equilibrium price OP_2 is set and this becomes the firm's new average revenue or demand curve. Equally, a similar change in the market and so in the individual firm's price could arise if new firms entered the market and caused the market supply to shift down. Clearly, in local building markets, when either general demand for building work falls or a number of new companies enter the market, the level of tender-bids is pressured downwards, along with the average revenue curve for each firm.

Imperfect competition

In contrast to perfectly competitive markets, imperfect competition involves some ability of a firm to control the price which it receives for its product. The greater the degree of imperfection, the greater the capacity of the firm to manipulate the price it receives. The monopolist has the most complete control over price. The oligopolistic firm has correspondingly less control and the smaller firm operating in general monopolistic conditions has the least control. (A fuller account of the different types of imperfect competition can be obtained elsewhere; see, for example, Lipsey[4].) Wherever the conditions of perfect competition are not fulfilled, imperfect competition exists.

The firm in imperfect competition always faces a downward-sloping demand curve. This demand curve is the firm's average revenue schedule, since for any given output the firm chooses to offer to the market, a market price is identified. In Fig. 3.10, if the firm offers quantity OQ_1 to the market it will obtain a price of OP_1 for each unit. Should the firm choose to restrict supply to only OQ_2 units, it will be able to obtain a higher price per unit of OP_2. Obviously, price elasticity considerations will be taken into account in deciding whether to increase or reduce price in imperfect markets. Usually firms in such markets tend to face demand schedules which are relatively price inelastic and so a combination of higher prices and lower sales volumes are normally preferred. Firms use advertising and marketing techniques to differentiate their products from those of competitors and in this way try to create brand loyalty and price inelastic demand for their individual product.

The large firms who dominate imperfect markets create barriers to would-be new entrants to effectively restrict competition. In manufacturing industry, the capital set-up costs for new plant are often prohibitively high. Frequently, patents are used to protect innovative technologies. Pilkingtons use patents very extensively to maintain their position in the UK glass industry. Where competition

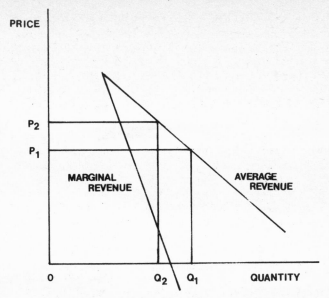

Fig. 3.10 *The firm's demand schedule in imperfect competition*

threatens, large firms often have the resources to either take over or merge with the would-be competitor. Large firms can also make trading extremely difficult for new entrants by temporarily cutting prices and expanding supply to try to eliminate any threat of new competitors. Construction firms in specialised sectors of the civil engineering market defend their market position against competitive threats by trimming down tender-bids to very low levels. Established firms usually have adequate resources to enable them to operate lower prices temporarily, in the interests of restricting competition and so ensuring longer-term profitability.

The marginal revenue schedule

Where a firm's average revenue curve slopes downwards it implies the existence of a marginal revenue curve below it. The relationship between these two schedules is illustrated in Fig. 3.10. Marginal revenue is the incremental change in total revenue resulting from the sale of one more unit. Unlike marginal cost, marginal revenue can become negative. A better appreciation of the relationship between the various revenue schedules can be gained from the data in Table 3.5. As price or average revenue falls, the quantity sold increases and between output values of 1 to 8 units the total revenue increases; thus marginal revenue is positive. Beyond 8 units, further reductions in price fail to bring about compensating increases in the quantity demanded, so that total revenue begins to decline and marginal revenue becomes negative. Up to a quantity of 8 units, demand is price elastic but beyond 8 units it becomes price inelastic.

4. The theory of the firm

A firm makes its decision on how much output to produce by using cost information together with demand knowledge. Neither the costs of production alone, nor the revenue schedules facing the firm on their own are adequate to reach a decision which will maximise the firm's profits. The theory of the firm says that in order to maximise profits the firm must produce at that output where marginal cost equates to marginal revenue. This fundamental proposition applies just as much to firms in imperfectly competitive markets as to those facing perfect competition. It is helpful to examine the theory of the firm separately for each type of competition. Thereafter, the relevance of this theory to firms in the building sector is assessed.

Profit maximising decisions for the firm in perfect competition

The firm's supply costs are those represented in Fig. 3.2, while the relevant revenue schedule is that derived in Fig. 3.9. When these

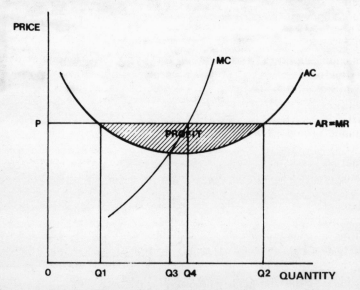

Fig. 3.11 *The short-run decision of the firm in perfect competition*

two sets of curves are combined the result is Fig. 3.11. This figure represents the position of the perfectly competitive firm in the short run. In this context the short run refers to a period in which it is possible for the firm to earn above normal profits. In the long run, these excess profits will be reduced if perfect competition continues to prevail.

In Fig. 3.11 if the firm chooses to produce at an output level either below OQ_1 or above OQ_2 it will incur a loss on each unit produced. Only in the output region Q_1Q_2 does average revenue (AR) equal or exceed average cost (AC). Thus only in this output range will any profit be made. Within the range Q_1Q_2, profit is made on each unit produced, but inspection of the figure indicates that the amount of profit varies across this range. It is clear that more profit per unit is being made towards the middle of the output range than at the extremes, where the gap between AR and AC is very small. Only one output level will produce maximum profit and the theory of the firm assumes that firms will systematically search this out.

Output level OQ_3 in Fig. 3.11 is the point at which marginal cost (MC) cuts average cost from below and so determines the point of minimum unit cost. At output OQ_3 significant profits are being made, but this is not the output which maximises profit. Consider output levels immediately to the right of level OQ_3: here AR exceeds AC, but more importantly marginal revenue (MR) lies above marginal cost. In other words, the additional revenue from selling one more unit exceeds the additional cost of producing one more unit, thus a positive contribution is being made to unit profit. This contribution continues until output level OQ_4 is reached. At this point MC equals MR and this is the output level which maximises profit. Beyond output level OQ_4, MC is greater than MR, so that further units of output bring about a negative contribution to unit profit. Hence, the profit maximising level of output for the firm in the short run is determined at output level OQ_4. This output level is greater than the output which leads to minimisation of unit costs.

It is clear from Fig. 3.11 that at output level OQ_4 a very significant margin of profit is being made. Usually, economists define normal profit as a small component already allowed for in the firm's average cost curve. Normal profit will be earned wherever AR equals AC. Excess profits are made when AR exceeds AC. With perfect competition the existence of such excess profits will attract new firms into the industry. The result of an increase in market supply is to force down the equilibrium price which each perfectly competitive firm receives. In the longer run, this equilibrium price will be forced down until each firm is only making normal profit. This situation is shown in Fig. 3.12. The profit maximising output level in

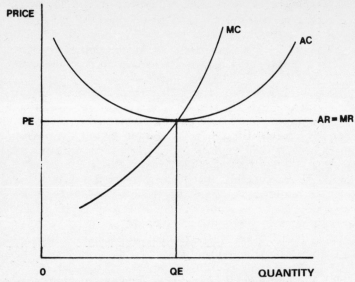

Fig. 3.12 *Long-run equilibrium for the firm in perfect competition*

the long run must coincide with the cost minimising output level, so
that AR = MR = MC = AC.

Profit maximisation for the firm in imperfect competition

This firm's supply costs are again those represented in Fig. 3.2, but
the revenue schedules are those shown in Fig. 3.10. The two sets of
cost and revenue curves are combined in Fig. 3.13. Once more a
distinction is made between the firm in the short run and the firm in
the long run.

The firm in imperfect competition uses the same profit maximising criteria (MR = MC) as its counterpart in perfect competition. In
Fig. 3.13 the best level of output (OQ) is determined by reference to
the intersection between MR and MC. Since for imperfect competition MR ≠ AR, it is necessary to extend the straight line through the
point of intersection to determine the price (OP) at which this
output will be sold. In the same way the unit cost (OC) of the output
can be identified and by definition the unit profit associated with
OQ units of output is PC. Whilst the procedure for identifying the
profit maximising level of output is the same for all firms regardless
of the degree of market competition, the chosen level of output
tends to be different. Comparison of Fig. 3.11 and 3.13 indicates
how for perfect competition, the profit maximising output lies to the
right of the cost minimum point; for imperfect competition the

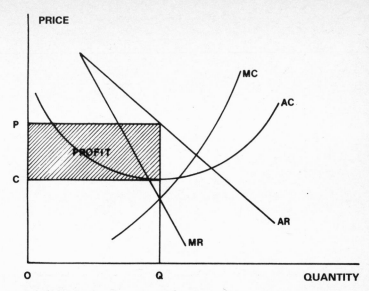

Fig. 3.13 *The short-run decision of the firm in imperfect competition*

preferred output lies to the left of this point. In general, imperfect competition leads to a lower level of output being chosen by the firm.

The nature of imperfect competition implies that barriers to new entrants to the market will tend to persist, so that the identified levels of excess profit may well continue—even in the longer run. Unlike perfect competition, there is no market mechanism which will necessarily lead to long-run equilibrium. However, where new firms are able to enter the market to compete for the excess profit, there will be a move towards a longer-run equilibrium position, as is illustrated in Fig. 3.14. The average revenue curve is shifted to the left as each firm has to settle for a lower market share. This process continues until a point of equilibrium is achieved where AR = AC, so that only normal profits remain. This long-run equilibrium output once more shows the firm in imperfect competition producing significantly less and at higher unit cost than its counterpart firm in perfect competition.

A full comparison between the output and price decisions of firms in the two types of competition is rendered difficult by the distinctive nature of the production costs of each type of firm. Most commonly, the firm in imperfect competition will be a relatively large unit and its short-run average cost curve might be expected to have a lower minimum cost point than the comparatively smaller firm in perfect competition. The rationale for this difference is illustrated in Fig. 3.4. While the larger imperfect competitor will

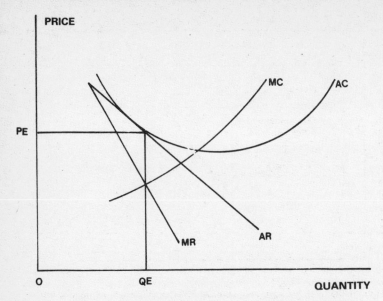

Fig. 3.14 *Long-run equilibrium for the firm in imperfect competition*

produce at a level below minimum cost output and thereby its unit costs will be above the minimum, nevertheless, these unit costs will in all probability be lower than those achieved by the smaller, more perfect, competitor.

Table 3.6 provides an example of the firm in imperfect competition determining its profit maximising output. This table combines the cost information given in Table 3.4 with the revenue data presented in Table 3.5. This table indicates how the marginal cost and marginal revenue schedules intersect close to an output quantity of 7 units. At this value, the average revenue or price per unit is £57, while the unit cost is £33. The minimum cost point where average and marginal cost coincide lies between 8 and 9 units. When changes occur in either production costs or market conditions, such that the average cost or revenue schedule shifts, the firm is likely to choose a new optimum level of output to ensure that it continues to maximise its profits.

The behaviour of building firms

The construction sector contains a very wide diversity of firms ranging from the small, sole owner type of firm to the large public company and the direct labour organisation. The objectives of each of these units are likely to differ significantly and many individual motives for continuing in business can be identified. However, the

3.6   The output decision of the profit maximising firm

Quantity	Average cost (£)	Marginal cost (£)	Average revenue (£)	Marginal revenue (£)	Total profit (£)
1	70	—	93	—	23
2	60	50	87	81	54
3	52	36	81	69	87
4	45	24	75	57	120
5	40	20	69	45	145
6	36	16	63	33	162
7	33	15	57	21	168
8	32	25	51	9	152
9	33	41	45	−3	108
10	36	63	39	−15	30
11	40	80	33	−27	−77
12	45	100	27	−39	−216

Explanatory notes
(1) Average cost and marginal cost are taken from Table 3.4
(2) Average revenue and marginal revenue are taken from Table 3.5
(3) Total profit = (average revenue − average cost) × quantity
(4) Profit maximising output is near to quantity level 7, where marginal cost cuts marginal revenue

most common objective which guides the behaviour of the typical building firm is the maximisation of profit.

Hillebrandt[5] examines the objectives of building firms and reaches the conclusion that the assumption of profit maximisation is the closest approximation to the behaviour of the building firm. The owners of firms are concerned with earning the highest possible return on capital employed; the maximisation of profit is seen as the first step towards realising this central aim. While at times other objectives, such as earning a minimum acceptable level of profit or maximising turnover subject to a satisfactory return on capital, may come to be important, profit maximisation remains the prime objective of the building firm.

The theory of the firm is most applicable to the firm in a manufacturing-type situation where a single homogeneous product is produced and where output is infinitely adjustable as production costs and market conditions change. As Chapter 1 makes clear, the product of most building firms is often unique and output cannot be easily varied in the short term. The larger building firm operates in many different markets, as Chapter 4 explains, and the nature of competition varies considerable between these markets. It is unlikely that the theory of the firm model can be simply applied to the situation of any building firm. Rather, it is the principles of marginal adjustment, as contained within the theory of the firm, that will be embraced by building companies as they strive to improve profitability and move towards a position of profit maximisation.

The average cost curve of the building firm will be U-shaped in the short run and firms will attempt to produce in an output range which enables them to realise lower unit costs of production. Firms will seek to avoid especially low outputs where unit costs are significantly higher. This tends to mean that larger sized firms pursue only the bigger contracts and that they mainly leave the less sizeable repair and maintenance jobs to the small firms in the industry. Where firms of limited size attempt to increase output significantly they can expect the law of diminishing returns to begin to apply and their unit costs will increase.

The shape of the building industry's envelope curve is rather uncertain. Large firms in the industry demonstrate how the curve falls progressively with increases in size and how it remains approximately flat over a wide range of higher output values. Improvements in necessary technologies suggest that this curve might be expected to continue sloping downwards as large firms invest and seek to lower production costs. However, shortages in management resources, along with diseconomies arising from the operation of large sites, may well cause the envelope curve to turn upwards eventually at very high output levels. Most firms in the construction industry would expect to achieve lower unit costs by increasing the size and scale of their operations over time.

Most building firms operate in predominantly competitive markets and it is relatively rare to find a contractor who will contemplate setting a price without regard to competitive pressures. Firms in the construction sector do not face perfect competition and therefore have some control over the price they are seeking to obtain. Housebuilders regulate their supply of units on to the market and other contractors do not bid for all the work available. In this way, supply is restricted in order to yield higher average revenues and firms thereby take advantage of any existing market imperfection. The construction industry remains a very open sector facilitating relatively easy entry to any new firm. This ensures that in the longer run, excess profits will be constrained. The prevailing state of competition is critically important to the construction firm's decisions with regard to output and price.

It is unlikely that any building firm will have a very clear appreciation of either its average or marginal cost curves; or of its average or marginal revenue schedules. Yet most firms will be aware of the importance of unit costs to their profitability; equally, they will recognise the limitations imposed on price by the nature of market demand and competition. The firm seeking to maximise its profits will vary its output levels in response to cost and demand changes. The theory of the firm provides a guideline, showing how a firm may be expected to change its output when production costs and demand schedules alter.

In the case of some of the larger house-builders, longer production runs of standard units are often possible. In many of the new town developments a high number of houses of the same basic type have been constructed around a common site. At Letchworth, John Mowlem built some 4000 units with only a handful of different designs. Frequently, the house-builders will attempt to alter the facial appearance of the units to convey an element of individuality. In practice, however, the product behind the veneer is the same. The growth of timber-frame construction in the early 1980s encouraged this trend towards standardisation. Although timber-framing subsequently declined in importance, contractors remain very aware of the cost savings to be gained from longer production runs. Many of the large developments being created in the London Docklands area in the late 1980s are based on the principles of minimising unit costs and pricing so as to maximise revenue. The theory of the firm has particular validity in the house-building sector.

Questions

1. Describe the structure of the construction industry and in so doing identify the importance of the small firm in the industry.
2. Distinguish the main forms of the firm operating in the construction sector.
3. In what way is the separation of ownership from control an important feature of the larger firm?
4. Outline the objectives of a firm and comment upon the central objective.
5. Explain why a distinction is made in the theory of the firm between short-run and long-run costs of production.
6. Discuss the economies of scale which are available to large construction firms.
7. Demonstrate your understanding of the law of diminishing returns and give appropriate examples found in the construction industry.
8. Plot the data provided in Table 3.4 in the form of a graph to distinguish average total cost, average fixed cost, average variable cost and marginal cost.
9. Discuss the main determinants of an individual's demand for a product and service and describe how market demand relates to an individual's demand.

10. State the law of downward-sloping demand and comment on why, in practice, it is often difficult to observe.
11. Define the price elasticity of demand for a product. Why does price elasticity vary along a straight-line demand schedule?
12. Using the data in Table 3.5 calculate the price elasticity of demand when price (average revenue per unit) falls from £63 to £57. In the same way do the same calculation for price rising from £57 to £63. Explain the difference between these two results.
13. Why is a knowledge of price elasticity useful to a construction firm who are about to change the price of their product?
14. Use diagrams to distinguish between price elastic demand and price inelastic demand.
15. Distinguish between perfect and imperfect competition and discuss the relevance of each for firms in the construction sector.
16. Identify the strict conditions necessary for perfect competition to exist, and comment on the nature of the firm's demand curve when in a state of perfect competition.
17. Explain why the firm in imperfect competition faces a downward-sloping demand curve.
18. Plot the data in Table 3.5 in the form of a graph to illustrate the relationship between average and marginal revenue. At what level of output does demand change from price elastic to price inelastic?
19. 'A firm wishing to maximise its profits will aim to produce and sell that output at which its marginal cost and marginal revenue are equal.' Use diagrams to fully explain this statement for the firm in perfect competition in the short run.
20. Distinguish between the perfectly competitive firm in the short run and the same firm in the long run. Why in the long run must the perfectly competitive firm produce at that level of output which minimises cost?
21. Contrast the way in which prices and output are determined under conditions of perfect and imperfect competition.
22. Use the data in Table 3.6 to plot average and marginal revenue and cost schedules in the form of a graph. Use this graph to determine the profit maximising output level.
23. Critically assess the relevance of the theory of the firm to firms in the construction industry.

Further Reading

BANNOCK, G., *The Economics of Small Firms*, Blackwell, 1981

Begg, D., Fischer, S. and Dornbusch, R., *Economics*, Part 2, McGraw-Hill, 1987

Blight, D. and Shafto, T., *Introduction to Microeconomics*, Pitmans, 1984

Burningham, D., *Understanding Economics*, Part 1, Hodder and Stoughton, 1984

Curwen, P. J., *The Theory of the Firm*, Macmillan, 1983

Harvey, J. *Modern Economics*, Parts II and III, Macmillan, 1983

Heilbroner, R. L. and Thurow, L. C., *Understanding Microeconomics*, Part 3, Prentice-Hall, 1981

Hillebrandt, P. M., *Economic Theory and the Construction Industry*, Chapters 9–14, Macmillan, 1985

Lipsey, R. G., *An Introduction to Positive Economics*, Parts 2, 3 and 4, Weidenfeld and Nicolson, 1983

Ruddock, L., *Economics for the Construction and Property Industries*, Sections B and C, Polytech Publishers, 1983

Stanlake, G. F., *Introductory Economics*, Parts 2, 3 and 5, Longman, 1983

4 Construction Markets

1. Alternative general market structures

In Chapter 3 a distinction was made between two very general market classifications: perfect competition and imperfect competition. The term 'imperfect competition' covers many shades of competition which fall short of perfection; further distinctions are usually made between monopoly, oligopoly and monopolistic competition. In Table 4.1 a summary is provided of the characteristic features of each of the main market forms. In practice, a large construction firm is likely to encounter all shades of competition, as it attempts to sell a wide range of products and services in a variety of different markets.

Monopoly

Examples of pure monopoly, where one firm has total control over the whole market, are rarely found in real life. It is unusual to find a firm, outside of the government-owned public sector, exclusively controlling the supply of a product for which there are no ready substitutes. A firm may well exert monopoly power in either a local or a regional market, but usually, within the national market, the firm will be exposed to competition from imports. The supply of some building materials, such as flat glass and plasterboard, approaches a monopoly market, but the existence of import sales serves to moderate the power of the sole UK supplier. In geographically isolated markets the supplying firm may well have a monopoly position, yet the firm will normally wish to avoid exerting its market power to prevent possible competitors—attracted by the existence of very high profits. A firm may sometimes have an apparent monopoly in a very specific product, but usually acceptable substitutes will be available. Hanson Trust, through their ownership of London Brick, have a monopoly of fletton bricks, but many other types of brick can be bought in their place, so in terms of

4.1 *Alternative market forms*

	Perfect competition	Monopolistic competition	Oligopoly	Monopoly
(1)	A large number of buyers and sellers	A large number of sellers	Only a few sellers	One seller only
(2)	Homogeneous product	Some differentiation of product	Differential products	One product with unique brand identity
(3)	Market-determined prices. Firm has no price control	Mainly market-determined prices, but some very limited control	Collusive pricing, determined by the largest firm	Complete firm control of prices
(4)	Freedom of entry to the market	Relatively easy entry, but some constraints	Strictly limited market entry	No entry to the market
(5)	No advertising or marketing	Some advertising and marketing	Extensive brand advertising and marketing	Advertising and marketing to prevent possible competition
(6)	Full buyer information and customer mobility	Limited buyer information and customer mobility	Restricted buyer information and mobility	No effective choice or alternative for the buyer

the total brick market, this firm is far from having a monopoly.

Most monopolies tend to be owned by the state, or at the very least they are tightly controlled by the government. In the UK many nationalised concerns, such as British Rail and the Post Office, are monopoly suppliers. In a large number of countries of the world, public utility concerns which supply water, gas, electricity, telecommunications and post services are state-owned and regulated. Many large-scale national transport facilities, such as airports, docks and harbours, also tend to be state-run monopolies. It is felt that a monopoly which is controlled by the government will not seek to operate against the interests of its customers and it will modify its profit objective in the interests of providing a regulated market supply. In some instances, the government actually creates a state-controlled monopoly, such as the various agricultural marketing boards, to regulate the market. Construction firms need to buy services from the nationalised monopolies and, at the same time, they may well be attempting to sell their products to a monopoly customer in the public sector.

Monopoly power may also exist in the provision of services and in the supply of labour to the firm. Many professions are very closely controlled by a single powerful institute. The architectural profession is regulated by the Royal Institute of British Architects (RIBA) and likewise the surveying profession is dominated by the Royal Institute of Chartered Surveyors (RICS). In so far as these bodies control entry to the profession, they can be seen to be regulating the supply of these skills and maintaining the price of labour in this sector. The professional bodies, by laying down schedules of fees and charges, seek to eliminate price competition between members and in this way they establish monopoly conditions. Trade unions may also seek to exercise monopoly power by regulating the supply of certain labour skills. A number of construction trades have historically been regulated by the unions to restrict the number of apprentices and thereby control the supply of skilled operatives. Widespread unemployment and a general lack of demand for construction skills has served to weaken this power, but construction firms are still occasionally confronted with this labour skill monopoly. Recent attempts to build a power station on the Isle of Grain were largely thwarted by the monopoly power of the unionised laggers, a minority but vital group.

Oligopoly

Much more common than monopoly is oligopoly, or control of the market by a few large firms. This type of market structure is probably the dominant form found in the UK manufacturing sector today. Prais[1] has shown how concentration of market sales is growing in a large number of UK industries. When the scales of the five largest firms in an industry are expressed as a ratio of the total sales for that industry, it is quite common to find that these five biggest firms between them control in excess of 70% of the market. Oligopoly is the characteristic market form of the building material supply industries. The markets for cement, ready-mixed concrete, most metals and most types of aggregate are all oligopolistic. Certain specialist building contracting markets may also be regarded as predominantly oligopolistic, although the oligopoly often only holds at the regional market level, rather than across the national market. Specialisation is more common in civil engineering than in building work.

Firms operating in an oligopoly usually seek to avoid competing on price; rather, they can be seen to collude on this, such that when one firm—the market leader—changes its prices, all the others follow. Common examples of such behaviour are found in the supply of petrol and in the setting of bank interest charges. The pricing of cement and ready-mixed concrete follows the same pattern. The oligopolistic firm competes for increased market share by differentiating its product from those of its rivals and it tends to use advertising to further its market position. Firms in an oligopoly pay close attention to their distribution networks and to the sales service they provide their customers. The overriding concern of these firms is to prevent new entrants to the market and to protect their profitability. Commonly, the oligopolistic firm restricts its supply in the interests of maintaining market price and profits.

Monopolistic competition

Monopolistic competition exists in a situation where there are a large number of firms supplying the market, but where potential buyers will usually not have complete information or mobility to enable them to eliminate any price differences which may exist. Clearly these are the conditions which characterise the markets for most contracting firms. There is usually some degree of product differentiation, reinforced with modest advertising. However, this type of market remains much more competitive than that in the oligopoly situation, and competitive price adjustments are common. Large firms may exist, but they will not be sufficiently powerful to exert a dominant influence. Urban markets and regions with relatively high population densities are more likely to experience monopolistic competition than are rural and sparsely populated areas, where monopoly and oligopoly market forms are more typical.

The range of contracting markets: an example

A large public company operating in the construction sector is likely to be confronted with all types of general market structures in its various activities. If Tarmac is taken as an example, it can be seen how this company operates a number of distinct divisions. In its quarry products division, Tarmac performs in highly oligopolistic markets, which in some regions approach monopoly conditions. The supply of aggregates, asphalt, tarmacadam and pre-mixed concrete is a highly concentrated industry in which the producing firms benefit from economies of large scale. In contrast, the markets for Tarmac's building products division are more competitive, although monopolistic elements can still be identified. Tarmac in this division operates a large number of smaller units producing roofing, cladding and insulating materials. The market competition is correspondingly greater and the profitability of this division tends to be less than that of the quarry products division. Tarmac's two contracting divisions, construction (civil engineering) and housing, operate in far more intensely competitive markets than either of the two products divisions. Tarmac operate a number of separate, but wholly-owned subsidiary companies, and regional specialisation is apparent in their activities in the housing market. Once again, the relatively lower levels of profitability indicate the more competitive nature of the contracting divisions. The remaining property and industrial divisions operate in a wide variety of markets where a range of market conditions are encountered.

Most large contracting firms are likely to operate in many different markets simultaneously. In the first instance these markets can be identified by the nature of the product or service being offered. Typically this will vary, as with Tarmac, from small-scale maintenance work through to large-scale civil engineering projects. Where the firm has diversified, it will be usual for it to produce building materials, construction plant or associated industrial equipment. Many medium- and larger-sized builders have developed property interests. The markets for each of these products and services are likely to vary in terms of degree of competition, and some unique features will be present.

Markets can also be distinguished according to both geographical location and type of client. The degree of competition varies significantly between a local, a regional, a national or an international market. The smallest firms restrict their operations to local markets, but as a firm grows it is likely to expand into the wider regional market. Larger firms operate nationally and they are likely to have separate regional divisions—or trading companies set up to enable the firm to compete effectively in all areas of the country. Only the very largest firms tend to pursue contracts in international markets, where the degree of competition is intense. As a firm grows in size, so the nature of the client who commissions the construction work is likely to change. Small firms deal predominantly with individual householders and perhaps carry out some work for the corporate sector. Larger firms also deal with house buyers, but much of their workload stems from the industrial and commercial sector, and also from local authorities. The largest firms carry out most government contracts; they are also the organisations who deal with overseas governments.

The character of construction markets is set by the product or service, the geographical location and the nature of the client. The exact type of competition experienced by the construction firm depends on all these factors.

2. Government intervention

The UK's economic system is generally regarded as a market economy, wherein the free interplay of the forces of supply and demand is allowed to determine market prices, and where this price mechanism determines how the nation's scarce resources are allocated. A market system, however, unless modified and monitored by the government, contains inherent weaknesses which are both economically and politically de-stabilising. In practice no market economy in the world is allowed to operate without some measure of government intervention. Most obviously, government intervenes to ensure that certain public services such as the road system are produced. Government also intervenes to try to ensure an equitable distribution of income, or at least, to make sure that everyone receives some income. More generally, government has been shown in Chapter 2 to intervene to try to realise central macroeconomic objectives. When fiscal, monetary and balance of payments policies are operated to realise these objectives, general interventionary forces come into play and their impact is felt in the market-place. The effect of such policy changes on construction markets has already been described.

Market intervention

Government is concerned to ensure that the markets for individual products and services work as efficiently as possible. In theory, this means that the firm should be as productive as possible, produce at the lowest unit costs and provide a regular supply of their products, at fair prices to the consumer. In order to generate such efficiency, at times it will be necessary for a government to intervene in the market. While all political parties subscribe to the goal of efficiency, they do not agree on the amount of intervention deemed necessary to realise this elusive objective. Conservatives tend to favour minimal intervention and relatively little regulation of the free markets; Labour favour a stronger measure of intervention and a greater role for the state in the control of the market. In practice, intervention which is carried out to try to ensure greater market efficiency is often indistinguishable from measures enacted to realise the macroeconomic objectives.

Construction markets are the recipient of much government attention. In this section, emphasis is placed on interventionary measures designed to make the supplying firms more efficient. It should be remembered that government agencies are a principal client of the construction industry and that construction demand is heavily dependent on disposable real income and the price paid for the property. Changes in fiscal and monetary policy can exert a strong effect upon demand. Equally, general changes of this kind can also influence the construction firm's supply costs and thereby change the underlying market conditions.

Monopoly legislation

Since 1948 the UK has operated legislation to deal with aspects of monopoly which affect commercial markets. This legislation has two main elements. The first aims to control the position of the dominant firm by investigating its powers of monopoly; more recently, this approach has been extended to monitor the use of mergers and takeovers as firms seek to extend their market dominance. The second element involves controlling the use of restrictive business practices. Large firms operating in oligopolistic markets frequently resort to collusive agreements on both price and supply of goods. Legislative Acts were passed in 1948, 1965, 1973 and 1980 to deal with the problem of domination of the markets by large firms. Acts dealing with restrictive practices were passed in 1956, 1964, 1968 and 1976. The most comprehensive piece of legislation on monopolies is the 1973 Fair Trading Act. Despite subsequent amendments, it is this act which determines the government's present approach to monopoly. The Fair Trading Act builds on and develops all the earlier pieces of legislation.

The Monopolies Commission

The 1973 Act established the Office of Fair Trading (OFT), whose Director-General has overall responsibility for all aspects of competition policy. The OFT is responsible for monitoring behaviour in markets generally, and for taking appropriate action to deal with monopolistic practices. It is the OFT which makes references to the Monopolies Commission, who may be required to investigate fully any firm which has a share of more than a quarter of any market. Equally, the OFT may deem it more appropriate to make a reference to the Restrictive Practices Court, especially if the issue is one of price-fixing or restricting supply, rather than market dominance. The OFT oversees the whole area of consumer protection, which involves monitoring firms to ensure that they are complying with existing legislation. If legislation is inadequate to protect the consumer, the OFT will initiate proposals for new legislation. Since 1973 the OFT has been a unifying agency for a more comprehensive approach to monopoly control [2].

The fact that a firm has more than 25% of a market does not in itself cause the firm to be automatically investigated, but it does mean that the OFT can refer the firm to the Monopolies Commission. In practice, the number of referrals remains small: until 1980 only about 40 monopoly firm situations had been investigated. These investigations covered a wide range of products and services. Firms supplying beer, cigarettes, colour film, soaps, fertilizers, breakfast cereals and—most significantly for construction—wallpaper, plasterboard and bricks were all subject to Monopoly Commission reports. Equally, firms and organisations in the service sector, such as architects, barristers, solicitors, stockbrokers and surveyors have been investigated. More recently, the Monopolies Commission has looked into the supply of services by publicly owned undertakings, such as British Rail, British Gas, the CEGB and the Severn-Trent Water Authority.

Firms operating a local or regional monopoly are just as likely to be investigated as those exercising a national monopoly. Contracting firms have, in the past, avoided investigation by the Commission, since individual construction firms rarely approach a position of market dominance. One early Monopolies Commission report, in 1954, did investigate the collective supply of buildings in the Greater London area, however.

An investigation by the Monopolies Commission does not infer that any action will necessarily be taken against the firm or authority in question. The Commission seeks to thoroughly investigate all aspects of a company relating to the firm's monopolistic behaviour and a report is produced with recommendations for changes. Often these recommendations have been found to be of a very low-key nature, suggesting for example the desirability of altering a firm's pricing system without necessarily lowering prices overall. In other instances the recommendations have been more stringent, and firms have been told to cut prices significantly, or free the market by establishing better conditions for supplying the product. It is generally felt that firms who have been investigated by the Monopolies Commission will wish to comply with the recommendations, since if they do not, the government can, in theory, pass legislation to compel them to do so. Usually, firms do meet the recommendations, as failure to comply creates uncertainty which often adversely affects the firm's share price.

The Monopolies Commission is a relatively small body, with limited resources. It is only able to carry out a few investigations at any one time and the preparation of these reports is very time consuming. Often the Commission's reports have been criticised for not condemning monopoly elements with sufficient vigour. The existence of the Monopolies Commission is thought to act as a deterrent to firms who seek to abuse their dominant market positions. Whether this deterrent effect is as strong as it ought to be and whether the actual investigations are as stringent as they might be remain open issues.

Merger policy

Since 1965, much of the Monopolies Commission's work has been taken up with investigations into the effect on the market of actual and proposed mergers and takeovers. While a large number of proposed mergers have been screened by the OFT, only a small proportion of these mergers have actually been investigated by the Monopolies Commission. Out of these investigations, only a handful of proposed mergers have actually been stopped; others have been allowed to proceed after certain assurances have been given. The Monopolies Commission can only investigate mergers where capital assets of more than £15 million are involved, so most smaller mergers can proceed without the threat of possible intervention. In recent years, the Monopolies Commission has investigated a number of proposed mergers with relevance for the construction sector. The Commission cleared London Brick's attempted takeover of Ibstock Johnson, another large brickmaking firm, and later it allowed Hanson Trust to take over London Brick—after this firm failed to effect its own takeover of Ibstock. Construction interests were also involved when Trafalgar House attempted to take over P&O, the parent company of Bovis. The major business interests of these two large firms lay in shipping and the Monopolies Commission saw fit to intervene. Such intervention served to delay the attempted takeover and subsequently it failed to take place. Despite the watchdog role of the OFT and the Monopolies Commission, mergers and takeovers have continued to produce higher levels of concentration in UK industry as a whole.

Restrictive practices legislation

It is generally felt that legislation on restrictive practices has been more successful than that on large firm domination and merger control. Prior to the first 1956 Act, price-fixing was widespread, but by the mid-1970s most known cases had been eliminated. Equally, a large number of registered agreements between suppliers of goods and services have now been abandoned—and many terminated voluntarily—as the results of a few key cases examined by the Restrictive Practices Court (RPC) became known. Successful RPC investigations have caused the abandonment of many agreements in the pharmaceutical and textile industries in particular. In the case of construction, investigations into practices involved in the supply of roadstone, sand and gravel, baths, pipes, electrical cable and sanitary ware have led to the abandonment of agreements. Initially, restrictive practice law concentrated on written agreements of a formal nature, but increasingly firms replaced such visible collusion with informal agreements and arrangements to exchange information. The 1976 Act takes account of such agreements and also extends its coverage to the supply of services, as well as products. Even where an agreement passes through one or more of the stipulated gateways of acceptability, the RPC must still be satisfied that on balance the benefits of the agreement outweigh its detriments. Only a few known agreements meet this criterion.

Despite the existence of the RPC, many firms continue to collude, and hitherto undisclosed agreements are entered into. Cartel arrangements are typical in an oligopoly market structure and it seems unlikely that the best efforts of the OFT and RPC will successfully eradicate such behaviour. In the late 1970s, the RPC uncovered illegal agreements on price-fixing and market-sharing in the supply of ready-mixed concrete and black-top road surfacing. The fines which the RPC imposed on the firms concerned were relatively small—and probably trivial in comparison with the excess profits generated by the agreements. In many ways, the RPC, like the Monopolies Commission, is a symbol of the government's intent to induce greater competitiveness into UK industry. These bodies do not have sufficient resources to do a more rigorous job of enforcing the monopoly legislation.

Nationalisation and privatisation

Where private enterprise is failing in its attempts to supply the market, and where this failure cannot be remedied by either monopoly legislation or temporary financial intervention, a government may take the industry into state ownership. When the industry becomes fully owned by the government on a permanent basis, it is regarded as a nationalised enterprise. However, other less permanent forms of public ownership exist. In 1975 the National Enterprise Board was created to provide state assistance to selected firms and to promote industrial re-organisation. The NEB temporarily owned large firms such as Alfred Herbert, British Leyland, Ferranti and Rolls Royce. When the Conservatives returned to office in 1979 they ended the NEB in its original form and began the process of returning state-owned enterprises, including some fully nationalised concerns, into the private sector, by means of a series of privatisations.

State takeover of a company is a very strong form of market intervention and the extent to which this should be used remains a political issue. Where an industry provides a key national service (public utilities or transportation, for example) and where large-scale investment is required to ensure adequate supply, the government may well be the only agent capable of financing this industry. Equally, where very large economies of scale are found to operate and private ownership creates the potential for excessive profit to be made, state ownership provides a safeguard against monopoly exploitation. In any event, the extra profit will accrue to the state and so, in theory, belongs to the public at large, rather than to any one private firm or individual. In other instances, the industry may be a key producer which, because of international market conditions, is incapable of making sufficient profit and so cannot attract private sector finance. In the 1970s the UK aircraft manufacturing and shipbuilding industries both came into this category and were taken into state ownership. If the alternative to government ownership is to allow large firms, often very significant employers and exporters, to collapse into liquidation, the social cost may be deemed too great and public ownership will be undertaken.

The direct labour organisations are the most obvious groups under public ownership in the construction sector. In 1977 the Labour government of the day published plans for a massive extension of nationalisation in the construction sector.[3] It was envisaged that the role of DLOs would be greatly expanded and that the state would acquire interests in one or more major contracting firms, creating around these interests a National Construction Corporation. At the same time, the 1977 proposals envisaged the government buying up a large number of key firms in the building material supply sector. Firms producing aggregates, flat glass, plasterboard, cement and brick were identified as possible candidates for nationalisation within the state-owned Building Materials Corporation. While this particular set of proposals has now faded into history, it serves to underline the fact that public ownership as a form of market intervention is just as pertinent to construction as to other sectors of the UK economy.

In the 1980s the arguments in favour of public ownership have been rejected and the trend is to return large parts of the nationalised industries to the private sector. The most significant of these privatisations has been the sale of British Aerospace, British Telecom, British Gas, British Airways and various state-owned oil companies such as Britoil and part of British Petroleum. It seems possible that other nationalised concerns will also be privatised in the late 1980s and early 1990s; these might include the electricity and water industries. The government argues that all these organisations will become more efficient as private companies and that they will no longer be constricted by public sector borrowing limits. The monopoly legislation remains the main means of controlling these new private sector companies, who in many cases have very strong market domination.

Forms of financial assistance

The government, having rejected public ownership and control as a means of market intervention, has come to rely on a complex mixture of financial schemes, aimed at encouraging the small firm and hence increasing competition through the growth of such units. Since 1970 successive UK governments have made more than a hundred changes in the legislation dealing with small businesses, all designed to create a market with advantages for the small firm. Small firms in the construction sector have benefited strongly from such financial intervention and these measures have been significant in the rapid growth of such firms.

Most of the financial assistance given to small firms has been in the form of tax relief, improving the liquidity of the small business unit and encouraging investment in this type of firm. Special lower rates of corporation tax for smaller firms have been introduced and the exemption limits below which firms do not have to pay VAT have been raised. Tax allowances for small building schemes have been established and arrangements have been made to allow the small firm to pay its rates by instalment, spread across the trading year. The Business Expansion Scheme provides tax relief for those prepared to invest in small businesses. In addition, various venture capital schemes have been announced which provide tax incentives for those making loans to small businesses. Under the Loan Guarantee Scheme, designed to encourage banks to support small firms, the government guarantees a high percentage of the loan up to a given limit. All these measures help the small firm to survive and grow, thereby making industry more competitive.

In addition to these special measures aimed at small firms, the UK government is also able to intervene more generally in private industry, influencing and restructuring selected sectors, and providing financial support for other key firms and industries. In the 1960s the Industrial Reorganisation Corporation was set up by the government to stimulate mergers which would make UK firms more efficient. The creation of British Leyland was directly attributable to this government initiative and it was representative of the policy of discretionary intervention which prevailed at this time. In 1972 the Industry Act granted the government power to provide selective financial assistance to companies. (The shipbuilding industry was a particular beneficiary of this act.) Generally, the construction sector has not been affected by this type of intervention—although it could be at a future date.

Beyond the special measures made on behalf of small firms and the highly selective interventions, there exists the more general range of tax reliefs which are available to all firms undertaking investment. When the government chooses to alter the rates of such allowances and to discriminate between different types of investment, it is varying the financial aid which it provides to industry. The construction sector is especially sensitive to investment allowances on building work carried out by firms.

The government also intervenes financially when it imposes taxes on goods and services—or, alternatively, where it offers subsidies. While such measures are a part of the wider fiscal policy, for the firms in the industry directly affected, the tax changes represent forms of market intervention. In the same way, the government's role in granting or withholding general trade credits, although a part of monetary and balance of payments policy, can have a pronounced impact on the individual firm in a market. Construction firms seeking international contracts will often require insurance in the form of an Export Credit Guarantee, which involves the government in underwriting the risk of the client defaulting on payment.

Less obvious forms of financial assistance occur in the government funding of general agencies providing free or highly subsidised information to the firms in a particular industrial sector. The various government statistical services (some of which were referred to on pp. 14–20) provide a good example of these. Government financial support for research and development organisations is another example of such funding. The construction sector benefits from work carried out in the Building Research Establishment. Small firms, who could not hope to fund their own building research, benefit from the ready availability of research reports produced at the BRE. In a similar vein, the British Overseas Trade Board, by providing financial assistance for exhibitors at trade fairs abroad, enables building material producers to expand into export markets.

These types of government financial aid are what might be termed 'benign intervention', but they can be a particular help to the small firm, and stimulate greater competition.

Planning controls

The supply of buildings and related works is strictly governed by planning controls, which serve to impose physical constraints on exactly where certain types of structures can be built and, equally, where they cannot. Local authority planning powers, which have been developed in a series of legislative acts from 1947 onwards, are used to ensure that developers and builders conform to laid-down local and structural plans for the geographical area. The granting or withholding of planning permission is a powerful form of local government intervention which indirectly serves to ensure the competitiveness of construction markets. By careful exercise of its planning powers the local authority can ensure that building work is well distributed amongst competing developers; in this way tendencies towards dominance of the market by large firms can be restricted.

In a totally free market, firms choose to locate in those areas which yield maximum private benefits to the firm, but often the consequence of these thousands of individual decisions is a marked imbalance in the regional activities within the country. In the UK during the post-war years there has been a persistent tendency for firms to locate in the south and east of the country and to neglect the north and west. There has been a resulting high demand for building work of all types in the south-eastern part of the country, but comparatively weaker demand outside this area. In response to this situation, the government has operated a set of regional policies designed to encourage investment in the depressed areas of low activity and discourage investment in the already highly developed areas[4]. Such policies constitute yet another type of government intervention in private markets, but the main impact has been to change the geographical balance of the market-place. Inevitably, such intervention changes the nature of construction markets in particular regions.

Regional incentives have varied a great deal, but the main thrust of the government's policy in recent years has been towards the availability of regional development grants to subsidise the cost of capital investment in buildings or plant and machinery (where the investment occurs in a designated development area). The definition of a 'development area' has changed frequently over time and the rates of grant have similarly varied. In addition to investment incentives, government agencies have been funded to provide advanced factory units in development areas. In this way, demand for construction work has been stimulated in areas in the north and west of the UK and construction firms based in these areas have received orders which, in the absence of regional policy intervention, would not otherwise have existed.

In addition to this overall attempt to produce a better balance of economic activity between regions, the government operated a new town policy after 1946, designed to induce a better distribution of population and activities across a region. New towns were conceived as a partial solution to overcrowding in the big cities and were therefore built to deal with overspill populations from the established urban centres. The new town building programmes created an important market for construction firms over a period of 40 years. Such programmes also switched the geographical balance of construction markets, thus providing another example of government intervention in the operation of the free market. In so far as the new town programmes are a form of regional planning, they have been regarded as a form of planning intervention, but they might equally well be viewed as an attempt by the government to increase the demand for construction activity. (A fuller account of how planning controls influence the building decision is provided on pp. 216–20.)

3. Markets for new housing

The market for the provision of all new housing in 1986 represented about 17% of all construction output in the UK. In historical terms, this percentage is relatively low: in the early 1970s new housing constituted between 25 and 30% of all construction output. Since this time there has been a switch away from new house-building towards the rehabilitation, improvement and conversion of the existing housing stock. When new house-building is taken together with the repair and maintenance of housing, all housing output represents some 40% of the total construction market. Although the distinction between a new-built house and an extensively improved property is sometimes not very meaningful, in terms of the value of work done it remains useful to separate the two markets. (Repair and maintenance is examined on pp. 130–5.)

Housing need

The markets for new housing are created in the longer term by the need for more houses than are currently available. Housing need, regardless of whether it is met by the private or the public sector, is determined by a number of long-run factors:

a) The rate of growth of the population and the distribution of this population critically sets the basic size of the housing market. In an area where population is increasing rapidly, either naturally or through internal immigration, pressure is put on the existing housing stock and such pressure will translate itself into a demand for new housing. In the UK, after the Second World War, rapid population growth, coupled with an increasing concentration of population within the urban connurbations, underpinned a continuously high demand for housing, which could not be met from the existing housing stock. Since the late 1960s population growth has slowed appreciably and pressure on the connurbations has been eased by policies of intra-regional population dispersal. Although some of the pressures on the housing market have been alleviated by such changes, there remains a substantial backlog of unfulfilled housing need, as the supply of housing in previous years has failed to keep pace.

b) Even in an economy where population growth and its associated distributional changes are relatively static, housing need can be generated by changes in the number of separate housholds in existence. In the UK, over the 30 years between 1951 and 1981, the average size of households has fallen from 3.2 persons to 2.7 persons. This has meant that the proportion of households containing only one or two persons has increased significantly. The rate of net new household formation has far outstripped the rate of population growth. Household growth also has a pronounced regional dimension: the rapid growth of households creates significant imbalances within the regional housing markets. In most parts of the UK, the need for smaller housing units to accommodate smaller-sized households has tended to outstrip supply in recent years. This need for suitable housing, however, has been most intense in the south-eastern region.

c) If the existing housing stock was sufficiently large and varied, it might be possible to accommodate population and household growth without any need for new house-building. In practice, it is usually the case that the existing housing stock is inadequate to fully meet current needs—yet alone to provide for future expected needs. While crude statistics sometimes show the number of physical housing units to exceed the number of households, such data fails to take account of the condition, location and intensity of use of the stock. The data provided in the *English House Condition Survey, 1981*[5] suggested that some two million housing units, or 11% of the total, were in a poor condition. A significant part of housing need arises from depreciation of the existing stock.

d) As economic growth leads to increasing standards of living, so expectations of minimal acceptable housing conditions also rise. Today's households will not tolerate Victorian housing conditions, and the UK government itself has sought to specify minimum standards of acceptability. There is a need to remove dwellings which are unfit—either by demolition and new build, or else by renovation. Such considerations create a requirement for upgrading the existing housing stock; further new housing is also needed to meet the higher standards of today's society.

Demand for houses to purchase

Housing need is a long-run planning concept which is defined without regard to the ability to pay for such dwellings. Demand is a short-run concept measuring the quantity of houses required which people are both willing and able to pay for. There exists both a demand for houses to purchase and a demand for houses to rent, although it is usual to treat the latter as a residual demand, arising only when the first preference of purchasing one's own home cannot be realised. The demand for owner-occupation is predominant in the UK housing market today and over 60% of dwellings are owner-occupied. The strength of demand for houses to purchase is the key determinant of the number of the private sector housing

4.2   *Permanent numbers of housing starts in the UK (000 starts)*

	Local authorities	New towns	Housing associations	All public sector[1]	Private sector	All dwellings
1972	104.9	11.4	9.7	129.1	232.7	361.8
1973	91.3	12.5	11.2	117.3	220.7	338.0
1974	124.4	12.6	11.8	150.4	109.6	260.0
1975	139.9	19.4	19.6	180.0	153.1	333.1
1976	133.7	14.9	29.2	180.1	158.4	338.5
1977	96.8	10.6	28.4	136.9	138.6	275.5
1978	79.5	9.6	20.9	110.9	161.6	272.5
1979	58.4	8.4	16.1	83.5	148.2	231.7
1980	37.5	6.8	15.0	59.4	101.5	160.9
1981	26.1	1.9	12.0	40.3	118.9	159.2
1982	35.9	2.3	17.8	56.1	144.6	200.6
1983	36.9	2.0	13.0	51.9	174.2	226.2
1984	29.0	1.1	13.4	43.9	161.0	204.9
1985	23.1	0.8	12.1	36.3	169.0	205.3
1986	20.8	0.6	12.4	33.9	179.2	213.1

[1] The total for all public sector includes local authorities, new towns, housing associations and government departments (not separately shown)
Source: Housing and Construction Statistics

starts made by building firms. The statistics presented in Table 4.2 show how private sector starts have fluctuated markedly over the period since 1972: the average level of such starts is significantly lower in the 1980s than it was in the 1960s and early 1970s.

Demand for houses to purchase depends primarily upon the real income of the would-be purchaser and the effective price which must be paid to buy the house. Because houses are comparatively expensive it will usually be the case that the buyer will need to borrow a significant proportion of the cost. This means that the buyer must initially be capable of raising the necessary loan and, thereafter, be able to meet the on-going interest and capital repayments to either the building society or the bank—or whichever institution has made the original loan. When real incomes are rising, would-be purchasers qualify for higher loans from the financial institutions and so they are able to enter the house-purchase market more readily. However, when real incomes are relatively stagnant and where significant unemployment means that many households experience reduced income, a great number of potential purchasers are unable to enter the home-owner market. The expectation of changes in future real income will also influence people's willingness to commit themselves to the purchase of a house.

Often the mortgage interest rate is a more critical determinant of demand for housing than changes in real income. House buyers make repayments out of current income to cover both capital and interest charges. Particularly in the early years of a mortgage, interest charges are the dominant consideration and a small percentage change in the mortgage rate can result in a sharp increase in the monthly repayment. For would-be first-time buyers, who typically need to take out large loans relative to their income levels, increases in the mortgage rate are particularly critical. This problem of the 'front-loading' of the mortgage has been widely described elsewhere.[6] When interest rates are increasing, demand for houses to purchase is likely to be reduced and this will feed back into the number of planned housing starts.

The number of new houses produced in any one year constitutes only a very small percentage of the existing housing stock and therefore, it is possible that any increase in the demand for home ownership could be accommodated from within the pool of houses and flats already built. Where there exists a large number of houses for sale in any area, new demand, in theory, need not necessitate new housing starts. Equally, demand for owner-occupation could be met by sales of dwellings from the existing rental stock. Since the 1980 Housing Act, sales of council houses have increased significantly and throughout the post-war years there has been a steady supply of dwellings for sale out of private rental stock. However, existing dwellings are not a perfect substitute for newly-built houses and even where there is a significant surplus of existing houses on the market, demand for new houses to purchase will exist.

A critical determinant of demand for houses to purchase is the number of first-time buyers to enter this market. While only a small proportion of first-time buyers purchase new dwellings, their entry into the market, usually at the lower end of the price range, allows existing home owners to 'filter up' the housing hierarchy. Few home owners are able to purchase another dwelling until they have secured a buyer for their existing property. When first-time buyers enter the market this frees other home owners to complete purchases of higher-valued houses, some of which will be new sales. Both the government and the building societies pay particular attention to the needs of the first-time buyer and many contractors market their products specifically for this type of client.[7]

Rental markets

In the early years of the present century the predominant form of housing tenure was the private rental. Private landlords—in the form of rich individuals, industrialists, developers and various charitable trusts—were the main clients of the house-building industry. Only about 10% of houses were owner-occupied and the proportion built for local authorities was negligible. As the century progressed, the private rental was increasingly replaced by both the owner-occupied dwelling and the public sector rental.[8] Today, there are very few new houses built specifically for the private rental market. Instead, the rental sector is provided for by various publicly-funded authorities, which jointly constitute the public sector for housing.

The data in Table 4.2 indicates the relative roles of the three main institutions in the public sector and their house-building performance over recent years; this is compared to the activities of private sector firms building speculatively. While in the mid-1970s the combined public sector agents started more dwellings than the private sector, by 1986 public starts were less than a fifth of those in the private sector. Of course, many of the dwellings built by the public institutions are flats rather than houses, and statistics of output value, such as those given in Table 1.1 (p. 4), may present a somewhat different picture.

The local authorities have long been the most important public sector housing client and although in recent years their programme of new housing starts has been subject to severe cut-backs they remain the most important source of new rental supply. In comparison, the housing associations have not suffered anything like the same decline, although their level of starts in the 1980s remains well below that achieved in the second part of the 1970s. The new town building programme has been progressively winding down over recent years and the number of new starts commissioned in 1986 was relatively tiny.

Although demand for rental housing is largely residual, determined by households who are unable to enter the purchasing market, the continuing rapid growth in the number of households has ensured that in most areas of the country this demand has been well sustained. In several urban authorities reports of long waiting-lists for council houses, as well as statistics on homelessness, testify to the excess demand for rented dwellings. As the stock of private rented properties has continued to shrink, pressure on the public sector rental organisations has been maintained. In the 1980s fewer local authority new houses are being built than are being sold from the stock.[9]

The number of new public sector starts commissioned in any year depends upon the ability of the public housing agents to arrange finance. Borrowing by the public housing agents constitutes a key element in the overall Public Sector Borrowing Requirement. The reasons for tight control of the PSBR were discussed in Chapter 2 above; the cash limits placed on PSBR have led to very tight borrowing limits for local authorities in particular, and their new house-building programmes have had to be trimmed accordingly. Where the authorities generate revenue from the sale of existing council houses, they are only permitted to spend a proportion of the proceeds on new building. In addition, any surplus income which is obtained from the operation of the housing revenue accounts can be applied to new house-building. In practice, however, the sums obtained from council house sales and the revenue accounts only yield a small addition to the capital borrowings.

Public sector house-building is the central pawn in the housing policies adopted by different UK governments. In general, Labour governments have favoured the public rental sector and have increased the borrowing provisions to permit higher levels of starts. The data in Table 4.2 shows a more favoured treatment of the public sector in the Labour years, 1974–9. The Conservatives give a very low priority to public sector starts in their housing policies, favouring the private sector instead. Again, data for the Conservative years 1979–86 demonstrates this point. The future balance between the private and public sector housing markets may well depend on the political administration in power.

Further studies of housing markets

Markets for housing exhibit many characteristics, but present limitations on space do not allow a fuller exploration. Housing is a complete topic in itself, but here it is necessary to treat it as just one element of the overall construction market. Inevitably, readers will wish to take some of the issues raised in this section very much further. Accordingly, some fuller references for housing markets and issues are incorporated in the Further Reading at the end of this chapter.

4. Markets for industrial and commercial work

The market for industrial and commercial new building work commissioned by the private sector has remained relatively stable in recent years. The data in Table 1.1. (p. 4) indicates that the amount of such work has fluctuated in line with the construction industry's total output. Private sector non-housing activity, on average, accounts for just over one-fifth of all construction output. However, while the combination of industrial and commercial building demand since 1970 has held up comparatively well, there has been a significant shift away from industrial towards commercial buildings. During the 1970s, both types of market experienced fluctuations in demand, but overall, they were equally important. By 1983, however, commercial work was 50% more important than industrial. Despite some recovery in the industrial market in the mid-1980s, it seems likely that commercial activity will remain more significant into the 1990s.[10]

The data in Table 4.3 shows how the predominant types of industrial building are the factory and the warehouse. As the UK's manufacturing industry base has continued to shrink, investment in new factories has declined, although there has been a substantial market for refurbishment and renovation of the existing factory stock. In contrast, the demand for offices, shops and entertainment complexes has grown steadily. The bulk of new investment in this area has been in the prosperous south-eastern region of the country. The UK economy in the post-war period has been changing slowly from a predominantly manufacturing to a service industry base. In recent years, the growth of financial and professional services has created a continuing demand for quality office space. At the same time, the movement away from corner shops towards larger multiple retailing outlets has sustained demand for shopping complexes.

4.3   *Contractors' new non-housing work in 1986*

Private sector	*£ million*
Factories	1,842
Warehouses	546
Other industrial	245
Offices	1,949
Shops	994
Entertainments	603
Garages	160
Agriculture	96
Schools and colleges	73
Other commercial	351
Total private output	6,858
Public sector	
Gas, electricity and mining	272
Rail and air transport	187
Education	293
Health	455
Factories and warehouses	231
Offices and garages	348
Roads	762
Harbours and canals	92
Water	108
Sewerage services	241
Other work	658
Total public output	3,646
All contractors' output of new non-housing work	10,504

Source: *Housing and Construction Statistics*

Demand for industrial buildings

The main factor behind the demand for industrial buildings is expectation of the future output of the product manufactured in those buildings. When product sales are rising, firms anticipate continuing growth and so a derived demand for more factory space is created. Such a relationship is at the heart of the 'accelerator model' which links investment to changes in product output (see Hillebrandt[11]). In recent years, demand for many of the products produced by UK manufacturing firms has been weak and erratic. Export markets have been lost and in many cases, significant import penetration into home markets has meant reduced sales volumes for UK firms. In particular, most of the metal-producing industries, along with the engineering, chemical and textile industries have suffered in this way. Inevitably, such weaknesses in final demand have had a derived effect on the manufacturing sector's demand for industrial buildings. Table 4.4 shows how the shares of certain manufacturing industries (numbers 3 to 8 in the table) have declined over recent years, despite signs of recovery in the mid-1980s.

4.4   Gross domestic fixed investment in UK new buildings and works (excluding dwellings)   *Industry percentages*

	1972	1985
1. Agriculture and fishery	4.6	3.8
2. Oil and gas	2.7	11.4
3. Chemicals and minerals	1.6	1.5
4. Metals	1.8	0.3
5. Motor vehicles	0.7	0.8
6. Engineering	1.3	1.4
7. Food, drink and tobacco	2.6	1.4
8. Other manufacturing industries	2.0	0.7
9. Construction	0.3	0.7
10. Wholesale distribution	1.9	1.9
11. Retailing	4.2	6.5
12. Hotels and catering	3.5	2.9
13. Banking and insurance	6.5	8.9
14. Business services	5.2	6.7
15. Other services	3.0	4.2
Total private industry	41.9	53.4
16. Electricity, gas and water	7.5	8.1
17. Coal mining	0.2	1.3
18. Railways	2.2	1.6
19. Other transport (sea, air)	2.8	3.0
20. Communications	2.0	1.8
21. Roads	13.4	10.4
22. Education	11.2	4.0
23. Health and sanitation	11.1	9.6
24. Public administration	7.7	6.8
Total public industry	58.1	46.6
Total industry	100.0	100.0

Source: Housing and Construction Statistics

Manufacturing industry has also experienced an increase in concentration of ownership, as markets have become more oligopolistic (see pp. 102–3). Concentration has inevitably brought about the rationalisation of production, leading firms to release significant amounts of unwanted factory space. The existence of surplus capacity is an effective constraint on the demand for new units.

Many firms seeking to expand will consider renting existing vacant buildings, rather than commissioning the construction of new ones. This will be a preferred strategy where doubts exist about the permanence of any increase in product demand. Equally, the existence of empty stock has caused other firms to opt for renovation and refurbishment as a cheap alternative to new build. Much industrial building work involves the conversion of large old factories into much smaller, upgraded units. The value of this work is appreciably lower than that generated by the new build alternative.

Impact of structural change

While declining markets in traditional manufacturing industries have led to recent reductions in industrial building activity, elsewhere in the economy structural changes have occurred, producing some compensatory increases. The growth of North Sea Oil activities has created a demand for new structures for the oil and gas exploration industries. Table 4.4 indicates how the proportionate share of the oil and gas sector, in investment in new buildings and works, has grown very significantly since the early 1970s. Another growth area has been within the new high technology industries of electronics, computer systems, robotics, telematics and bioengineering. Such industries tend to require small, high quality factory units, with better standards of space and environment than those traditionally associated with industrial buildings. These high technology industries have stimulated a demand for new, purpose-built factories, since conversion and up-grading of existing stock will not meet their exacting needs. Such factories have been built mainly in the south east of England, along the M4 motorway, in the 'Silicon Glen' area of Scotland or else on selected science park sites, mainly associated with university campuses. New technology is a key factor underpinning the need for investment in new industrial building and in other instances, for the extensive refurbishment of existing factory space.

Much of the existing stock of industrial buildings is old and in relatively poor condition. It follows that a lot of present market demand stems from the need for replacement. However, many manufacturing firms planning to replace deteriorating buildings will not necessarily want to rebuild on or near the original site. Firms may wish to locate elsewhere, near to a main centre of population for example, where transport facilities are at a premium. Equally, firms may be influenced by any financial inducements resulting from government interventionary policies, such as those on offer in enterprise zones. Industrial building activity has tended, in recent years, to be concentrated on the southern and eastern areas of the UK, in the more prosperous zone around London.

The role of financial factors

In addition to factors determining the willingness to invest, the market for industrial buildings is also governed by factors controlling the firm's ability to finance their investment. Where high profits are being generated, there is a ready availability of funds to accommodate this, but, in the absence of such internal profits, firms must look for external sources of capital. Industrial buildings— unlike their commercial conterparts—are not usually viewed as desirable investments by the financial institutions, so the sources of funds for the building or purchase of industrial buildings are more limited. (The overall problem of raising investment finance is the subject of Chapter 10.) When tight monetary policies are being operated, such that bank loans are more strictly controlled and interest rates are relatively high, this will serve to depress the market for industrial buildings, as new investment is delayed to wait for more favourable borrowing conditions.

Government intervention is also an important factor determining industrial building investment. Frequently, in the recent past, industrial buildings have not been treated as favourably for tax purposes as investments in plant and machinery. The decision to phase out initial tax allowances on industrial buildings after March 1986 has made investment in such buildings even less financially attractive. On the other hand, local authorities, who in the past have often adopted a rather inflexible approach towards industrial development—especially in areas of mixed residential and industrial use—are now showing signs of a more flexible attitude, as demand for industrial buildings has faltered.

Demand for commercial buildings

As manufacturing industry in the UK has contracted, so the services sector has expanded to partially fill the employment gap. This has prompted a switch in demand away from the factory towards the office. The data in Table 4.4 indicates how the main service industries (numbers 11 to 14 in the table) have increased their proportional share of investment in new buildings and works in the 1980s. Banking, insurance and professional services have grown significantly over the last decade and this has led to a derived demand for more office space. Elsewhere in the services sector, stagnation in the overall market for consumer expenditure has prompted sweeping changes in the retailing industry. Large organisations, led by the food retailers, have sought to realise large-scale economies by creating 'superstores' at the expense of a larger number of smaller units. This change has sustained a demand for shopping complexes, many built outside the urban core areas so that access by car can be accommodated. The entertainment sector has benefited from the drift out of manual factory employment into non-manual office work, where people have more time for leisure pursuits. Growing demand for tourism, the arts and especially sports and leisure has produced an increased demand for building work from the entertainment sector.

As in the case of industrial buildings, so the commercial requirement is for buildings of higher quality, reflecting the need for improved space and services provision. Offices, in particular, must accommodate new technological machinery, such as desk-top computers and word processors, and many of the older office blocks constructed in the 1950s and 1960s are not suitable for this purpose. The market for new office buildings is greatly enhanced by a market for refurbishment of the existing stock. Also, there is a significant market for buildings which combine office space with either warehousing facilities or workshop space. The majority of service sector firms only employ a few people in any one office and so the demand of the market is for a larger number of predominantly small-scale, high technology office units.

The location of the commercial building is frequently a critical consideration in making the decision to invest. Offices, shops and entertainment centres need to be located near urban centres and, in the case of offices, demand is strongly orientated towards central London, a fulcrum for service industry activity. During the 1980s this has meant that despite some attempts by central government to disperse office activity into the provincial centres, demand for suitable office space has remained strongest in the south-eastern area. In other parts of the country the demand for office accommodation has not been so strong and this is reflected in the lower overall levels of office rents outside London.

Development demand

Whereas most industrial buildings are commissioned by the firms who intend to use them, the majority of office buildings—and also many shopping units—are built speculatively by property developers. Commercial buildings have proved an attractive investment proposition to financial institutions looking for a sound investment for their savings deposits. Throughout the post-war period, the property market has proved an attractive investment alternative to the share and bond markets. When commercial rents are rising more rapidly than interests rates, commercial buildings are a favoured investment. In the period after 1973 there was a significant slump in this market as escalating interest rates and falling rentals brought about the collapse of a number of development companies and their financiers. Since the late 1970s, the commercial building market has recovered and despite high average interest rates it has continued to expand.

One of the central restraints on the market for commercial buildings is the availability of suitable sites and the granting of planning permission. Very few commercial buildings are built on virgin sites as almost all commercial construction takes place in urban centres where most sites have been previously developed. Not all proposed commercial developments can expect to obtain local authority planning permission; others may be significantly delayed by the process of obtaining planning approval. The wider aspects of the process of property development are examined in Chapter 7; the economics of specific location decisions are discussed in Chapter 8.

5. Markets for public non-housing work

The market for public non-housing work consists of all civil engineering, buildings and works commissioned by various public sector clients in central government, local government and the nationalised industries. In recent years, this market has experienced very significant declines in output. The data provided in Table 1.1 (p. 4) shows how in the period since 1972 the output of public non-housing work declined by over 40%. While this sector, like others, has been subject to cyclical fluctuations, the dominant feature has been a downward trend in output. In the early 1980s there were some signs that demand for this type of work was exhibiting greater stability, some consistency of output is expected in the period until 1990.[12]

Public sector non-housing work covers a wide diversity of building activity, with the one common link that all such work is commissioned by a public client. In Table 4.4 public sector building is mainly represented by numbers 16 to 24 inclusive. This table demonstrates how several areas of the public sector have experienced a reduction in their percentage share of fixed investment in new buildings and works. Both the public energy authorities and the water boards have restricted their building programmes and most of the public corporations have experienced significant cutbacks. However, the largest decline in building activity has occurred in those markets directly controlled by government, such as road construction, and building for the educational sector. Where industries such as British Telecom have been sold off from the public into the private sector, this will result in a switching of building demand between the two sectors. The impact of such changes is likely to increase, as more and more public sector assets are sold.

Short-term demand factors

The central determinant of demand for public non-housing work is the government's willingness to advance investment funds in the form of grants, spending approvals or borrowing sanctions. As was made clear in Chapter 2, UK governments since the 1970s have been increasingly concerned to limit the PSBR and this has usually meant that funds for public sector capital investment have been severely restricted. As current expenditure has proved difficult to contain, the percentage share of capital investment in the public expenditure budget has declined. Moreover, buildings and works have had to compete with plant and machinery for a share of the declining total investment expenditure. Against this background, the volume of new public building work has been the most obvious casualty of the policy of stringent control of the PSBR.

Despite this recent pattern of reductions, the need for further investment in this sector remains strong. A recent NEDO report[13] has drawn attention to the poor state of much of the existing public-sector-built infrastructure, a good deal of which is very old and in need of improvement. It is unlikely that the work involved can be met by small-scale repair and maintenance allocations out of current expenditure budgets. Rather, extensive new capital expenditures are required to upgrade the nation's stock of roads and bridges, water mains and sewers, national health service estates, school buildings and central government civil estates. Although not specifically covered in the NEDO study, it seems likely that similar considerations apply to the buildings and structures owned by the Central Electricity Generating Board and the various area electricity boards, as well as those belonging to British Rail, the National Coal Board, the Post Office, the British Steel Corporation and various other smaller public corporations.

Longer-term investment factors

While financial constraints applied by the government determine the short-term level of public sector non-housing output, in the long term, the need for new investment is informed by wider considerations. In the case of most public corporations, it is the demand for their final product or service from which the need for building is derived. As demand for electricity has grown, so the industry has had to increase supplies; this has meant an expanding investment in installation plant, as well as in commercial buildings to accommodate office and sales staff. In this respect the public corporation's building needs are similar to those of any private sector firm. However, several of these public corporations have for many years been operating at a loss; thus without government support, they are not in a position to raise the funds required to pay for new investments. This is true of both British Rail and the British Steel Corporation. Without new investment in both building and works, and plant and equipment, such industries will have to struggle to survive, yet no simple mechanism exists for determining how much borrowing the government should sanction for these loss-making activities. The same problem does not arise with profitable ventures, such as the CEGB and the electricity boards, but the government—as owner—applies these profits to supplement the national revenue and so these industries, too, are subject to investment sanctions when they come to determine their building programmes.

Investment in areas such as the National Health Service, education, roads and defence is required to maintain an essential supply of these key public goods. These services, however, unlike the output of the public corporations, make no revenue, so there is no single criteria for evaluating the appropriate level of capital spending within them on buildings and works—as well as on other investments. In the provision of hospital buildings, the government will have some idea of how many beds per thousand of population it will want to provide. Similarly, notions of the 'right' number of places in all levels of education will establish a guide to the amount of space required in educational establishments throughout the country. The number of vehicles using Britain's roads will partly determine the number of new roads which must be built to accommodate expected traffic flows. Such guidelines, nonetheless, are variable, and a government committed to restraining public investment can easily reduce the planned minimum number of beds and educational places, and limit the amount of road space. While countries with relatively higher levels of gross national product usually spend more on public investment goods, there is no clear relationship between these two variables. Long-term public need may be slow to translate itself into effective demand for public buildings—unless the government of the day has the political will to speed up the process.

Local government is responsible for providing a wide range of buildings and works to serve the needs of the local community.

These include local roads and infrastructure, schools, community buildings, as well as leisure complexes such as libraries and swimming pools. Different local authorities are likely to have varying perceptions of the need for such investments within their community. Frequently, the costs of some of these projects are easy to identify, but the benefits which result are not so readily measurable. Investments in such local projects may often be delayed for several years—without any tangible disadvantages for the community. Once again, the local government's decision with regard to investment may depend more upon the political will of the authority than on the urgent need of the community.

Fuller consideration of investment decisions in the public sector is provided in Chapter 9; the method of cost-benefit analysis is examined as a guide to making the best investments in public buildings and works.

Characteristics of the public sector client

The public sector incorporates a wide diversity of clients to the construction industry. All of these clients are, to some extent, constrained in their ability to finance new building activity by central government borrowing sanctions of one form or another. The degree of autonomy each type of client enjoys varies significantly. In some cases, such as that of the Property Services Agency, the public client is a governmental department. In others, such as the case of public corporations, government control is less immediate and the organisation can select building programmes within the wider borrowing constraint. A fuller account of the public client and the construction sector is provided by NEDO[14].

In a number of important ways, the public client differs from the private sector client. The public sector has a marked preference for competitive tendering, especially selective competition. In contrast, the various forms of negotiated contract are far more prevalent in private sector markets. Public clients are more concerned to be seen to be competitive in letting the contract and in securing the lowest competitive bid, than in negotiating the lowest duration times—and possibly greater cost savings.

Public clients commonly employ their own design staff; most public authorities have architects, surveyors and engineers in their employment. In consequence, it is far more usual in the public than in the private sector to find design work being carried out in-house. Where projects arise beyond the experience of the authority's staff, use will be made of external design consultants. From a contractor's standpoint, this means that the firm is less likely to be able to offer a design-and-construct package deal to the client.

The existence of large numbers of design staff working for the public client tends to mean that the contractor's work is monitored more rigorously on public sector than private sector contracts. It also tends to mean that these same design staff have a high propensity to issue variation orders while construction work is in progress. In consequence, contractors working for public clients have become accustomed to submitting a large number of claims and to experiencing many more disputes than are usual with the typical private client. Because of the variations and claims, it has become usual for public clients to be quite late in agreeing final settlements for payment to the contractor. The NEDO study found that out of a sample of some 2000 public sector contracts, in 12% of cases the final payments were made more than two years after completion. In these ways the public sector market differs from its private sector counterpart.

6. Markets for repair and maintenance activity

While the markets for new construction work have experienced a significant decline in the period since 1970, those for repair and maintenance activity have increased. Over the period 1972–86 overall repair and maintenance output has increased by almost 28%. The most pronounced increase has been in the market for housing renovation, although the repair and maintenance market for both public and private non-housing work has also grown strongly. There has been an increase in the demand for refurbishment of industrial and commercial buildings, but some of the resulting output is likely to be recorded as new work, rather than repair and maintenance.

The basic output statistics for repair and maintenance trends are provided in Table 1.1 (p. 4). A further insight into this market is provided in Table 4.5, where three statistical series highlighting selected aspects of housing repair and maintenance are given. This table shows how grants given for housing improvement increased significantly until 1984, both in number and in value. At the same time that the government has been encouraging greater expenditure on housing repair and maintenance through its grant policies, it has also drastically reduced the number of housing units demolished or closed down. The data in this table confirms the shift away from demolition and new build towards renovation and improvement. While no comparable data exists for non-housing markets, the same trend away from new build towards renovation and refurbishment is apparent.

4.5 Statistics of housing repair and maintenance activity

	Number of dwellings improvements (1980 = 100)	All grants paid to private owners (£ million)	Number of demolitions or closures (1980 = 100)
1972	135	76.0	251
1973	184	136.3	236
1974	175	198.5	156
1975	80	77.9	175
1976	80	78.2	159
1977	87	75.2	139
1978	90	92.4	112
1979	99	122.4	103
1980	100	159.3	100
1981	88	187.1	82
1982	126	350.9	57
1983	205	826.1	40
1984	214	1078.9	35
1985	159	677.9	32
1986	130	527.6	—

Source: *Housing and Construction Statistics*

The need for repair and maintenance

Demand for repair and maintenance is conditioned by a wide variety of factors, central to which is the existing condition of the building stock. In the case of housing, regular surveys are carried out to establish the condition of the stock and to record how aspects of the stock's condition are changing over time. The *English House Condition Survey 1981* indicated that some 11% of housing units were unsatisfactory, lacking basic amenities or needing substantial repairs to bring them up to an acceptable standard. In comparison to five years earlier, the number of housing units which were unfit or were lacking basic amenities had fallen, but the number requiring extensive repairs was increasing. In 1981, almost 40% of the English housing stock, some 7 million units, required over £1000 per house to be spent on returning them to a 'good' condition. Inflation will serve to raise the number of housing units exceeding this threshold. Comparable surveys of the Welsh and Scottish housing stocks paint a similar picture to that of England.

The majority of housing units in need of substantial repair and maintenance expenditure are located within the private sector. Such houses are predominantly privately rented terraced units, with low rateable values, built before 1919. A survey carried out at the end of 1986 showed that about 28% of all houses in Great Britain were built before 1919 and that a further 20% were built in the inter-war period. This means that almost half of the housing stock of Great Britain is more than forty years old, and that one in seven of such houses is more than a hundred years old. Inevitably, the age profile of the housing stock ensures that there is a high potential demand for renovation work.

In the case of public sector housing, age of stock is not the only determinant of repair needs. A recent DOE survey[15] into the condition of local authority housing stock in England has identified that over 80% of units are in need of attention. Simple decrepitude is the central cause of the need for repair, and a widespread problem exists with hastily-erected units, constructed in the immediate post-war period. Significant problems exist with some non-traditionally built high-rise flat blocks of relatively recent vintage. Faults with the industrialised building systems of the 1960s have led to substantial repair requirements on some properties of only twenty years age or less. Overall, it was estimated that the local authorities would need to spend some £19,000 million at 1985 prices to bring their housing stock up to a satisfactory standard. If the houses and flats in the private sector were to require similar attention, then the national total repair bill would be about £76 billion. The annual recorded expenditure on housing repair and maintenance was nearer to £6 billion in 1985.

The large potential market for housing repairs is also matched by a substantial potential market for refurbishment in the case of industrial and commercial buildings. Although no surveys comparable to the DOE's have been carried out, it is known that much of the industrial stock is relatively old and in poor condition. Many factories are too large for today's industrial requirements and the standard of their amenities is low. There is a high potential for the conversion of old buildings into smaller workshop units and the upgrading of some to accommodate high-technology processes and modern services. Similarly, many office buildings constructed in the 1950s and 1960s are now well below the standards required in the 1980s and, if developers are to obtain good revenues from rental, then refurbishment of the interior and some up-grading of the exterior cladding is called for. Many office developments occupy sites on which it would now be impossible to obtain planning permission, so there is a strong case for refurbishing the property to take advantage of the strong demand for newer accommodation in the 'best' locations.

Financing repair and maintenance

Repair and maintenance needs will only be translated into demand when the potential client is able to finance the work. Obviously, the income level of the individual and the profitability of the corporate sector involved are important in determining the ability to pay for repairs. Smaller repairs can be paid for out of current accounts, but where such acounts are under pressure, building requirements will often be the item most easily deferred. Frequently, only the most essential repairs will be carried out where budgets are limited. General changes in disposable income influence the short-term demand for repair and maintenance.

Larger needs, such as improvement and conversion, will often have to be paid for by borrowing, in the same way as new construction is financed. For the individual client, the availability of mortgage finance and the level of the mortgage rate will determine the basic ability to fund this improvement work. For the public client, it is the availability of government grants (together with the borrowing sanction) which sets the limits on repair and mainten-ance activity. The industrial and commercial client will finance this type of work either out of profit reserves or by use of bank loans. High interest rates are a disincentive to repair the maintenance activity.

Successive Housing Acts since 1949 have given the local authorities the power to pay grants to both public and private house owners to subsidise the cost of carrying out various types of repair and maintenance. The 1969 Housing Act contained a major policy shift towards spending on housing rehabilitation, rather than on new development. This act contained a government commitment to providing a higher level of state funding for repair purposes. The 1969 Act also established General Improvement Areas, in which *all* housing units qualified for particular grant assistance. In the 1974 Housing Act, this concept was extended to create Housing Action Areas, which were narrower sets of houses qualifying for extra grant aid. This act led to fewer grants being awarded in total, but the value of each grant was significantly increased. The impact of the 1974 legislative change is apparent in the data given in Table 4.5. The 1980 Housing Act attempted to make grant awards more flexible, in order to hasten the pace of housing rehabilitation.

The role of housing grants

The present system governs a variety of different housing grants, with availability mainly restricted to those owning houses built before 1961, with relatively low rateable values. Only the inter-mediate grant, to cover standard amenities such as the installation of baths, sinks and basins, as well as essential basic repairs, is mandatory. All the other main grants, with the exception of the low-valued insulation grant, are discretionary and so are conditional on the existence of sufficient total funds in the coffers of the local authority. There is an improvement and conversion grant, a special grant and a repair grant, whose availability is usually restricted to housing units in General Improvement and Housing Action Areas. Each of the grants has a stipulated upper limit and is usually only for a percentage of this. The percentage typically varies between 50% and 90%; up-to-date details about this are published by the Department of Environment[16].

Grant finance is undoubtedly important in subsidising repair and improvement expenditure on dwellings in the worst condition. However, the grant system has a number of significant limitations. One central problem is that grant finance is subject to the same restraints as public sector investment in general. Both the number of grants and their average values have varied over time, as the government has alternately expanded and contracted overall funding. The impact of cuts in grant expenditure in the period 1985–6 is clearly seen in Table 4.5. Most grants are paid through the local authorities and it is clear that quite a high proportion of the funds available for grants are applied to public sector housing stock. In 1984 some 46% of grant finance for the renovation of dwellings in England was taken up by the combined local authority, new town and housing corporation sector. Although the dwellings in the worst condition are predominantly those in private ownership, government expenditure on repair and maintenance is not always concentrated on this sector.

Grants to private owners and tenants cover a significant proportion of the cost of basic repair and maintenance, but there still remains the problem of financing the residual cost. Those living in the very worst housing are frequently those on the lowest incomes, and many are unable—or unwilling—to accept this expenditure. This problem of ensuring that the housing grants are applied to the dwellings in the worst condition is often compounded by the restrictive approach of the local authority. Before grants are paid, the local authority may require satisfying on many aspects of the repair work; the standard of the work will need to be checked and the grant will not normally be paid until the job is completed and approved. Restrictions on the subsequent short-term sale of the dwellings may also be imposed. Many house-owners who qualify for aid may be discouraged by such bureaucratic stipulations. Others may not be aware of the existence of the grants—or the procedures for securing this type of financial assistance.

Future changes in grant finance

In a recent Green Paper[17], the government put forward suggestions for changing the future basis of grant-aided housing improvement.

Briefly, it was suggested that grants should be more highly selective, and that mandatory grants should only be available subject to means-testing and a more rigorous definition of the standard of fitness of the dwelling. It was further suggested that all discretionary assistance with repair and maintenance should take the form of a government loan rather than a grant. The government would take a financial stake in the ownership of the dwelling, proportional to the repair loan, and this stake would be realisable upon the sale of the property. Where dwellings are deemed unfit and the owner is unwilling or unable to take any remedial action, the local authority would be empowered to make compulsory purchase and so rectify the problem more rapidly. Overall, it seems likely that future government expenditure on repair and maintenance will decrease and it is expected that private owners will make a larger financial contribution to the renovation of their properties.

7. Overseas markets

As UK markets for new building work began to decline in the 1970s, the larger contracting firms looked increasingly to overseas markets. In particular, contractors looked for market opportunities in the Middle East, where higher world oil prices had produced a sudden increase in wealth. African countries, such as Nigeria, also offered considerable potential for new construction investment.

4.6   *British construction work overseas: the value of work done*

| | £ million | | | Percentage by region | |
	Total work	Middle East	Africa	America	Europe
1972/3	312	17	23	20	16
1973/4	363	16	32	17	15
1974/5	458	32	28	11	14
1975/6	859	44	27	10	9
1976/7	1,253	49	27	9	5
1977/8	1,597	51	24	6	7
1978/9	1,678	51	25	6	6
1979/80	1,384	50	17	12	8
1980/1	1,271	42	16	16	11
1981/2	1,478	39	21	23	4
1982/3	2,314	32	23	19	5
1983/4	2,344	31	24	20	3
1984/5	2,433	30	20	25	4

Source: Housing and Construction Statistics

Table 4.6 shows how, over the period 1972–9, the value of work done by British contractors overseas grew five-fold in terms of current prices. Even after allowing for inflation, this represented a very significant growth in real output, such that by 1979 overseas turnover accounted for almost 9% of total UK construction work. Three-quarters of this work was carried out on contracts in the Middle East and Africa.

After 1979 the overseas market declined briefly, before recovering strongly in the mid-1980s. However, the Middle East, while still the dominant market, has become relatively less important and with the prospect of declining oil prices in the final quarter of the 1980s this pattern is likely to continue. The share taken by the African countries and also the Latin American nations has increased in recent years, but once again oil wealth has been the key to increased construction investment. Although they are not shown separately in Table 4.6, Australasia and the Far East have become important markets for some UK contractors. The demand for industrial and commercial buildings in Hong Kong, Malaysia and Indonesia has been particularly significant. It is noteworthy that, despite UK membership of the European Economic Community, British contractors have not found much success in the EEC countries.

Some difficulties in overseas contracting

While a number of UK contracting firms have entered overseas markets, not all have prospered there, and for many profits have proved elusive. Few firms have experienced success in all their ventures and some—prominent amongst these are Tarmac and Laings—have encounters high losses on specific contracts. This points to some of the peculiar difficulties with which contractors may be confronted in overseas markets. Perhaps the central difficulty is the intense competition which exists for the potentially lucrative overseas contracts. The degree of competition is very much fiercer than that customarily met in domestic markets. UK contractors frequently confront West European rivals, as well as those from Japan and the USA. More recently, Korean contractors have entered the Middle Eastern market, which again has served to cut back profit margins. Where ventures entail a high degree of risk, UK contractors have sometimes formed consortia with their international rivals. While this type of market behaviour serves to reduce the risk of losses, it also leads to a sharing out of the profits.

Most international contracts involve large financial risk. The scale of international contracts frequently requires the tendering contractor to organise a package of extensive credit to finance the work in progress. Sometimes, the overseas client goes bankrupt during the project, while on other occasions problems arise when the client simply refuses to pay for work already done. Usually, contracts are negotiated in the currency of the client's nation and if exchange rates move against this particular currency, the contractor finishes up earning considerably less than had been hoped for. In order to win the contract it might prove necessary to guarantee a fixed price, without full provision for recovering costs. Where unseen difficulties arise on such a contract, the losses will be borne by the contractor. The financial risks on overseas contracts are generally much larger than those encountered domestically; thus usually only larger firms can afford to gamble in these markets.

The public client in a developing country will often seek to impose quite stringent conditions on foreign firms who gain access to the market. Commonly, firms will be required to use local sub-contractors and suppliers, and the firm may be expected to enter into joint working arrangements with domestic engineers and surveyors. Firms need to ensure that such local services are adequate to their needs, and where shortcomings are identified, alternative sources of supply will need to be organised. When firms are obliged to start importing significant amounts of labour, plant and materials into a country, their costs rise rapidly and the profitability of the venture is threatened.

Another source of difficulty arises from overseas contractors having to work within the constraints of the local environment, taking heed of local customs and practices. Problems sometimes arise with national bye-laws and building regulations, which may exhibit aspects unique to the particular overseas country. Equally, local employment practices will need to be accommodated, and account taken of cultural differences in relationships with the workforce and the sub-contractors. Allowance must also be made for intervention on the part of the national government concerned. All these factors serve to render overseas contracting a demanding exercise for the inexperienced firm. A fuller account of the trials and tribulations of contracting in overseas markets can be found elsewhere.[18]

Questions

1. Distinguish the main features of monopoly from those of oligopoly and imperfect competition.
2. Outline the operations of a large public contracting firm in several different types of market.
3. Why do governments consider it necessary to intervene in the workings of the market-place?

4. Describe the workings of the Monopolies Commission and provide examples of areas of recent investigation.
5. How successful has monopoly legislation been, overall, in regulating the market behaviour of large firms in the UK?
6. Discuss some of the financial measures applied by government to encourage small firms to compete in the market.
7. Identify those factors which determine the level of future housing need.
8. Assess the importance of the first-time buyer to the house purchase market, and is so doing comment on the difficulties which such a buyer has on entering this market.
9. What are the main determinants of the supply of rental housing units onto the market?
10. Describe recent trends in the demand for:
    a) new private industrial building work
    b) new commercial building work
11. What factors lie behind the persistent demand for office buildings?
12. Account for the strong decline in new public non-housing construction in the period since 1970.
13. In what main ways do public sector clients differ from those in the private sector?
14. Describe the causes of the marked growth in repair and maintenance activity since 1970.
15. Discuss the condition of the English housing stock, as revealed by recent surveys.
16. How important are housing grants for ensuring a continuing demand for repair and maintenance activity in housing? Identify the main limitations of such grants.
17. Analyse recent trends in British construction work overseas.
18. Identify some of the peculiar difficulties which confront contractors operating in overseas markets.

Further Reading

BALCHIN, P. N., *Housing Policy: An Introduction*, Croom Helm, 1985
BARBACK, R. H., *The Firm and its Environment*, Philip Allan, 1984
GEORGE, K. D. and JOLL, C., *Industrial Organisation*, George Allen and Unwin, 1981
HILLEBRANDT, P. M., *Analysis of the British Construction Industry*, Chapters 2 and 4, Macmillan, 1984
HILLEBRANDT, P. M., *Economic Theory and the Construction Industry*, Chapters 4, 5 and 6, Macmillan, 1985
NEDO, *Construction for Industrial Recovery*, Building and Civil Engineering EDC, HMSO, 1978

NEDO, *Construction to 1990*. Building and Civil Engineering EDC HMSO, 1984

PASS, C. and SPARKES J., *Monopoly*, Heinemann, 1980

RUDDOCK, L., *Economics for the Construction and Property Industries*, Section D, Polytech Publishers, 1983

SHORT, J. R., *Housing in Britain*, Methuen, 1982.

5 Economics of Supplying Construction Markets

In Chapter 3 the theory of the firm, by which companies determine the quantity of goods and services they will produce, was established. The output decision was seen to be determined by the joint influences of market demand and the costs of production. Chapter 4 analysed the nature of construction markets and the different demands which originate in different markets. This chapter looks more closely at the cost factors underlying a construction firm's willingness to supply these various markets.

Initially, a construction firm has to decide which market or combination of markets it is going to enter. This is the output decision and it will be taken with regard to the firm's size, its expertise and its availabe financial resources. Generally, small firms are more restricted in their output decisions than large companies, who tend to operate in several markets—but not to the same degree in all of them. Once a firm has determined its market and identified the nature of its output, it must consider how to organise the input factors to achieve supply cost-efficiency. For the construction firm this will mean attention to its material, labour and plant costs. Control of these three key inputs is critical to the firms's profitability.

1. Output decisions

The structure of the construction industry, described in Chapter 3 (pp. 61–69), accommodates a larger number of very small firms as well as a small number of much larger organisations, including those in the public sector. Inevitably, such a structure leads to market specialisation, both geographically and in terms of the decision to produce particular products and services. Table 5.1 provides a broad indication of the market specialisms adopted by firms of different sizes. Using the traditional definition of small firms as those employing less than 25 people, it can be seen that such firms concentrate relatively more on repair and maintenance work than the larger companies, especially in the private housing market. In contrast, medium- and larger-sized firms do much more new work, although over time the medium-sized firms especially have found it necessary to do increasing amounts of repair and maintenance work. Where larger firms do engage in repair activity, they tend to favour non-housing work, which is more suitable to their scale of operations. Direct labour organisations engage in very little new work, so that their role is predominantly restricted to repair and maintenance work on public sector housing stock, and civil buildings and infrastructures.

5.1   Size of firm by type of work done, 1985

Percentages of total

| | Private contractors employing | | | |
	0–24	25–114	115+	DLOs
All new work	41%	64%	81%	9%
Housing repair and maintenance	38%	14%	7%	47%
Other repair and maintenance	21%	22%	12%	44%
Total	100%	100%	100%	100%

Source: *Housing and Construction Statistics*

Small firm decisions

The advantage of the small firm resides in its flexibility and in its ability to carry out smaller construction tasks more efficiently than a larger firm. Small firms operate in very local markets which ensure low travel costs and enable word-of-mouth recommendations to be used to extend their business. Many are capable of giving a speedy response to a customer's repair and maintenance needs, and in areas such as plumbing and electrics this is clearly very important. Most small firms have low capital requirements, both in terms of plant investments and day-to-day working capital. Few of the specialist trades require extensive equipment and usually such tools of the trade as are necessary can be acquired progressively. Small firms tend to maintain minimal inventories and they make wide-spread use of trade credit at the builders' merchant or plant hire shop. Since most of the jobs undertaken are of relatively small scale, these firms rely upon rapid payment to avoid maintaining extensive bank loans and overdrafts. Repair and maintenance jobs, therefore, are especially suitable for small firms.

Most small firms are sole traders or partnerships and as such they have comparatively simple management structures. Most commonly, the owners are working proprietors who exercise a high degree of personal control. The workforce is kept to a minimum and any extra manpower is either recruited on a temporary basis or else the work is sub-contracted out. It is unusual to find trade union members amongst the employees of the very small firms, where working conditions tend to be highly flexible. Frequently, long hours will be worked without formal overtime being paid. In the same way, the premises maintained by the small firm will be unpretentious; often, space in the proprietor's home will serve as an informal office. The transport needs of such firms will be very simply met and it is unlikely that any permanent office staff will be employed until the firm starts to grow significantly. In this way, the small firm seeks to avoid fixed cost overheads; indeed, virtually all of its costs are kept variable.

Small firm trades

Apart from repair and maintenance work, small firms carry out a considerable amount of new work in their function as specialist sub-contractors. Hillebrandt[1] identifies the key dependence of the construction sector on the small specialist firm. Table 5.2 provides a breakdown of the distribution of private sector firms across various types of trade. While small firms remain the dominant represent-atives in all trade categories, they have virtual total domination of the group of specialist trades. Here, except in a few trades which require extensive capital plant for such activities as asphalting and tar-spraying, most firms employ less than 25 employees. Regardless of whether it is the number of firms or the amount of work done, it can be seen that the small specialist firm is very important to overall construction output. Over time the balance in trade specialisms has tended to shift. The number of some traditional trade firms, such as painters and decorators and plasterers, has been declining in recent years, but newer trades, such as heating and ventilating engineers, have increased. Firms specialising in roofing and glazing have increased in number to meet the demand for this type of repair and maintenance.

The small, specialist sub-contractor flourishes because, with its low overheads, the firm can usually carry out the work at a lower unit cost than the main contractor. The small firm's workforce will be highly productive as a result of extensive repetition of the standard task. In some trades, such firms may also possess specialist knowledge and equipment which the larger general contractor could only acquire at considerable expense. Commonly, many

5.2   *Private contractors: trade of firms by number and value of work, 1985*
Percentages of total

Main trades	Number of firms	All work done[1]
General builders	40.0	33.0
Building and civil engineering contractors	2.0	16.0
Civil engineers	1.5	8.0
Specialist trades		
Plumbers	9.0	3.1
Carpenters and joiners	6.5	2.2
Painters	9.0	3.8
Roofers	3.3	3.2
Plasterers	2.4	1.1
Glaziers	2.6	2.0
Heating and ventilating engineers	5.2	6.7
Electrical contractors	9.2	7.2
Asphalters	0.5	2.2
Plant hirers	2.2	2.3
Other trades	6.6	9.2
Total	100.0	100.0

[1] Based on the third quarter, 1985
Source: *Housing and Construction Statistics*

small specialist firms develop working relationships with their larger counterparts, who generate the workload for these sub-contractors when making their own output decisions.

Some small firms engage in new speculative house-building in addition to their repair and maintenance and sub-contracting activities. Statistics compiled by the National House Building Council[2] suggest that the majority of its active member firms produce very few dwellings each year. Typically, it is found that more than 80% of its active member firms build less than three housing units in a year. These firms purchase very small plots of land, build a few houses and use the proceeds to finance further small-scale developments. In this way, small firms are responsible for about 20% of all private sector new housing starts.

Decisions of larger firms

As a firm increases in size so it is likely to increase its range of construction activities and, as Table 5.1 illustrates, it will seek to do a higher proportion of new work. Medium-sized firms, who employ between 25 and 114 people, concentrate primarily on private sector new work, both speculative house-building and industrial and commercial building. The largest firms, those employing over 115 people, carry out the largest contracts, usually in the public sector, including work on housing, civil engineering and larger government building projects. Typically, the larger construction firm will be active in all sectors of the market, but its output decisions will be geared towards new work markets. In 1985, larger firms employing more than 25 people, although constituting less than 3% of all construction firms, were responsible for carrying out some 72% of the new work done.

Large firms invest in a relatively high proportion of fixed cost overhead items. Typically, such firms have significant investments in offices, vehicles, plant, laboratories and office equipment, including computers. The larger firm will employ specialist staff at its head offices and these staff salaries will need to be met, regardless of the volume of work carried out. Larger contractors employ their own surveyors, engineers, accountants, legal staff, and purchasing and estimating specialists. They may also employ their own architects if they are offering a comprehensive design service. There is a need to back up such staff with clerical and technical support and to lead the corporation with a board of directors. The advantages of the large firm must lie in putting all this potential expertise to best use across a range of larger contracts which are able to absorb the fixed cost overheads. The specialist staff and equipment are wasted on smaller contracts where they tend not to be cost efficient.

Large firms attempt to spread the risks inherent in operating in only one type of building market. Most of these firms are active in a number of geographical markets and frequently engage in work across the complete range of construction output. As described in Chapter 4 (pp. 104–5) the large contractor will often create separate divisions to try to maximise its opportunities in the different markets. The dictates of profit maximisation, however, will require the firm to make fine output adjustments as resources are switched between markets. Neither the rate of growth of demand nor the level of competition from other suppliers is likely to be the same in any two markets. Firms striving to increase profits will attempt to anticipate these differences and they will plan their output decisions accordingly.

The role of demand forecasts

A firm's output decisions will try to anticipate the direction of market demand. Assumptions about the future are necessary for most types of decision, especially those concerned with construction output. The short-term cyclical variation of demand for most types of construction work renders forecasting a rather hazardous exercise. Nevertheless, most of the larger firms find it necessary to form some view of future markets as a basis for forward planning.

Two short-term forecasts of construction output, analysed by main market divisions, are regularly published by the Joint Forecasting Committee of the Building and Civil Engineering EDC[3] and by the National Council of the Building Material Producers[4]. Both forecasts attempt to project output for between two and three years ahead. The approach used to generate the forecast combines the subjectives judgements of a group of construction experts in order to produce a panel consensus. Reasons are advanced to justify the reported set of projections and it is always open to the firm or individual to modify these forecasts for a particular application. These short-term forecasts often turn out to be inaccurate to some degree, and in the past, many of the published projections have proved to be over-optimistic. However, many firms take heed of the forecasts and while the exact magnitude of changes in market demand remains difficult to predict, the general trend in construction demand can usually be pinpointed. A fuller account of the problems encountered in short-term forecasting is given in Hillebrandt[5].

In addition to exercises in short-term forecasting, a number of longer-term projections for the construction sector are produced from time to time. Both NEDO[6] and the Institute of Marketing Construction Industry Group[7] have looked in detail at the future of construction markets over the next ten years. These studies are primarily concerned with the need for construction of different types—together with the nature of the factors governing the likelihood of this need being met. Such forecasts may provide a basis for larger contractors in making longer-term planning decisions about what markets they should be in over the next decade.

2. Materials management

Materials typically account for about 40% of the cost of all construction work; this percentage can be much lower in the case of repair and maintenance jobs, but appreciably higher for some new large building projects with a high services component. Materials in use on a construction contract cover a very wide spectrum and the type of material varies according to the nature of the work being undertaken and the exact method of construction. A fuller account of the various materials and components utilised by the typical contracting firm is provided in a NEDO study[8] of the flexibility of the construction sector.

Often the difference between a profit and a loss on a building contract is attributable to the efficiency with which materials are procured and utilised. Larger firms, who typically produce higher profit margins, pay much more attention to purchasing materials. The medium-to-large building firm will often employ specialist staff to carry out purchasing and to ensure that materials are procured at the lowest possible cost. Efficient material management involves purchasing the right quality of materials in the required quantities, and ensuring their availability on site at the right time. Moreover, sound management requires that the contracting organisation knows the building material supply industry and understands the channels of distribution for commonly used materials. If a firm is to acquire its materials at the best price and on the best terms and conditions, it will need to research the structure of the supplying industry and identify alternative sources of supply.

Quality aspects of materials

Quality in construction materials refers not only to their chemical and physical dimensions but also to their properties in use. Within a commonly used material group, such as brick, there is considerable diversity in terms of hardness, strength, surface finish and colour. Inevitably, those bricks exhibiting superior characteristics will enjoy a large price premium over their lower-grade counterparts. A high-grade engineering brick may cost three times as much as a common brick. Contractors will often have to make decisions about which quality of material to adopt. While in general, firms will be anxious to avoid paying more for a material when a lower-cost alternative will suffice, too many compromises on material quality can lead to poor standards in the finished building. Frequently, the standards of some materials will be rigorously specified by the designers, but in other areas choice of material is left to the discretion of the contractor.

Historically, many construction materials have become favoured by contractors because of their well-known properties and comparatively reasonable cost. Technological changes in recent years, however, have created many potential substitutes. As the brick came to replace stone and timber, so in turn brick has been increasingly replaced by the concrete block. In many countries the timber frame is preferred to its brick counterpart because of its insulation properties. For other applications, such as flooring and shelving, solid wood has come to be replaced by timber products such as chipboard and fibreboard. These newer materials exhibit the same properties as the traditional substitute, but their unit cost is much lower. Elsewhere, plastic products and components have come to be preferred to traditional metals. Plastics are now widely used in plumbing and guttering—as well as in electrical fittings.

If contracting firms are to maximise profits, a full knowledge of possible substitutes both between and within material groups is essential. Firms need to continually search for alternative materials which either match all the existing properties of the current material but yield a lower unit cost, or else provide additional properties for the same unit cost. However, the introduction of new materials and components must be handled with caution as the construction client is traditionally very conservative and often resistant to innovation. Frequently, attempts to replace traditional construction materials with newer pre-fabricated components have led to problems. The widescale use of pre-fabricated concrete panels for cladding high-rise flat blocks in the UK in the 1960s is one such example. Another is the quality problem revealed in timber-frame housing in this country in the early 1980s. (The general problem of introducing new materials and components into the construction sector is more fully explored by Stone[9].)

The ordering and delivery of materials

Ideally, contractors will require materials to arrive on site just at the time when they are needed and in sufficient quantity to avoid waste on the one hand and shortage on the other. Where materials arrive too early, they may well be subject to deterioration on site; equally, they may be depleted by pilferage—or cause access problems around the site. In addition to the cost of storage and insurance, valuable working capital may become tied up in stocks of materials—a situation the contractor will be very anxious to avoid. Where materials and components are late in arriving on site, costly delays in the construction programme may result. The contractor could face on-going labour costs which often will have to be met, even though the workforce remains idle because of non-delivery of key materials. Serious delivery delays can result in late completions and this may lead to financial penalties from the client and higher interest charges on borrowed capital as the time period is extended.

With most commonly utilised materials, there is unlikely to be any severe problem in obtaining satisfactory delivery. Most types of brick, timber, cement and glass are widely available from local suppliers and very little forward planning of orders is necessary—except, perhaps where large quantities are required at relatively short notice. Materials of a special quality or non-standard types of components, however, can pose acute ordering problems.

Frequently, architects working on large buildings will specify a special grade of material, which may only be available from a single source of supply—possibly outside of the UK. The contractor must then ensure that orders are placed sufficiently early to allow for delays in delivery.

Occasionally, when materials and components arrive on site they are found to be defective, or else they are the wrong specification to that which was ordered. In this situation, unless a safety margin has been allowed for, significant delays may result. Few projects of any magnitude in the UK manage to avoid this type of problem. Where the distance from the site to the source of the material production is very large, as in some international contracts, the need to closely monitor ordering and delivery times is especially important. A close knowledge of the conditions of the building material supply sector is a valuable aid to the contractor in making his purchasing decisions.

Building material supply industries

Building materials are supplied by a wide range of firms in several different industries. In some cases, as in the provision of aggregates, the firms are mining natural resources, whereas in others, such as glass and steel production, the firms are manufacturing specific products. Some material supply industries, such as that of ready-mixed concrete, produce a material and provide a service at the same time. Other supply industries, such as timber merchants, are predominantly carrying out a distribution service, often supplying imported products. Indeed, within the building material supply sector, there exists a large number of middlemen, merchants and fabricators, who form a key part in the distribution link of moving the product from its original source to the contractor client.

While the material manufacturers cover a range of diverse industries, they mainly tend to operate in markets which are characterised by monopolistic and oligopolistic features (see pp. 100–103). Most of the supply of manufactured building materials is dominated by large firms. Monopolistic trends are fostered by the economies of large-scale production on the one hand and by local monopolies of distribution on the other. A study by the Labour Party[10] clearly identified the importance of the building materials sector to the construction industry and it also drew attention to the degree of large firm dominance in the individual material industries.

Supply of key construction materials—such as aggregates, cement, ready-mixed concrete, bricks, steel, glass and plasterboard—depends upon the policies of a few large firms. NEDO[8] has described how such firms attempt to plan their production on the basis of predicted construction outputs, but the amount of allowance they build into these plans for unexpected variations in demand is usually quite small. Manufacturers are anxious to avoid creating excess industrial capacity which would threaten their profitability. Most manufacturers retain enough capacity to accommodate short-run increases in demand of up to 10%, but should demand for a particular product increase by more than this, supply difficulties would arise. New production plants take several years to bring into operation, and once an existing plant has been closed and put in mothballs it is extremely expensive to bring it back into active operation. A further constraint on the ability of a material producer to increase short-term supply is the size of its existing road transport fleet—and the limitation this imposes on deliveries.

As construction output has declined from the peak years of the early 1970s, so the capacities of most of the building material supply industries have been adjusted downwards. While no national shortages of key materials have occurred, local shortages do arise from time to time, particularly where construction activity is concentrated in a narrow geographical area, as in some parts of the south-east. As already observed, shortages of less popular qualities of material or product are quite possible. Products which are provided mainly from import markets are more likely to experience supply shortages, when increases in total world demand may not be matched by increases in world supply. Shortages of any material will usually lead to price increases; this, of course, will create unanticipated increases in costs for the contracting firm.

Material prices and conditions of supply

The price of any material is determined by the interaction of market demand and supply. In the period since the early 1970s demand for most construction materials has been relatively weak, as output has been constrained. However, there have been continuous increases in the costs of supplying most materials and these increases have caused the average cost schedule to shift upwards. In Fig. 5.1, price indices of some selected building materials are given. The graphs indicate how the price of most materials increased sharply following the oil price increases in 1973 and 1979. Manufactured materials such as brick and cement consume a high proportion of fuel in the production process, so higher energy costs will be passed on in the form of increased prices. Throughout the last decade, persistently rising labour costs and high average interest rates have also caused material prices to increase.

The graphs in Fig. 5.1 indicate how different materials have experienced significant variations in their respective rates of price

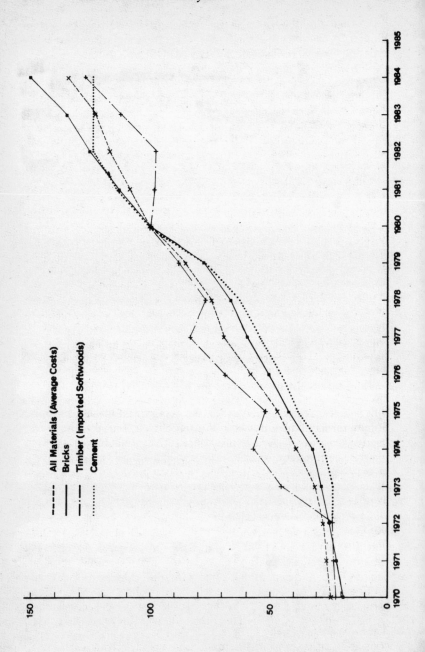

increase. While overall both brick and cement have shown steady price increases, since 1980 the price of bricks has increased more rapidly than that of cement—which has experienced stable prices in response to lower levels of demand. The price of timber, as measured by the price of imported softwood, has shown much more variation than the other materials and, in some years, prices have actually fallen in absolute as well as relative terms. Worldwide market factors, along with variations in the UK exchange rate, account for the behaviour of the price of timber and its related products. Where significant price differentials arise between competitive materials, cost-conscious contractors will actively seek to substitute certain materials for others, in order to produce at the lowest unit cost. The falling price of imported timber in the early 1980s encouraged the growth of timber-frame housing at this time.

Contractors will try to obtain their material requirements at the lowest price available. The received material price to the contractor is likely to deviate from the published average market price, depending on the discounts and rebates which are offered. Most large contractors will seek to buy materials direct from the manufacturing or importing company and thereby obtain a lower unit price on bulk purchases. Where materials are bought through a merchant or similar distribution outlet, the unit price will have to be higher to allow for the middleman's margins. Merchants are most suitable for smaller purchases, such as are made by the small construction firm.

While contractors will evaluate all alternative sources of supply to ensure that they purchase their materials at the best possible prices, they will also be concerned with more general conditions of supply. Supply terms involve not only the price itself, but also the credit facilities for payment which are offered; such credit is a vital source of working capital for most contractors. In addition, contractors will be concerned with the reliability and timing of deliveries, as well as the quality of the delivered product. Moreover, the range of items available from stock and the extra services offered—such as the cutting of materials to size—will also influence the choice of supplier. Sometimes contractors will be prepared to pay slightly higher prices for their materials if the chosen supplier can provide a reliable and comprehensive service in these other respects.

3. Labour decisions

The cost of labour can often be the largest cost item incurred by the contractor in supplying construction output. While on new non-housing contracts the combined costs of materials and plant will

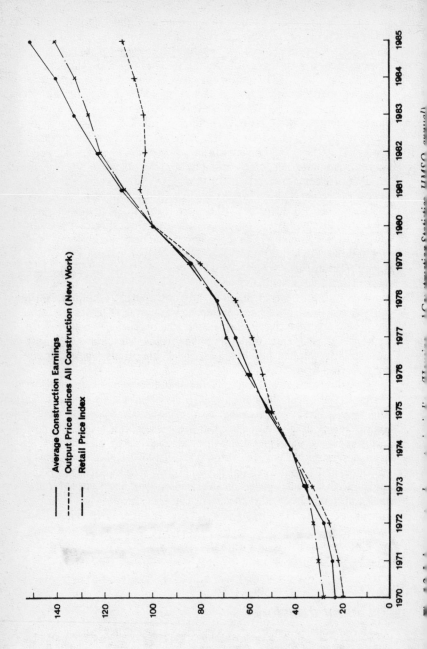

Average Construction Earnings
Output Price Indices All Construction (New Work)
Retail Price Index

usually outweigh labour costs, as the scale of construction falls, labour costs become relatively more important. In most types of repair and maintenance work the cost of labour is the most important cost element governing the price of output.

Over recent years, labour costs in the construction sector have been rising more rapidly than average material costs. In Fig. 5.2 an index of average earnings for the construction sector is graphed against the price of output for all new construction work and the retail price index for all the economy. Whereas in the decade up until 1980 increases in construction earnings were broadly matched by increases in the price of new construction work, since 1980, earnings increases have not been paralleled by output price increases. Indeed earnings in construction, despite the relatively low levels of demand, have been increasing more rapidly than average prices. Inevitably, contractors have become concerned to try to minimise their labour costs.

A contractor has a choice of either employing direct labour or of sub-contracting the job to another firm or individual, who will provide the labour resources. The construction sector has a very high propensity to sub-contract work out. As labour costs have risen in recent years this propensity to sub-contract has increased. Many large contractors now employ relatively few direct operatives and as Table 1.2 (p. 5) indicated, self-employment has increased significantly, at a time when the number of direct employees has been falling.

The costs of direct employment

When a contractor decides to take an operative into direct employment, the initial cost will be one of hiring, establishing and training the new employee. Such costs are likely to vary extensively depending on the skill involved, the location of the site and the experience of the operative. The firm may have incurred both advertising and interviewing expenses already; such expenses are likely to be most significant in the case of managerial and supervisory appointments. The firm may need to provide protective clothing or basic tooling for the new operative. Equally, some introduction to the working practices of the firm may be appropriate. In any event the firm will normally incur the CITB training levy—whether or not it actually carries out any training. With apprentices the cost to the firm can be quite marked, as more senior staff will need to devote valuable time to training and, despite the availability of CITB grants, there remains a net cost to the firm carrying out apprentice training. In recent years, the levels of trainee employment in the construction industry have fallen rapidly and some of the larger firms have virtually ceased to take on apprentices.

Once an employee has been hired, the major on-going cost is the commitment to pay the agreed wage for the basic working week. As long as the operative presents himself for work the employer is obliged to pay him the contracted wage, whether any work is carried out or not. Often adverse weather conditions or shortages of materials and plant may mean that the operative is unable to work all the hours for which he must be paid. The basic wage, which usually also includes a component of guaranteed minimum bonus, either derives directly from, or is related to, one of the various working rules agreements, negotiated by construction unions and their employers' federation counterparts.[11] In addition to the basic wage, the employer will also have to pay the national insurance employers' contribution and any associated surcharges and pay roll taxes. When the employee is absent from site, or off sick for short periods, the employer may also be obliged to continue the basic wage payments, depending on the exact circumstances.

Beyond basic wages, contractors will often need to make additional payments to their direct workforce. Overtime hours above the agreed basic weekly hours are paid at time-and-a-half. Bonus payments, in addition to the guaranteed minimum, are also wide-spread in the construction sector. Enhancement payments to particular operatives, or to groups with special skills, are also quite common in some construction firms. Usually, where operatives are required to travel and perhaps to live outside their own locality, expense allowances will need to be paid. In some areas of construction, workers may be required to work special shifts; appropriate extra payments must then be made to these employees. On some construction jobs all these extra labour costs—which are over and above the basic wages—can amount to more than the basic wage bill.

Firms who employ direct labour may also have to meet other associated labour costs. Where operatives are casually employed the firm will need to pay for the employees' weekly holiday stamp, or else they will pay directly for the holiday period. Employees who are continuously employed by the construction firm may well belong to a pension scheme to which the firm makes a financial contribution. The firm will also need to pay insurance premiums for its own employees, as protection against accident. Managers within the firm may receive a number of benefits or 'perks' such as canteen meals, paid for by the company. All of these payments substantially add to the costs of directly employing labour.

When the firm decides to dispense with the services of an employee, significant costs can also arise. In some cases, agreed amounts of severance pay will be made; in others, where the employee has worked for the firm for more than two years, legal levels of redundancy payments must be met. In the event of a dispute arising over the unfair dismissal of an employee, the firm may be left with legal costs and payments to the wronged employee. In addition to such costs, the firm will also have to pay the wages of someone to handle the paperwork associated with the employee, as appropriate returns are made to the Inland Revenue, the National Insurance Fund and the CITB.

At the same time that these costs associated with direct employment have continued to rise, there has been an upsurge in the amount of legislation governing the employment of direct labour. Various pieces of employment legislation have defined the employee's rights in redundancy, unfair dismissal and lay-off situations. The Health and Safety at Work laws have laid more stringent safety responsibilities on the shoulders of the construction employer. The firm, to a lesser degree, may also have been influenced by legislation governing minimum pay and by the implications of the sexual and racial discrimination laws. Faced with this growing body of legal obligation towards their potential employees and the escalating cost of direct employment, many construction firms have turned to the external labour market and sub-contracted to meet their labour requirements.

Advantages of sub-contracting

The decision to sub-contract a construction task must be based on the conviction that the job can be carried out more efficiently (and so at lower unit cost within a specified time period) by a sub-contractor than by the contractor using direct labour. This concept of greater efficiency entails many dimensions; the advantages of the sub-contractor stem from the economics of comparatively small-sized operations as described earlier (pp. 141–3).

Often, the main contracting firm will be a larger organisation, pursuing several contracts in parallel. Such a firm will possess the managerial ability to handle many contracts, but it will not have sufficient direct labour resources to fulfil all its obligations simultaneously. It will usually be more economical to sub-contract work to smaller local firms than to attempt to stretch its limited direct labour across several jobs in different geographical areas. Frequently, time may be an important consideration on a contract, and the use of sub-contractors to supplement a firm's own workforce will enable deadlines to be met. In this way the main contractor can save its own direct employees to work on the more difficult contracts, where the potential for profit is greatest. Increasingly, many larger contracting organisations are favouring management contracting, wherein the construction work is sub-contracted entirely and the main contractor carries out a management-only function for a set fee.

Traditionally, some types of construction work, such as electrical and plumbing services, have nearly always been sub-contracted. Small specialist firms have developed expertise and high productivity in these areas, enabling them to tender a price that may fall below the main contractor's own estimate for doing the job. Often, competition between local sub-contractors ensures keen tender prices which serve to minimise costs. The low overheads of the smaller sub-contracting firm are also an important consideration. In the 1980s it has become commonplace not only to sub-contract more specialised work, but also to sub-contract most of the brickwork, carpentry and decorating.

When main contractors sub-contract work they are able to avoid much of the uncertainty that surrounds their own direct labour costs and at the same time avoid most of the responsibility that attaches to direct employment. Sub-contractors agree to carry out the work required for a lump sum; thus the contractor can be more certain about costings. Variations and normal inflation adjustments may bring about increases in the original tender-bid figure, but unexpected increases in labour costs will usually have to be absorbed by the sub-contractor. In this way, sub-contracting helps to spread the risk involved in carrying out a contract and the main contractor is prepared to sacrifice some of the potential profit in return for being able to offset a few of the risks of possible losses.

It is clear that sub-contracting offers considerable potential advantages to the main contractor. Indeed, on larger jobs it is quite common to find several levels of sub-contracting, as small sub-contracting firms themselves sub-let part of their work to even smaller firms or to self-employed workers. The sub-contracting system encourages operatives to become self-employed and it also helps to explain the existence of such a large number of small firms in the construction sector. Many workers have a strong preference for self-employment and many contractors prefer to deal with self-employed operatives, rather than to engage in direct employment.[12]

Potential pitfalls of sub-contracting

Although sub-contracting has always been widely practised in the construction sector, it has often proved a source of problems. When labour-only sub-contractors (in receipt of lump sum payments, not declared for tax purposes) were extensively used in the industry in the early 1970s, sub-contracting became identified with the 'lump' and with poor standards of workmanship. Certainly some sub-contractors, anxious to maximise their earnings by carrying out construction work as quickly as possible, will cut corners and, unless closely scrutinised, the quality of work done may suffer. Where a premium is placed on speed, quality may be sacrificed and faulty workmanship can be very expensive to rectify. In some cases, faults may not be revealed until after the sub-contractor has been paid and has left the site. The problem of so-called 'cowboy' work has long dogged the industry and it has most commonly been attributed to 'lump' workers. The majority of sub-contractors, however, are recognised firms and legitimate self-employed workers, who have an interest in maintaining standards in order to ensure future work.

The small size of the majority of sub-contractors tends to mean that most of these firms operate on a relatively narrow basic working capital. In consequence, the liquidity position of many sub-contractors is finely balanced and it is quite common for a firm to go into liquidation or be declared bankrupt in the course of a contract. Where sub-contractors have tendered a particularly low price in order to win a contract, the firm may not be making sufficient profit to enable it to stay in business. When sub-contractors do go out of business in the course of a job, the consequences can often be damaging for the main contractor. Inevitably, delays result and usually there will be significant cost increases involved in securing another sub-contractor to pick up the pieces. The main contractor can take some steps to avoid this situation by checking the liquidity position of the would-be sub-contractor. Such checks, however, can rarely be comprehensive and the system which awards the contract to the lowest bidder may often result in work being sub-contracted to firms or individuals who have insufficient working capital to complete the job. Some of these issues are more fully examined in Chapter 11.

Where several sub-contractors are engaged on a contract, it is important that each sub-contractor carries out the required task at the agreed time. Failure to commence work at the planned date, and failure to complete the job within the scheduled time, can lead to expensive delays on the overall contract. Frequently, one firm of sub-contractors cannot commence work until another firm has completed its task. Not all firms of sub-contractors are equally reliable. Problems of absence from site, poor supervision of labour and lack of attention to detail in the ordering of their materials and plant are common failings amongst small firms of sub-contractors. Obviously, main contractors seek to minimise such difficulties by using only known, reliable sub-contractors, but often the contract requirements will lead firms to use unknown companies.

In their attempt to increase productivity and make as much profit out of the job as possible, sub-contractors may not only seek to cut corners on the quality of work done, but also to disregard safety needs and engage in working practices inferior to those normally expected by the main contractor. Many labour-only sub-contractors ignore the requirements of the Health and Safety at Work Act, and accident levels are found to be highest in small sub-contracting firms and in the ranks of the self-employed. Equally, many small sub-contractors do not conform with working conditions established in the various working rules agreements. Where other site operatives, either direct employees of the main contractor or employees of conforming sub-contractors, are required to work alongside non-conforming sub-contractors, labour difficulties can easily arise and damaging stoppages may occur, until the differences in working practices can be resolved. When non-union labour is put together on site with unionised operatives, industrial relations disputes may result unless management can ensure reasonable conformity in working practices.

Widespread use of sub-contracting involves the delegation of work across a number of independent firms. Almost inevitably, arguments and disputes are likely to arise over who has authority to issue instructions and who is finally responsible for specific parts of the job. The existence of different types of organisation—the nominated sub-contractor, the domestic sub-contractor, the labour-only sub-contractor and the self-employed operative—can lead to a complex workforce which is difficult to manage. Much can be done in the drawing-up of contracts to clearly establish structures of command and lines of responsibility. Equally, arguments over systems of measuring and paying for work done or for changes to the work can be kept to a minimum by careful preparation of contractual documents. (These issues are fully dealt with elsewhere; see for example the Aqua Group[13] and Hughes[14].)

4. Plant decisions

After the cost of materials and labour, the next most important supply cost for the construction firm is that associated with the acquisition and operation of plant. In construction, the term 'plant' is used to cover everything from very small items such as wellington boots and paint brushes, through to larger items such as excavating machines and cranes. Most firms will purchase smaller, perishable items of plant, as well as routine types of non-mechanical building plant such as scaffolding. There are few real decisions to be made with regard to the acquisition of these lower-valued items.

Mechanical plant, however, which is usually distinguished by the need for some sort of power unit and the services of an operator, is much more expensive and the contractor will need to carefully evaluate whether to invest in this capital equipment.

On smaller building jobs it will often be possible for the contractor to manage with a minimal amount of plant. In the absence of readily available plant, a labour intensive approach to construction is adopted. Operatives can be put to work with picks and shovels and in this way labour costs are increased, while machine costs are minimised. Whether this substitution of labour for machinery is an economically efficient solution depends on the relative factor productivities, as well as the relative factor costs.

Frequently, contractors will seek to extend the use of existing plant and equipment to meet the requirements of a new contract. However, it may not always prove economic to transport large items of plant between distant geographic sites. Existing plant may not always be adequate for the demands of the new contract. The available machines may be too small for the job or because of deterioration in use, they may not be sufficiently reliable. In these circumstances the contractor will need to supplement the existing stock of plant and new plant will need to be acquired, through hiring or leasing, or through purchase.

On larger contracts for high buildings and especially for civil engineering work, specific items of plant will often be essential. The contractor will have some choice in the exact specification of the required machinery, but the option of substituting labour for capital will be very limited. The availability of the right items of plant on site becomes every bit as important to the progress of the job as does the availability of materials and labour. As the scale of construction increases, so the value of the items of mechanical plant in use will also increase. It follows that the investment decisions on plant become very much more critical on large-scale jobs. With overseas contracts, there is the additional consideration of high transport costs in moving excavating and lifting equipment to distant locations. Incorrect assessments of plant needs on overseas contracts can prove critical to the final profitability of the venture.

Hiring and leasing of plant

For most small firms, the decision to acquire an item of mechanical plant means entering into a hiring or leasing agreement. The alternative option of purchasing is often ruled out because of an inability to raise the necessary finance. For larger firms, who tend to have much greater plant needs, hiring or leasing may also be the preferred mode of acquisition, despite their easier access to investment funds. During the 1970s plant hire and leasing became extremely popular in the United Kingdom, as many construction firms suffered low levels of profitability. The plant leasing industry grew very rapidly in the period 1960–80, to the extent that about one-third of all contractors' plant was subject to some form of agreement by the early 1980s.

The essential difference between hiring and leasing is one of time. Plant is hired on a relatively short time basis; smaller items may be hired on a daily basis, whereas larger items often have minimum specified hire periods of weeks and months. Leasing, on the other hand, normally involves the plant being leased for a fixed period of time, usually not less than three years. Under a leasing agreement the lessee enjoys exclusive use of the item of plant for the whole period of the lease and, in return, makes a commitment to pay the agreed lease charges for this period. The monthly leasing charge for plant will be significantly less than the equivalent hire charge, which must be set to cover the costs of those periods when the plant is not on hire.

Where a contractor anticipates continuing usage of an item of plant over several years, leasing is clearly more advantageous than hiring. Not only are hiring rates steeper, but there is less certainty about the instant availability of plant and its condition. Some items of hired plant are only available complete with an operator and this raises the costs quite appreciably. Specialist equipment, which is only likely to be used for a very short period on a contract, is more likely to be hired than leased. Similarly, very small firms, who may only need general items of plant for one contract, are likely to favour hiring rather than leasing. By definition, the firm which hires or leases plant never owns it; thus it does not qualify for any of the tax advantages conveyed on the original investors. Sometimes, under a leasing agreement, the lessee may get the chance to purchase the plant after the end of the lease period, but this is not a central consideration in the decision. Both hiring and leasing costs are normal operating costs and they will be deducted from revenue in arriving at the amount of net profit on which the firm pays tax. Indeed, the firm is able to use the hired plant to generate revenue and to use these revenue proceeds to pay the rental costs. In this way the firm avoids borrowing debts and does not tie up working capital in the form of fixed assets. The hired items of plant do not appear as fixed assets in the firm's balance sheet, although they are contributing to the firm's revenue. (A fuller appreciation of these points is given in Chapter 11.)

The purchase of plant

For construction firms earning good profits and for larger firms who are able to secure bank loans for investments, the possibility of purchasing plant, rather than leasing it, is a real option. Purchase involves a large capital outlay, made to secure net revenue returns over a succession of future years. When capital is invested in plant purchases there is either an interest cost incurred, or an opportunity interest cost foregone and capital resources tied into the fixed item of plant for several years ahead. Obviously, unless the firm can see sufficient usage for the plant and unless the future net revenue estimates are adequate, it will not contemplate making a commitment to purchase.

Ownership of plant brings with it a number of important financial advantages which are not available to lessees. Most of these advantages accrue through tax savings. Firms who own plant are able to write off against tax a proportion of the plant's value each year as a normal depreciation allowance. Until 1986 firms investing in plant were also able to claim initial allowances, which permitted the cost of the item of plant to be written off in its year of purchase against the firm's tax assessment on its profits. Over the years, the exact value of such initial investment allowances has varied, but, until recently, 100% allowances made the tax offset against profits especially attractive. For small contractors, who do not earn much profit, such allowances provide little incentive to purchase, but for larger, more profitable firms and particularly financial institutions they provide a strong incentive to purchase. Much of the plant available to lease is owned by large contracting firms and by companies operated by financial institutions. In 1986 the initial allowance was discontinued in favour of a lower basic rate of corporation tax; such a change is likely to make plant purchase less attractive.

For some firms investing in plant for use in development areas of the country there is a possibility of regional grant aid to subsidise the purchase cost. However, such grants have mainly been made to manufacturing firms creating permanent jobs in an area. The possibility of cheap loans being made to firms buying plant for use in selected areas also arises. In general, regional incentives have not favoured investments made by construction firms; rather they have provided assistance to client industries of the construction sector.

The firm which owns its own plant will have to meet the costs of servicing and maintenance, but such costs remain small in comparison to on-going hiring or leasing charges. As long as the plant is adequately utilised, the net revenue returns to the firm which owns it will be higher than those to the leasing firm. In addition, most plant will have some scrap or resale value after its book value has been reduced to zero. Inflation tends to raise scrap value, meaning that plant can often be resold after several years use for only slightly less than its historic purchase price. However, the cost of replacing it with equivalent new plant will have increased appreciably.

The firm's investment decision

No simple guidelines exist with regard to the best methods of acquiring plant. The optimum decision depends upon the financial position of the individual company, general levels of interest rates and the specific levels of plant rental and leasing charges. External factors, such as changes in corporate taxation and the level of inflation, will also influence the decision. A fuller exploration of the nature of the firm's investment decision is provided in Chapter 6. (A wider discussion of the economics of acquiring and managing construction plant is provided in Harris and McCaffer[15].)

Questions

1. Outline the relationship between size of firm and market specialism in the construction sector.
2. Describe the advantages enjoyed by small firms in carrying out repair and maintenance work.
3. Assess the importance of the small specialist firm in supplying construction output.
4. Why are larger construction firms best suited to new work markets?
5. Comment on the value of demand forecasts for the output decisions of construction firms.
6. Explain why it is important for a construction firm to exercise good management over the procurement and use of its materials.
7. What factors account for the substitution of one type of material for another in construction? Provide some recent examples to illustrate your answer.
8. How will greater information on the building material supply industries help the contractor to make better material purchasing decisions?
9. Describe the main factors which have brought about price increases in construction materials since 1970.
10. Discuss the reasons for the rapid growth in self-employment and the increase in sub-contracting in recent years.
11. Identify the main costs to the contractor of directly employing labour.

12. Outline the main advantages which can accrue from the use of sub-contractors.
13. What are the most commonly encountered pitfalls that can arise in the widespread use of sub-contractors?
14. In what ways do the nature of plant decisions differ between small and large construction firms?
15. Identify those factors which have made leasing an increasingly popular method of plant acquisition.
16. Distinguish the relative advantages of plant hiring and leasing as opposed to plant purchasing.

Further Reading

BAILY, P. J. H. and FARMER, D. J. *Purchasing Principles and Management*, Pitman, 1985

CALVERT, R. E., *Introduction to Building Management*, Chapters 9, 11 and 12, Butterworths, 1986

CLEGG, H., *The Changing System of Industrial Relations in Great Britain*, Chapters 3, 4, 5 and 6, Blackwell, 1979

FARMER, D., *Purchasing Management Handbook*, Part 1 and Chapter 26, Gower Publishing, 1985

HARRIS, F. and McCAFFER, R., *Modern Construction Management*, Chapter 7, Granada, 1983

HILLEBRANDT, P. M., *Economic Theory and the Construction Industry*, Part 3, Macmillan, 1985

NEDO, *Construction for Industrial Recovery*, National Economic Development Office HMSO, 1978

NEDO, *How Flexible is Construction?*, Building and Civil Engineering EDC HMSO, 1978

WARD, P. A., *Organisation and Procedures in the Construction Industry*, Part 2, Macdonald and Evans, 1979

Part Two

More Advanced Economic and Financial Analysis

6 The Investment Decision

1. The need to invest

The process of investment is one of increasing the real capital stock of the economy. Frequently, when people save out of their incomes and put savings into financial institutions they speak of 'making an investment'. However, until these savings are actually applied to purchase a capital asset, the true investment cannot be said to have taken place. Investments are made in fixed assets, such as buildings and dwellings, plant and machinery and vehicles, as well as in inventories and work in progress. Our present concern is with fixed investments, made to add to the capital stock.

The implications for construction

The construction industry is directly concerned with investment behaviour for two main reasons. First, construction firms need to carry out investment decisions in order to create productive capacity. The importance of plant decisions has been discussed earlier (pp. 158–62) and most construction firms, except the very smallest units, have to determine their investment needs for items of plant and machinery. In addition, firms will often need to make decisions regarding the purchase of plots of land for development or of existing sites for redevelopment. Larger construction firms invest in buildings both for their own use and for their rental potential. Several of the larger firms operate divisions which specialise in property development, as distinct from general contracting. In common with most other firms, construction companies also need to invest in vehicles, as transportation of materials, plant and personnel between sites is of critical importance.

The second main reason for the concern with investment behaviour is the construction sector's unique role as the supplier of new buildings and dwellings for the rest of the economy. The general nature of this derived investment demand for construction

6.1   Gross domestic fixed capital formation in the UK in 1985 (£million)

Sector	New dwellings	New buildings and works	Purchases net of sales of land and existing buildings	Plant and machinery	Vehicles	Total
Personal sector	9,462	893	3,980	1,012	1,131	16,478
Industrial and commercial firms	126	5,410	428	14,599	2,920	24,373
Financial companies	0	1,240	791	4,044	1,766	7,841
Public corporations	288	2,713	−351	2,458	610	5,718
Central government	50	2,346	−55	742	68	3,151
Local authorities	2,189	2,382	−1,677	441	122	3,457
Totals	12,115	14,984	3,106	23,296	6,617	60,118

Source: UK National Accounts: CSO Blue Book

output has already been described (pp. 7–9). In Table 6.1 details of gross investment for 1985 are analysed according to type of asset and sector of the economy. This table shows how the investment demand for new dwellings arises from both the private individual and the local authority sector. Demand for other types of new building and works arise mainly in the corporate and general government sectors. While some of this investment demand is met from the existing stock of buildings and dwellings, most is accommodated by the output of the construction sector. Construction output critically depends on investment behaviour in other sectors of the economy.

This chapter is predominantly concerned with the corporate investment decision, as opposed to the individual and local authority housing decision, examined in Chapter 4. Companies, whether industrial, commercial, financial or public corporations, all need to invest in fixed assets to enable them to supply the marketplace. However, the amount of investment spending undertaken by any firm in a given time period is determined by a number of complex factors. It is useful to distinguish between those factors which govern the willingness and the basic need to invest from those which control the ability to carry out the required investment. This second set of factors is predominantly financial. The various sources of investment funds available to the firm are examined in Chapter 10.

The firm's willingness to undertake investment

Firms will invest in order to enhance their productive capacity when they expect the future demand for their product or service to be strong. Industrial and commercial buildings are required to accommodate production activity and when this is increasing, the demand for such building space will also grow. Often, the demand for a firm's final product is highly variable and uncertain, to the extent that the firm will be reluctant to commit itself to new investment in buildings. Many firms delay investment until demand is revealed to be more permanent. The link between investment in buildings and growth in final demand is a well-known economic relationship which can be formally modelled. This 'accelerator' model of investment behaviour has been widely described elsewhere.[1]

With commercial buildings, many of which are commissioned not by the final user, but by the speculative developer, the willingness to undertake the investment relates to expectations about net rental income. When demand for office space is increasing, developers are able to obtain growing revenue from rentals, and this will provide the basic incentive for investment. Firms undertake investment on the basis of positive expectations about the future net revenue produced by the investment asset.

Where there is a large amount of existing buildings and plant currently under-utilised, this will inevitably be a disincentive to new investment. Frequently, unused capacity can be modified and upgraded to accommodate an increase in final product demand. It will often prove more economic for a firm to utilise an existing building, possibly with some refurbishment, than to invest in a new building. During the 1980s most urban areas have had a significant number of unused industrial—and, to a lesser extent, commercial—buildings. Firms facing an increase in product demand may decide to rent temporarily a vacant building, while they wait to see whether their increased sales can be permanently sustained. Older building stock may prove an imperfect substitute for new purpose-built premises, however. Existing buildings may well be in poor condition, with a low quality of services, and sometimes in an unsuitable location. Nevertheless, the lower cost of such existing premises, even after allowing for a significant amount of refurbishment work, may turn out to make them an attractive option when compared to new build investment.

With the passage of time, many buildings deteriorate so unless they are regularly maintained and up-graded, they will become increasingly unsuitable for the activities which they accommodate. Technological change has been especially rapid over the last decade and new factory and office processes have rendered many existing buildings prematurely redundant. The advent of computer-controlled processes and robotic operations has meant that factories in the 1980s need to accommodate more machinery than men and most of this machinery requires better environmental conditions than were necessary before. Similarly, the high-technology office contains a wide range of sophisticated business machines, which have different requirements to those of their predecessors. Many offices built in the 1960s are being extensively refurbished in the 1980s to take account of these technological changes.[2]

Few firms are able to ignore investment decisions if they wish to stay in business and remain profitable. Some investment decisions can be delayed, especially those associated with buildings which have a much longer economic life than most items of plant and equipment. However, capital spending on the building stock will often be necessary to take account of normal depreciation and obsolescence. A firm may have very limited funds, and investment decisions are usually irreversible commitments to buy assets which will serve the firm for a long time. It is therefore vitally important that investment is made in the projects which will yield the highest net income returns in future years.

2. Investment criteria

Firms need to carefully evaluate alternative investment projects to ensure that they select those schemes which provide the highest return on the capital invested. Various methods of investment appraisal are available to help firms make the best decision on the basis of the available information. However, these appraisal techniques only serve to guide the decision-maker in choosing between alternatives; the actual decision may be based on other factors which cannot always be taken into account by the appraisal method. The techniques facilitate a systematic comparison between alternative schemes, and all rely upon forecasts of future income flows. Inevitably, the investment decision is subject to considerable uncertainty and risk.

The first two methods of appraisal to be described are often referred to as 'traditional' or 'rule of thumb' techniques. Both the *pay-back approach* and the *rate of return approach* are regarded as comparatively crude methods, which fail to take account of the time profile of the net revenues generated by the investment. The other three techniques are variants of the *discounted cash flow (DCF) approach*, which has the major advantage of allowing for the time value of net revenue and for any other significant effects on the firm's cash flow over time. Today, most firms use one or other of the DCF methods.

The pay-back method

The objective of this method is to identify the number of years it takes to pay back the cost of the original investment out of net cash flows arising from the project. The firm may either set some minimum number of years for an investment to be acceptable, or it will choose the project yielding the fastest pay-back from the alternatives available. Table 6.2 provides an example of how this method might work. It can be seen how Project A takes four years to pay back the original £100,000 investment; Project B pays back after three years and Project C pays back after only two years. By this simple criterion, Project C is to be preferred. However, further study of the data in the table shows that by the end of year 4, Project B has produced an additional £100,000 over its original outlay, whereas the favoured Project C has only yielded an extra £50,000. It is clear that this technique attributes little importance to time and the value of total cash flow. It must, therefore, be seen as a very limited method of investment appraisal.

6.2   An example of pay-back appraisal

Project	A	B	C
Year	Cash flows (£000)		
0	−100	−200	−80
1	10	50	40
2	10	60	40
3	40	90	30
4	40	100	20
Payback period (years)	4 years	3 years	2 years

The rate of return method

This method calculates the average annual level of net revenue or profit yielded by each investment and expresses this average return as a percentage of the capital employed in the project. Various definitions of profit and capital may be adopted, but usually the average net return is taken as a percentage of the initial investment. In Table 6.3, project Z yields £90,000 profit over its three-year life and this amounts to an average rate of return of 30% on the initial investment of £100,000. Although both projects X and Y yield more profit in total, when averaged out over longer life and account is taken of higher initial investments, X and Y produce lower rates of return than Z.

6.3   An example of return on capital employed (rate of return) appraisal

Project	X	Y	Z
Initial investment (£000)	200	200	100
Annual profit flows			
Year 1	50	80	10
Year 2	50	60	10
Year 3	50	40	70
Year 4	50	20	—
Total profits	200	200	90
Average annual profits	50	50	30
Rate of return	25%	25%	30%

While project Z is seemingly preferred on the average rate of return criterion, it is worth noting that on the basis of pay-back it would not take precedence over the other projects, as it fails to return its total investment. A further difficulty with this appraisal method is its failure to distinguish between projects X and Y, which both give an average rate of return of 25%. Project Y generates more profit in the first two years of its life and this suggests that the time profile of profits and cash flow is of some significance.

The concept of discounted cash flow (DCF)

The basic idea behind the DCF method is that a sum of money received today is worth considerably more than the same amount received at some future time. Basically, a sum of money received today can be applied to earn interest and it can increase in value over time. By definition, money which has not yet been received cannot be applied to earn more money.

If a sum of money, say £1000, is invested and left to grow at a constant interest rate of 10%, it will increase in value to £1100 at the end of the first year. If the interest is added to the capital and another year's interest is added, the value of the investment becomes £1000 $(1.10)^2$ or £1210, at the end of the second year. Assuming compound interest at a constant rate, i, the value of any investment sum £A after n years may be given as: $S = A (1 + i)^n$. If this formula is reversed, it is possible to ask what the value of the amount S receivable in n years' time is worth today. The reverse process of compounding is discounting and it may be written: $S/(1 + i)^n = A$. In terms of the example above the following question can be asked: what is £1210, receivable at the end of year 2, worth today, if an interest rate of 10% is assumed? Clearly, the answer is £1000.

By using the discounting technique it is possible to put sums receivable at some future date into their present values. It is obvious from the formula given above that the present value will vary according to the value of n, the exact period when the money is received, and according to i, the predetermined rate of interest. In general, the present value of a sum declines as both n and i increase. Discounting tables are widely available to permit present values to be rapidly calculated. This book does not contain any such tables because they are so easily obtainable elsewhere.[3]

It should be noted that the basic DCF concept owes nothing to changes in the real value of money. It is true that inflation affects the real value of money receivable in the future, but since future rates of inflation are notoriously difficult to predict, inflation is often treated separately to the basic DCF calculation. When considering the effects of inflation in project appraisal, the most important requirement is that all estimates are made on a consistent basis. This point is taken up later (p. 182).

The net present value technique (NPV)

With this technique, all cash flows are discounted by a pre-determined rate of interest and the resulting present values are compared. Usually it is assumed that the initial investment is the only significant net outflow and this occurs at the outset of the project. Cash inflows from the investment occur over the life of the project and these sums have to be reduced to their present values, to facilitate comparison with the investment outflow. When all the sums are in present values, the initial investment is subtracted from the aggregate inflows to produce the net present value of the project. Only investments which give positive net present values will be acceptable; where it is a question of choosing between options, the project which gives the highest NPV will normally be preferred. If *At* represents the annual cash flow from the project and *i* is the predetermined annual rate of discount then:

$$NPV = \sum_{t=o}^{n} \frac{At}{(1+i)^t}$$

In Table 6.4, an example of net present value appraisal is given. Here two projects are under consideration and when the methods of pay-back and return on capital employed are used, it proves impossible to distinguish between them. Both projects achieve pay-back in the fourth year and the average rate of return is 30% on each. However, when the cash flows from the respective projects are reduced to present values and the total net present value is

6.4   An example of net present value appraisal

Year	Cash flows (£000)		Discount factors i = 10%	Present values (£000)	
	Project A	Project B	(From tables)	Project A	Project B
0	−200	−300	1.0	−200.00	−300.00
1	50	150	0.9091	45.45	136.47
2	60	90	0.8264	49.58	74.38
3	60	80	0.7513	45.08	60.10
4	70	50	0.6830	47.81	34.15
Totals	40	70		−12.08	5.00

obtained, it can be seen that only project B gives a positive NPV. The NPV for project A is negative, indicating that by this criterion, using a 10% rate of interest, the project is not worthwhile. Closer examination of the cash inflow profiles of the two projects shows how project B receives a higher relative share of its total cash inflow in the earlier years of the project.

If, in the example given in Table 6.4, a discount rate smaller than 10% had been adopted, a positive NPV might have been achieved with project A, although it would remain smaller than the NPV arising from project B, wherever a consistent rate was used. If, instead of 10% a rate of 6% were applied, the NPV for project A would become £6390 and that for project B would be £28,380. One of the difficulties with using NPV appraisal is this need to predetermine an appropriate rate of discount. In some cases, where capital has to be borrowed to finance the initial investment, the rate paid on the borrowed funds is deemed the appropriate rate to apply. In other instances, where the firm is using its own profit reserves to finance the investment, it is not so obvious what rate should be adopted. Some firms will choose to pre-set a relatively high rate of discount, which will serve to eliminate from consideration all except the most highly profitable investments; others will entertain a wider set of options, by choosing a lower rate of discount. (Choice of an appropriate discount rate is widely discussed elsewhere; see for example, Balchin and Kieve.[4])

The internal rate of return technique (IRR)

With this method, it is not necessary to specify a market rate of discount for generating the NPV. Rather, the aggregate cash flows are discounted by an unknown rate of return which reduces the NPV of the project to zero. This internal rate of return, designated r, is derived from:

$$\sum_{t=o}^{n} \frac{At}{(1+r)^t} = 0$$

where r is that interest rate which renders the total discounted cash flow equal to zero. It is easy to see how r is derived, if a simple one-period cash flow example is adopted, where $Ao = -£2000$ and $A_1 = £2400$. The formula becomes:

$$\frac{-2000}{(1+r)^0} + \frac{2400}{(1+r)^1} = 0$$

$$\begin{aligned}
-2000 &= -2400\,(1+r)^1 \\
2000r &= 2400-2000 \\
r &= 400/2000 = 0.20\%
\end{aligned}$$

It is obvious that if the cash flow in this example is discounted by a rate of 20% then the NPV will be zero. In practice, cash flows extend over many years and this results in complex polynomial equations, which need to be solved to obtain the value of r, the internal rate of return for the project. Hence, a two-period cash flow investment involves solving a quadratic equation and in general, the number of roots of the equation increase with the number of time periods.

In practice, a good approximation of a project's IRR can be found through linear interpolation, and a large number of computer packages are available today to make the task of determining the precise value of r relatively easy. An example is provided in Table 6.5. Here, two projects, X and Y, are considered; in terms of pay-back and average return on capital employed, it is virtually impossible to distinguish between them. However, when a discount factor of 8% is applied to project X its NPV is reduced to zero, while for project Y the appropriate discount factor is one of 9%. The IRR for X is 8% and that for Y is 9%; on this criterion, project Y is the preferred option. In general, the internal rates of return generated by this method of appraisal should be compared to the market rate of interest (i), such that the investment project will only be considered worthwhile when $r > i$.

6.5   *An example of internal rate of return appraisal*

Year	Project X			Project Y		
	Cash flow (£000)	*Discount factor $r = 8\%$*	*Present value (£000)*	*Cash flow (£000)*	*Discount factor $r = 9\%$*	*Present value (£000)*
0	−250	1.0	−250	−310	1.0	−310
1	50	0.9259	46	100	0.9172	92
2	100	0.8573	85	130	0.8416	110
3	150	0.7938	119	140	0.7722	108
Totals	50	IRR=8%	0	60	IRR=9%	0

The equivalent annual cost method

Some investments are undertaken without any clear concept of financial return, where these are essential expenditures in plant and works, necessary to the maintenance of production activity. Particularly in some public sector investment decisions, it is necessary to evaluate which of several alternative methods of approaching the job will minimise the cost of the project, assuming each yields the same overall benefit. The technique of equivalent annual cost reduces all cost expenses to a uniform basis. A predetermined interest rate is chosen and this is applied to produce an equivalent annual cost for each item. In Table 6.6 an equivalent annual cost of a single item A is calculated by reducing each year's cost to its present value and averaging out across four years, using a cumulative discount factor. This method is suitable where cost flows are regular and follow a well-defined pattern. When all such cost items are totalled together, an equivalent annual cost for each investment option can be determined. In principle, the same method can also be applied to income flows generated by the investment, where these are identifiable.

6.6   *An example of equivalent annual cost (cost item A)*

Year	Annual cost (£)	Discount factor $i = 10\%$	Present value (£)
1	500	0.909	455
2	600	0.826	496
3	700	0.751	526
4	400	0.683	273
Totals	2200	3.169	1750

Cumulative discount factor = 3.169 (4 years)

$$\text{Equivalent uniform annual cost} = \frac{1750}{3.169} = £552.2$$

A problem arises with determining the appropriate equivalent annual cost for an item of plant which is to be used in the investment project. Machines have a limited life, but frequently they yield services over a number of years; often too they will have a significant salvage value at the end of the project. In Table 6.7 an example is provided to show how the annual capital recovery costs of a machine can be calculated, once the cost of the machine and its expected salvage value, after a number of years of operation, are known. Use is made of a uniform series capital recovery factor, the expression in the square brackets in the table. The value for this factor is obtainable from standard discounting tables and a fuller account of its derivation is provided in Pilcher[5]. As the salvage value becomes realisable after a given number of years—in the example, after five years—it is only necessary to charge to each annual cost the interest on that amount.

When all the costs associated with an investment option are

6.7   The annual capital recovery cost of a machine

$$
\begin{aligned}
\text{Cost of new machine} &= £250{,}000 \\
\text{Anticipated life} &= 5 \text{ years} \\
\text{Anticipated salvage value} &= £50{,}000 \\
\text{Market interest rate } (i) &= 10\%
\end{aligned}
$$

$$
\begin{array}{l}
\begin{array}{c}
\text{Annual} \\
\text{capital} \\
\text{recovery} \\
\text{cost}
\end{array}
=
\begin{array}{c}
\text{Initial cost} \\
- \text{ salvage value}
\end{array}
\times
\begin{array}{c}
\text{Uniform series} \\
\text{capital recov-} \\
\text{ery factor}
\end{array}
+
\begin{array}{c}
\text{Salvage} \\
\text{value} \\
\times \text{ interest} \\
\text{rate}
\end{array}
\end{array}
$$

$$
= £200{,}000 \times \left[\frac{i(1+i)^n}{(1+i)^{n-1}} \right] + (50{,}000)\,i
$$

$$
= £200{,}000\,(0.2638) + 5{,}000
$$

$$
= £57{,}760
$$

reduced to an equivalent uniform annual basis, a choice between options can be made. This technique, like the NPV approach, requires the predetermination of a suitable market rate of interest. It is possible to use different rates of interest appropriate to individual cost items, but in general it will be simpler if a single rate of interest is assumed, as in the examples provided. The equivalent annual cost method is more suitable to making decisions, where the firm or institution is concerned with minimising the cost of the investment, than in maximising the return.

Incremental analyses

Not all of the investment criteria described above necessarily lead to the same decision. In general, the decisions indicated by those techniques based on DCF appraisal are likely to take precedence over those based on simpler methods such as pay-back and average return on capital. However, it sometimes occurs that the NPV technique indicates one investment option while the IRR method favours another. Different results can occur, because neither of these discounting methods makes allowance for the total capital involved in the project. In addition, neither method allows for the time over which the capital is exposed to risk. An example of such conflicting results is given in Table 6.8.

In Table 6.8, by IRR computation B is preferred to A, as it yields a much higher rate of return, but by NPV calculations, using a 10% market rate of interest, A is preferred to B. The essence of this seemingly conflicting result is that no account is taken of the relative scales of the two projects in the IRR estimate. In project A, much

6.8   *An example of incremental analysis (all sums are in £000)*

Year	Project A	Project B	NPV A $i = 10\%$	NPV B $i = 10\%$	Project A – B	NPV A–B $i = 10\%$
0	−400	−100	−400	−100	−300	−300
1	300	50	272.7	45.5	250	227.3
2	216	104	178.5	85.9	112	92.6
NPV total	—	—	51.2	31.4	—	19.9
IRR	20%	30%	—	—	15.6%	—

more capital is at risk than in project B. The dilemma can be overcome, when only two investment options are being considered, by examining the incremental yield between the two projects. In the table, the difference in the cash flows for A–B is examined and the IRR for this incremental flow is obtained. Since the incremental IRR is a relatively healthy 15.6% as long as the additional £300,000 of investment capital can be obtained at a rate less than this, it will be worthwhile proceeding with project A.

Further analysis

It should be clear from the above that choosing between investment schemes is no simple matter. While the techniques are relatively well-known and easy to apply, the information required to operate the selection methods is often poor and unreliable. If future revenue estimates are subject to considerable uncertainty, it will not be easy to make a clear choice. Where two schemes yield rates of return which are relatively close together, as for example in Table 6.5, it would only require slight differences in the cash flow profiles to reverse the order of the yields and so signal a different investment decision. It is very important to produce the best estimates of future net income flows and it is also desirable to test the sensitivity of the data on which the calculations are based.

In the following sections, specific elements affecting the investment in plant and buildings respectively are briefly appraised. The subject of sensitivity analysis lies outside the scope of this book and the interested reader is referred elsewhere.[6] Indeed, a much fuller appreciation of investment appraisal and capital budgeting can be obtained by consulting texts in the Further Reading at the end of this book.

3. Investment in plant

In Chapter 5 (pp. 158–62) the wider economic aspects of the decision to invest in plant were examined and particular attention was paid to the best means of acquiring the chosen items. Our present concern is with the detailed evaluation of information allowing a firm to make the optimum choice. Alternative items of plant not only cost different amounts, but also yield differential financial returns. The plant investment decision involves calculation of the various costs and revenue flows associated with each item of plant, so that this data can be applied according to the chosen investment criteria. In the case of plant, information on the expected life of the item, its likely salvage value, the income returns it will generate, the running costs, the impact of taxation and the effect of inflation is extremely important.

The life of plant and its salvage value

Most items of plant have a useful life of 5–10 years but in some cases, the life-span is much shorter. As plant begins to age, its operating costs usually increase and its resale value declines. Unlike buildings, plant is a much shorter-term investment and the time period over which it is operated becomes a critical consideration in the investment decision. Most firms will be able to estimate the useful life of an item of plant from experience, although not all firms will want to continue operating plant until it is totally exhausted. Indeed, firms will typically retain new plant investments for only a few years; thereafter, they will sell the plant on the second-hand market and aim to recover its scrap or salvage value. This value, as was demonstrated in the example in Table 6.7, is an important component in the investment decision.

Over time, plant loses value through depreciation. There are many different causes of depreciation, as well as of diminished performance due to wear and tear, but essentially it is a change related to time. There are several different methods available for allowing for depreciation; a fuller account is given by Harris and McCaffer.[7]. All the available methods attempt to relate the so-called 'book value' of the item of plant to its actual value, which is realisable upon sale. The longer the firm retains an item of plant, the lower will be its resale value, usually regardless of the degree of use to which the plant is put. The extensive market in second-hand plant provides the firm with information on the likely resale value for items of given age. While inflation may serve to raise the salvage value eventually realised, only present values need enter the investment decision.

Income returns and plant costs

In most of the examples given in the previous section on investment criteria, positive cash flows were identified as the net income returns from the purchase of the asset. However, in practice, it may not be such an easy matter for the firm to clearly attribute annual sums of revenue to any specific investment item. Plant is used together with other factors of production, such as labour, to produce saleable output and frequently several items of plant may be used on a contract, so that the returns to a single piece of plant may well be impossible to estimate. In this situation, the firm's approach will be to use its own full cost estimate for the item of plant and to assume an agreed profit margin on this amount. Thereby, the net income flow is the firm's expected profit margin from operating the plant. A similar approach makes use of published hire rates for individual pieces of plant and, after allowing for a realistic level of plant hire utilisation, income return can be calculated. Many contractors, of course, do purchase plant for the purpose of hiring, rather than explicitly for their own use.

The overall costs for an item of plant fall into two main categories: direct operating costs and semi-fixed indirect costs associated with ownership of the plant. The direct costs are obvious—for routine servicing and maintenance, transport charges, fuel and operator wages. These costs vary directly with the amount of use that is made of the plant. The indirect costs arise from ownership alone and they tend to be invariant with respect to use. They include interest charges on the capital used to acquire the plant, depreciation charges over time, insurances and licences and any fixed overhead charge the firm may decide to apportion to the item of plant. In general, the firm is likely to be better able to predict the future costs associated with a plant investment than to estimate income flows from the investment. Costs are commonly used as the basis for establishing profit and so net income flows are calculated in this way.

Taxation

The payment of tax constitutes an operating cost like any other expense and so it is a negative cash flow; since tax is levied in respect of profit, however, it is a particularly complex cost component. Firms do not pay tax on the profit yielded by any individual item of plant, but capital allowances (written-down depreciation) are applied to plant investments. Until recently, government investment incentives allowed the full purchase price of an item of plant to be deducted from company profits in the year of purchase. This reduction in corporation tax was recovered in later years out of the profits generated by the investment. The effect of full capital allowances was to alter the pattern of cash flows for the firm and so improve its overall return on capital. The decision to discontinue initial capital allowances after April 1986 significantly changed the cash flow profile from investments, with lower net returns in the early years offset by higher net returns later. (Examples of how taxation affects cash flow, and hence modifies DCF computations, are given by both Harris and McCaffer[8] and Samuels and Wilkes[9].)

Inflation

Inflation changes the level of prices, and affects both the income flow and the costs associated with any investment; thus the net income or profits stream is changed. Unfortunately, inflation cannot be predicted with any degree of precision and often its impact is to distort relationships between financial variables as prices change at different rates. Frequently, firms will want to make some allowance in their investment decisions for the impact of inflation. If the future rate of change of prices is expected to be small, and the life of the item of plant is relatively short, inflation adjustments will not make much difference to the evaluation exercise. Where the life of plant is taken to be much longer, and where inflation is likely to affect income returns (including salvage value) differently from running costs, explicit account needs to be taken of inflation.

The most obvious way of allowing for inflation is to carry out a number of different DCF exercises assuming alternative levels of inflation. In particular, different assumptions should be made about the running costs of plant, its likely salvage value and, most importantly, about the prices which are used to value the income attributable to plant, such as the effective hire rates. The competing plant investment proposals can be assessed for different inflation assumptions and the sensitivity of the optimal choice to these assumptions can be evaluated.

Another way of taking account of inflation is to adjust the market rate of interest (i) in those techniques where an external discount rate is applied. If the expected rate of inflation is subtracted from the rate of interest, the resulting discount rate is the real rate of interest and this can be used directly to calculate net present values. This method is simpler to apply than the previous approach, which involved detailed re-calculations of the cash flow. However, if a single real rate of interest is applied, it fails to allow for the differential inflationary impact on costs and income flows. Whichever method is used to allow for the effects of inflation on project appraisal, the key requirement is that all estimates should be made on a consistent basis.

4. Investment in buildings

The decision to invest in a building is usually much more complicated than the decision to invest in an item of plant; this is partly because a building usually has a much longer life, and partly because it is so difficult to estimate future income flows. In this section, only the decision to invest in buildings already in existence will be examined. The decision to develop a building, by carrying out works involving a change in use or in intensity of use of land, is examined separately in Chapter 7. Here, our concern is with the firm's decision to invest in completed buildings, with known purchase prices but uncertain net income flows.

Income flows from buildings

The majority of firms purchase buildings for their own use, although some developers and institutions purchase commercial properties in order to gain rental income. The existence of this property rental market sets prices for floor-area in buildings of different types, in different locations. Thus it is possible for potential investors to use market rents to estimate the hypothetical income flow from a building of a given size. In theory, the rateable value of a building is based on the rental value of the property; however, since base rate values are updated very infrequently, this measure may not prove particularly useful.

Estimates of future rental levels are subject to a high degree of uncertainty. The general level of rent for properties is set by total supply and demand for buildings of a particular type, in a given location. Firms moving into an area can create upward pressure on rentals of existing buildings; this has occurred in recent years in the market for most commercial buildings in the central London area. However, as new buildings are brought into the market, the balance between supply and demand is likely to shift and there is no guarantee that rentals will continue to grow at the same rate as they have been. Buildings are appraised according to the services they contain, their age and condition, their exact location and the use for which they have been designated. Within the average level of rents, there exists a wide dispersion between the newer, high-specification properties and the older stock.

The rental income from a building, whether real or hypothetical, is a critical parameter in the investment decision. It will be shown, in the next chapter, how this rental income also helps to determine the gross development value of a property, and hence the price at which it can be sold. Buildings, unlike construction plant, are not subject to rapid depreciation; the re-sale value of a building will usually increase rather than decrease. Investment in buildings and the land attached to them may be carried out on the basis of longer-term capital gain rather than maximum net income yield. Current rental levels determine the income flow from a building, so the investment decision will be particularly sensitive to changes in rents.

The operating costs of buildings

The owner or occupier of a building will be responsible for a number of significant on-going costs; these will need to be offset against the income flows when carrying out the DCF appraisal. (A comprehensive listing of such costs is provided by Dent[10].) Occupancy of a building involves the payment of rates—including water rates, insurance premiums, fuel and power charges, as well as telephone rental charges. Routine servicing of any mechanical and engineering equipment and the provision of security services and general caretaking facilities will also have to be paid for. The owner of a building is responsible for the management of the estate and costs will arise in respect of rent collection and tenancy renewal. Most significant will be the costs arising from repair and maintenance. Generally, such costs are likely to increase with the age of the building, and where cash flows are to be calculated for many years into the future, allowances may need to be made for the cost of renovating and up-grading the building over time.

Choice of a discount rate

The average life of a new building is typically in excess of 60 years and often the expected life-span of a renovated building is more than 30 years. If the NPV method of appraisal is applied to evaluate alternative building investments, and if a commercial rate of interest is used, it can be readily shown that net income receivable in, say, 30 years is likely to be worth relatively little in present terms. A sum of £100,000 receivable in 30 years' time has an NPV of only £420 when an interest rate of 20% is used; this sum rises to £5730 at a rate of 10% interest, and to £23,130 at 5%.

Clearly, if today's relatively high rates of interest, which are typically closer to 20% than to 5%, are used in investment appraisal, it will not be worthwhile estimating income flows for many years into the future. Use of a high discount rate significantly reduces the contribution of income received in the distant future and such rates emphasise the key role of income flow over the first few years of the project in the NPV decision. If the net income returns on buildings more than 20 years hence are to carry any weight in the investment choice, lower rates of discount should be used. The general problem of choosing an appropriate rate of discount is examined again as part of Chapter 9.

Questions

1. Explain the relationship between gross fixed capital formation in the economy and the demand for construction output.
2. Identify those factors which determine a firm's willingness to undertake investment.
3. Discuss the role played by new technology in a firm's need to invest in new industrial and commercial buildings.
4. To what extent are decisions to invest in plant and buildings subject to uncertainty and risk?
5. Describe the appraisal techniques of 'pay-back' and 'return on capital employed', and in so doing assess their limitations as criteria for making an investment decision.
6. Explain your understanding of the concept 'discounted cash flow' and provide simple numerical examples to illustrate it.
7. Distinguish between the techniques of 'net present value' and 'internal rate of return' for appraising an investment decision.
8. Assuming a market rate of interest of 6%, calculate the net present values for project X and project Y in Table 6.5. Which project should be preferred?
9. Using the data in Table 6.4 calculate the respective internal rates of return for the two projects, A and B.
10. Discuss the circumstances under which the 'equivalent annual cost' method of investment appraisal might be used.
11. For the data given below
    a) calculate the IRR for each project and determine which project is preferred
    b) apply incremental analysis to resolve whether it is worth proceeding with the larger project, when the market rate of interest is 10%

Year	Project 1 (£)	Project 2 (£)
0	−2000	−3050
1	1000	1500
2	1000	1500
3	1000	1200

12. Outline some of the practical difficulties encountered in estimating the net cash flows associated with particular items of new plant.
13. Explain how taxation and inflation serve to complicate the plant investment decision.

14. Discuss why the decision to invest in buildings is sensitive to changes in the level of property rents.

Further Reading

CORMICAN, D., *Construction Management: Planning and Finance*, Chapter 12, Construction Press, 1985

DAVIS, E., and POINTON, J., *Finance and the Firm*, Part II, Oxford University Press, 1984

DENT, C., *Construction Cost Appraisal*, George Godwin, 1974

FERRY, D. J., *Cost Planning of Buildings*, Chapters 11 and 12, Granada, 1972

LEECH, D. J., *Economics and Financial Studies for Engineers*, Part 1, Ellis Horwood, 1982

LUMBY, S., *Investment Appraisal*, Van Nostrand Reinhold, 1984

MERRETT, A. J. and SYKES, A., *Capital Budgeting and Company Finance*, Longman, 1973

PILCHER, R., *Principles of Construction Management*, McGraw Hill, 1976

PILCHER, R., *Project Cost Control in Construction*, Collins, 1985

7 Economics of Property Development

1. Property versus other investment opportunities

Real property refers to buildings and other structures standing on land which by definition is physically immovable. An investment in property involves the acquisition of rights and interests in the land and the buildings which stand upon it. Many individuals, firms and institutions actively invest in existing property; no new construction will be involved in such transactions. Indeed, given the large size of the existing building stock compared to the number of new buildings produced in any given year, the majority of property investments are likely to be concerned with existing stock, rather than with new buildings. Many construction companies are actively involved in this property market and a significant percentage of their revenues arise from property exchanges, as distinct from construction activity.

Property interests

Investments in real property involve the acquisition of various packages of legal rights to the land and buildings. The most complete interest in property is the so-called 'fee simple absolute' which provides the owner with an unencumbered freehold estate. All the rights inherent in this type of ownership can be separated out and individually transferred to other people and institutions. For example, a lease may be granted to an individual to erect a structure on the land and to enjoy the rights to this building and land for a specified time period, in return for annual payments of ground rent. In addition, the lessee may also be entitled to sub-let and so sell his own leases in return for regular rental income. The owners of the freehold of the propery may wish to borrow through a mortgage; in this case the freehold will be used as collateral for the loan, thereby giving the mortgagee rights and interests in the property.

In the property market the exact rights and interests available can be finely adjusted to meet the individual needs of buyers and sellers; the price at which the property is exchanged will reflect this differentiation. Many institutions acquire interests in property not because they wish to occupy the property themselves, but because they see an opportunity to make profit out of the division of the rights to the property. Hence, many pension funds and insurance companies purchase the freehold to existing office blocks, with a view to leasing out a number of individual units within a particular block to several smaller firms. In this way, real property is an investment asset, rather like stocks and shares. Certainly, investment in a property will only take place as long as there will be a demand from an end-user. This end-user may not always be known at the time of the property purchase and often there may be a significant delay before a suitable occupant is found.

Property markets

In practice, there is not *one* property market in the UK, but rather a whole series of specialist sub-markets involving houses, shops, offices, factories, warehouses and agricultural estates. Within each sub-market there are likely to be a large number of transactions, involving a wide diversity of units. Such markets will often be characterised by unique locational factors, thus regional variations in the state of supply and the intensity of demand may exist. In the 1980s, demand for most types of property has been much stronger in the south-eastern region, around London, than elsewhere. This has been the main cause of the relatively higher market prices in this region. Not all types of property have experienced such marked imbalances between supply and demand, and the price of industrial premises has increased relatively slowly compared to the price of dwellings and offices in the south-east.

It is not uncommon for a building in a given area to fetch a significantly different price to a similar structure in the same area. Such differentials reflect either the expertise or the lack of experience of the respective sets of vendors and purchasers. Not surprisingly, in such markets, a state of short-run disequilibrium may persist, where minimum selling prices are set above maximum buying prices, so that until price flexibility is introduced, the property market will not clear itself. It can often happen that in times of high and rising demand for particular types of property, some units remain unlet or prove difficult to sell at the required price. As Balchin and Kieve[1] have pointed out, the Centre Point office block in Central London, completed in 1966, remained largely unlet until 1980 because the minimum rental demanded by the owners was set higher than the maximum rental bids of potential occupiers.

The determination of price in the property market is often the result of a complex process of offering and counter-bidding. The transaction is frequently carried out through the services of professional middlemen such as estate agents and solicitors. The vendor will not always know the exact price he is likely to obtain for the property. Some properties may be sold by open auctions and others by tender-bidding, but most sales are determined by more limited negotiations and the final selling price of the property is rarely made public. Properties are advertised for sale at prices which commonly exhibit marked differences from the prices finally obtained.

Institutional investors

Since 1945, investment in property has increased significantly. Private individuals have purchased their own houses in increasing numbers and the case for holding wealth in the form of real property has become widely accepted. Apart from private individuals, the post-war property market has come to be dominated by financial institutions such as banks, insurance companies, pension funds and similar organisations. These institutions have looked to the property market in the UK as an area in which to place their investment funds, ensuring a good return on their capital. In particular, the institutional investor has been attracted to commercial property; office blocks and shopping complexes in what is termed 'prime locations' have been much in demand.

Statistics compiled by Rose[2] show that between 1963 and 1973 institutional investment in property increased by over 700% in current price terms, and that between 1973 and 1982 a further increase of almost 300% occurred. After allowance has been made for the rates of inflation which prevailed over this time-span, the real increases will have been more modest, but, nevertheless, this growth in property investment is marked. Further data collated by Harvey[3] indicates that both insurance companies and super-annuation funds favoured land, property and ground rents as a category of investment during the 1970s.

In Table 7.1 statistics of institutional investment transactions for the year 1985 are given. The major investors in property were the insurance companies and pension funds, who invested, respectively, 15.3% and 5.6% of their funds in property. In comparison to earlier years, these percentages represent an overall reduced importance for property as a major investment category. In the late 1970s and early 1980s both types of institution were regularly committing about 15% of their investment funds to property. During the mid-1980s, the markets for company shares became relatively more attractive and this led to a lower demand for property investment. Institutional investment in property is volatile and changes in relative yields will lead to switching between the main categories of investment.

7.1   Institutional investment: transactions in 1985

(£ million)

| Type of investment | Institutions | | | | |
	Pension funds	Insurance companies	Investment trusts	Unit trusts	Building societies
British government securities	2,705	2,077	67	22	247
UK ordinary shares	3,489	2,152	117	1,073	—
Overseas shares	2,041	1,041	126	1,002	—
Land, property and ground rents	485	955	1	−4	87
Total transactions	8,720	6,225	311	2,093	334

Source: *CSO Financial Statistics*

In addition to the insurance companies and the pension funds, other institutions also invest in the property market. Table 7.1 indicates the interests of investment trusts, unit trusts and building societies. Since the 1960s, both property bonds and property unit trusts have appeared, enabling the small investor to acquire a financial interest in commercial property. Amongst other institutional investors in property, the Church Commissioners figure prominently, with total investments in excess of £700 million by 1980. Property development companies, set up primarily to organize the construction of new developments, frequently retain a stake in the completed property. Some of these property firms have strong links with the larger contracting companies.

Banks are another type of financial institution frequently investing in property. Direct investment from banks tends to exhibit high variability, as they switch funds in and out of property markets as financial yields change. Indirectly, the banks are major providers of loans and advances to individuals and firms wanting to invest in property. Banks also give loans to other financial institutions, as well as industrial firms and service companies, for the acquisition of property interests. In addition, banks advance mortgages, provide bridging finance for property transactions and grant loans for improvement work on land and buildings. More general aspects of such sources of finance are dealt with in Chapter 10.

The unique aspects of property investment

It is clear from Table 7.1 that property represents only one of several alternative channels for investment funds. As well as government bonds and company shares, both domestic and foreign investors may decide to keep funds in the form of cash or its close equivalents. All these options constitute viable alternatives to property investment and the potential investor is likely to examine in fine detail the relative merits and disadvantages of any specific property investment.

Ownership of property frequently involves managerial and maintenance costs, which are generally not associated with other types of investment. Often, the owner of a building will appoint management agents to take care of rentals and general maintenance, but the fees payable to such agents are a significant and on-going expense. When the property becomes vacant, problems can sometimes arise in reletting, and at such times rental income may become erratic. Older properties with inferior service specifications, perhaps located in less fashionable parts of a city, may prove difficult to let even with appropriately reduced rentals; yet rates and service charges on the property will continue to be incurred. The income from property is often less secure than that from other investments, such as government bonds.

Another aspect of property which makes it a very distinct type of investment is its inherent illiquidity. The markets for stocks and shares allow the investor to convert investments into cash very easily, but the process of selling property is usually long and it may take many months—or even years—to realise the cash proceeds from a property sale. Even in the market for dwellings, it is not always easy to sell a house or flat to realise cash in the short-term. Investments in properties are undertaken for their longer-term prospects, rather than for the likelihood of any short-term gains.

Institutional investors in property commonly look for longer-term capital growth, which will serve as a protection against inflation. In the post-war period, property values have increased significantly in real terms. Balchin and Kieve[4] have demonstrated how between 1962 and 1980 property capital values increased almost nine-fold, whereas the all-share index grew just over two-fold; retail prices increased by a factor of almost five in the same period. The increase in capital values has been brought about mainly by rising rental levels, which have persistently increased more rapidly than the rate of inflation. Most institutional investors are willing to trade-off lower present levels of rental income for the prospect of higher long-term capital growth. Not all properties have enjoyed capital appreciation to the same extent and the risk of capital loss on any particular property remains. However, compared to company shares, the risks of capital losses on property tend to be less and the average gains on property have proved to be much higher.

Generally speaking, the system of taxation in the UK tends to favour property investment, as capital appreciation is taxed at a lower effective rate than income receipts. Tax rates vary according to the status of the investor, and both pension funds and charities are exempted from corporation and capital gains taxes. Offsetting such favourable treatment is the on-going local authority rates levy, which serves to reduce the net income from property. In addition, until recently, some real property investments were subject to land development tax. The general issue of government intervention in urban land markets is dealt with more fully in the next chapter.

Yields from property investment

The concept of an investment yield was established in Chapter 6 (pp. 175–6), where the general principle of calculating the yield or rate of return was presented. The yield from an investment serves as a measure of comparison guiding the potential investor to the best decision. The precise calculation of property investment yields is a rather complex exercise, dependent not only on the currently received rentals, but also on the length of rent review periods and on investors' own expectations. (A full appreciation is obtainable from Frazer[5].) Here it is sufficient to note that different types of property investment have substantially different yields and that these mainly reflect variations in risk and growth expectations. Schedules of different property yields are regularly published by financial analysts, and while yields in general tend to follow the trend set by market interest rates, short-run discrepancies are observable.

A simple approach to property yield is to compute the net rental income yield by employing the following formula:

$$\text{rental yield } \% = \left(\frac{\text{current net rent}}{\text{property market price}} \right) . 100$$

Such a yield is only strictly appropriate where the rental income is fixed, such that any rent revisions are so far in the future that the present value of any rental increase is negligible. It is clear from this equation that when current rents increase, yields also increase, but when the market price of property rises without any corresponding increase in rents, then yields must fall. When interest rates begin to rise in the economy, investors will begin to switch away from property towards other investments with higher guaranteed interest rates, such as government bonds. The reduced demand for property will serve to lower the market price and so property yields will increase in line with general interest rates, although there may be some lag in the response.

Throughout the post-war period until 1973, property yields remained relatively stable, fluctuating narrowly around a value of 6% for prime office buildings. In late 1972, faced with accelerating inflation, the government imposed a freeze on the rents on all business property and this had the effect of reducing rental yields. During 1973 the inflationary spiral accelerated when oil prices increased four-fold. The government response was to significantly increase interest rates; this had a rapid and strong effect on the property market. Investors moved out of property and shares, into cash and overseas markets; the all share index—and shares in property companies in particular—fell rapidly. The market value of commercial property plunged, by about 30%, in a few weeks. There was a strong resulting upward boost to property yields, so causing them to follow interest rates to new high levels. Many property companies collapsed as the property share price index declined, over the 12 months from November 1973, to a quarter of its former value. The property market recovered slowly in the second part of the 1970s and institutional investment demand led to increasing market values and lower property yields.

2. The property development decision

While investment in property means essentially the purchase of rights to property, development entails the carrying out of construction to effect a change in the use of land or buildings. Usually, the developers are different agents from the investors, who seek to become the owners of the property which the developers bring into existence. The development industry in the UK is concentrated around some 100 publicly-quoted specialist property companies[6]. The precise numbers fluctuate and additional development is carried out by major contracting firms. In the public sector, both central and local government agencies are active in the development process and joint development ventures between private sector firms and public sector authorities are quite commonplace.

The development process has many different dimensions, but it is generally agreed that it entails three main phases. The first of these is the acquisition of the land and the securing of the planning permission; the second is the actual designing and production of the buildings, while the third centres on the disposal of the completed development. All these phases are beset by uncertainties, which lead to the developers incurring risks in their decision-making. One major element of uncertainty is time, as property developments usually take years, rather than months, to complete and many of the economic variables on which the development decision is based can change significantly in the period between inception and completion.

Acquisition costs

In Table 7.2 a representative cost breakdown of a typical development budget is provided. From this table it can be seen how the major cost of site acquisition is likely to be the purchase of the land itself. Initially, the price of the land which enters the development budget will be the price at which it is offered for sale. However, once all the other cost items have been estimated, and assessments of expected revenue from the development determined, this price for the land may need to be re-examined in the light of the revealed yields and profits for the scheme. The cost of the land in practice is a

7.2   *Cost elements of the developer's budget*

Cost item	Basis	£(000)
1. Price of land	Asking price for site with planning permission	1,000
2. Site assembly fees	Agents, solicitors, taxes, at 4%	40
3. Interest charges on loan for land purchase	15% interest rate for 2-year period	323
4. *Total acquisition costs*		*1,363*
5. Building costs	£ per square metre of estimated space	2,000
6. Professional fees	Architect, engineer, QS Fees (say) 15%	300
7. Interest charges on loans for building finance	Loan of £1m over 1 year at 15%	150
8. *Total production costs*		*2,450*
9. Advertising costs	Fixed sum for national advertising	10
10. Agent's letting fees	10% of Rental income (see Table 7.3)	40
11. *Total disposal costs*		*50*
12. *Total development cost*	Items 4 + 8 + 11	*3,683*

residual cost, which will usually be susceptible to negotiation. Where the asking price for land is such that it produces an unacceptably low profit projection, the potential developer will attempt to negotiate the price downwards with the landowner. Failure to strike a satisfactory bargain on the land price may lead to the abandonment of the project.

Developers are rarely able to obtain sites which are ideal for their precise requirements. Sites vary enormously in terms of the space they provide, the public utility services they offer, their accessibility and their precise physical characteristics. Ground conditions are highly variable and many sites contain existing buildings, which will need to be cleared before new development can be undertaken. Frequently, developers may need to assemble an appropriate site by negotiating with a number of landowners, where adjacent plots are owned by several different parties. Such separate negotiations can take quite a long time and investment funds may be tied up in land assembly for many months. The actual price paid for a site will reflect all these factors and it will also take account of any competitive bids seeking to acquire the site for an alternative use.

The public authorities are invariably closely involved in land acquisition, and, at some stage, in its assembly and development. Local authorities have the power of compulsory acquisition and they can be used by developers in some situations to overcome problems which arise in obtaining the necessary leasehold and freehold interests. Planning authorities control the use to which the site may be put and the density to which it can be developed. Planning permission is required for most forms of development and unless this has already been obtained for the acquired site, delays may arise while such permission is sought. The asking price for the land is likely to reflect whether or not planning approval already exists. Beyond local government controls, development of the land may also entail permissions from central government agencies such as the highways authorities and, possibly, the Department of the Environment, where any listed building of special architectural or historic interest is involved.

While the price of the land is the prime acquisition cost, significant costs may also be incurred in the payment of fees to various estate agents and to solicitors for their conveyancing work. There may be stamp duties to be paid as a tax on the land transaction and, certainly, there will be VAT costs. An estimate of the magnitude of such costs is provided as item 2 in Table 7.2. In general, this cost component will form a relatively small proportion of the total development cost.

It often takes quite a long while to assemble a site for development and the developer must commit funds to the land investment, until the project is completed and the sales proceeds are realised. The interest charges incurred by holding land over the full length of the development will usually be a highly significant item of cost. In our example, the straightforward assumption has been made that a loan for the full asking price of the land is required for a two-year period and a constant rate of interest has been applied. In practice, the developer can rarely be so precise about the period for which the loan will be required. The length of time taken to complete construction can be very variable and, equally, the length of time it takes to dispose of the completed development is subject to uncertainty. The actual rate of interest payable on the loan may well be variable over the period and it is quite likely that a loan of one million pounds will need to be financed from several sources. The terms and conditions on which the various loan packages are obtainable will differ, so that several different rates of interest will apply. Changes in market rates of interest may cause this component of the acquisition cost to vary significantly from the initial estimate.

Production costs

The single most important element of cost in the whole development budget is usually the actual cost of construction, as is shown in Table 7.2. A developer will make use of published building unit rates per square metre of floor area for particular types of building. These rates will be used by the quantity surveyor to estimate the cost of producing a development of specific size. Inevitably, many factors influence the final cost of a building, and many of these factors are difficult to predict with any degree of accuracy.

The time taken to complete construction is a key determinant of cost, as projects which overrun their planned schedules usually incur higher costs than those which are budgeted correctly. When the period of construction extends beyond the 12-month horizon, uncertainties arise in the costs of materials and in labour services. Unanticipated problems can arise in the implementation of design, and communication difficulties between all the participating parties in the construction process can lead to cost divergences. A study by NEDO[7] has investigated the key factors influencing construction times and costs in industrial and commercial building projects in the UK. This study revealed a very wide divergence in average construction times for projects of a similar size; moreover, more than half the projects studied overran their planned completion dates by more than one month. These aspects of the construction process are discussed in Chapter 12.

Professional fees are usually charged as a percentage of the overall cost of construction. Fees for the architect and the surveyor cover the preparation of design drawings and contract documents, as well as supervision and financial control of the contract. Depending on the exact nature of the project, fees for engineering specialists may also be incurred. Where the cost of construction varies from the original budget estimate, fees which are charged on a percentage basis will vary in line. Otherwise, professional fees may be regarded as one of the more certain cost elements in the total budget.

In the same way that funds have to be borrowed to finance the acquisition of land, so additional finance is required to pay for actual construction. In Table 7.2, item 7 assumes that half the estimated cost of construction will be borrowed for one full year. In practice, the size of the loan will depend on the length of the construction period, as well as the credit arrangements which are made with plant hirers, materials suppliers and sub-contractors. The prevailing rate of interest is the other main variable contributing to the uncertainty surrounding this estimate. Cost elements 3 and 7 jointly constitute some 19% of the total development cost, and this component is subject to much variability.

Disposal costs

In comparison to other cost elements, these expenditures are relatively small, thus they can usually be established with some certainty. The advertising cost will incorporate the placing of advertisements in newspapers and trade journals, as well as the preparation of all the relevant sales particulars. Unless the property proves particularly difficult either to rent or to sell, advertising costs will constitute only a small proportion of the total development cost (0.25% in Table 7.2).

The major disposal cost arises with either the letting of the property—if the development is to be retained for rental—or its sale, where the developer plans to realise the capital value upon completion. In either case, estate agents will probably need to be employed and their fees taken into account. Generally speaking, the agent's scale of charges will be related to the annual rental income on the property or to the realised selling price. The agent's letting fees are usually known in advance and the only element of uncertainty arises from fluctuations in the obtained rental or selling price. In Table 7.2, letting fees have been based on an assumption of 10% of the annual rental.

Development yields

When an estimate of total development cost has been determined, it will need to be examined in the context of the expected revenue and capital returns from the project. Some representative revenue calculations are combined with the obtained development cost in Table 7.3. The rental income is an estimate of the rent that will be achieved once the development is completed, which in the present example is in two years' time. Obviously, a large measure of uncertainty must surround this key parameter in the development decision. Existing property rentals will provide the best guide to future expected levels, but many factors are involved in the final determination of the obtained rental. Aggregate demand for floorspace of particular types of property, in specific locations, can fluctuate quite markedly and this may lead to movements in rental prices. Equally, aggregate supply of floorspace is governed by the activity of all developers and, where a large amount of new property is made available in a market in which demand is relatively stable, a downward pressure on rentals will result. While new developments will normally be able to command higher rentals than existing properties, the obtained rental will be conditioned by the total market supply and demand.

7.3   *Profit estimates in the developer's budget*

Item	Basis	£(000)
A. Estimated annual rental income	£ per square metre of rented space	400
B. Gross development (capital) value	Rental income ÷ market investment yield, (say) 8%	5,000
C. Total development costs	Table 7.2	3,863
D. Estimated developer's profit	Item B − Item C	1,137
E. Developer's yield (%)	$\dfrac{\text{Rental income}}{\text{Total development cost}}$	10.3%
F. Developer's profit (%)	$\dfrac{\text{Estimated profit}}{\text{Total development cost}}$	29.4%

The estimated rental income is used to determine the gross development or capital value of a project, as shown by item B in Table 7.3. The rental income is capitalised by using the appropriate market investment yield, as discussed above (pp. 192–3). Strictly speaking, the investment yield which is likely to prevail upon completion of the development in two years' time is the rate which should be applied. In the absence of certain information on future market yields, present published investment yields for particular types of prime-property will be used. This choice of a suitable investment yield introduces another key area of uncertainty into the property investment decision, as yields can change significantly over a two-year period.

In the example given in Table 7.3, use of a market yield of 8% produces a gross development value of some £5 million and a resulting profit to development cost ratio of 29.4%. If a yield of 6% had been assumed, the gross development value would have risen to £6.7 million and the profit to cost ratio would have been 72.5%. However, had a yield of 10% been applied, gross development value would have fallen to £4 million and the resulting profit to cost ratio would have declined to only 3.5%. The sensitivity of the property development decision to market-determined investment yields is clearly demonstrated.

The decision on whether or not to proceed with the property development hinges on the acceptability of the developer's yield (item E) and the developer's profit (item F) ratios. These ratios are based on a number of estimated values which are all subject to uncertainty. In particular, the values assumed for the interest costs on holding land and loans to carry out construction, the costs of building, the rental income and the market investment yield are each capable of significant variation. A fuller appreciation of how the property decision can be formally tested for its sensitivity to changes in these key underlying variables is provided by Byrne and Cadman[8].

3. Redevelopment decisions

Frequently, the developer contemplates a project which is based on a site containing existing buildings, which are still in use and generating rental income. In this situation, the decision becomes one of redevelopment and account must be taken not only of the predicted profits from the new project, but also of the revenues arising from the existing use. In general terms, redevelopment will occur when the present value of the site in current use falls below the capital value of the cleared site.

Present value of the site in existing use

The capital value of a building in existing use is estimated by discounting the net annual revenue returns by an appropriate market investment yield, as in Table 7.3. Over time, this capital value will change as its net annual revenue varies. When the building is new, the rental income will be relatively high and maintenance costs will be insignificant. Inflation will frequently cause net revenues to increase and for a number of years this will lead to increasing capital values. But after a while, capital values will begin to decline as the building ages. Inevitably, newer competing developments will appear and these buildings will command higher rents, so pushing down the obtained rents on the older building. At the same time, the costs of maintenance and repair will begin to increase markedly, so that revenue net of cost will be squeezed. The older building will be less adaptable and less well equipped than its newer counterparts and it may well become increasingly difficult to rent, so leading to further falls in net annual revenue. The consequences of such changes over the lifetime of the building for its capital value are represented, in Fig. 7.1, by the quadratic curve.

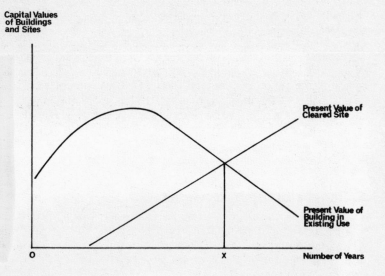

Fig. 7.1 *The economic life of a building*

Present value of the cleared site

The capital value of the cleared site is determined by the new and best alternative use to which the site can be put. This capital value is estimated by discounting the net annual revenues from the alternative use and deducting the costs of clearing the site and rebuilding. In the early years of the existing building, the costs of clearance and rebuilding are likely to outweigh the net revenues from the alternative application, but over time these net revenues can be expected to rise appreciably. A new building will be better planned; it will contain higher levels of services and it will use space more efficiently. All these factors will serve to increase rental income and so create higher capital values, even after allowing for site clearance and new building costs.

In Fig. 7.1 the present value of the cleared site is shown as a rising trend; initially, the capital value is negative, but thereafter it becomes positive as the potential gains from redevelopment begin to outweigh clearance and new build costs. There comes a point after OX years, when the capital value of the cleared site with a new alternative use exceeds the value of the existing site. It is at this time that the site is considered ripe for redevelopment.

Extending the life of the existing building

It frequently happens that the life of existing buildings on a site is extended beyond their economic span of OX years. Fig. 7.2 shows that if methods of increasing the present value of buildings in existing use can be found, the point of redevelopment can be delayed. In this example, the timing of redevelopment is delayed by XY years.

One device which serves to bring about an extension to the life of existing buildings is the use of a higher rate of yield for discounting

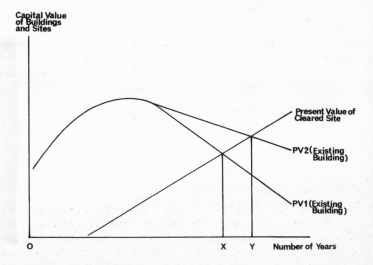

Fig. 7.2 *The extended life of a building*

annual revenues. This procedure reduces the capital values of both existing buildings and cleared sites, but it lowers the cleared site schedule by more than the existing building schedule. In particular, higher interest rates serve to raise the costs of clearance and new build. In the 1980s, higher yields and interest rates have served to keep many older buildings in existing use and so delay the date of redevelopment.

Often, as the rental incomes on existing buildings begin to fall, owners look at ways of using their properties more intensively to increase revenue. Harvey[9] has noted how, in twilight or transition zones of cities, all sorts of existing buildings, including small factories, shops and dwellings, have a run-down appearance and a tendency to over-crowding. Owners reduce maintenance and repair costs to a minimum, while they attempt to accommodate as many tenants as possible to boost flagging revenues. Frequently, sites are put to temporary uses, such as warehousing and car parking, as the time for redevelopment approaches. In the terms of Fig. 7.2, such activity serves to push the point of redevelopment beyond year X towards year Y.

Another factor which can prevent redevelopment occurring in year X is the use of conservation orders on old buildings and sites of potential historic interest. Sometimes, the use of current net revenue to estimate capital value seriously underestimates the true value to society of the existing building. Demolition of a historic building removes an asset which cannot be replaced and future generations may come to place a higher value on the old building than it enjoys today. Indeed, where an existing building is preserved for a sufficient number of years, it may eventually experience a resurgence in net revenue, as people will pay to view structures of historic interest, in the same way that tourists are drawn towards museums. Only a few such existing sites can expect to avoid redevelopment on these grounds, however.

Further obstacles to redevelopment

During the period 1950–70, redevelopment occurred on a very large scale in most urban areas of the UK. In more recent years, the scale and the pace of redevelopment has slackened appreciably and in particular, large-scale or comprehensive programmes of redevelopment have become much rarer. Today, redevelopment is on a much smaller scale; usually schemes are restricted to a single site, rather than covering large areas and several adjacent sites. In particular, the local authority has reduced its role as a major agent in the redevelopment process and this has been the prime factor in the scaling-down of redevelopment schemes.

Probably the central obstacle leading to a reduced local authority involvement in major redevelopment programmes has been restrictions on finance. As Chapter 2 made clear, a key element in the fiscal constraint of the 1980s has been strict limitations on public sector borrowing. The tight constraints on the local authorities' ability to raise investment funds has reduced the public sector's role in the redevelopment process to that of a secondary partner. Indeed, in more recent years, the emphasis has been on partnership schemes, with the private developer taking the major initiative.

The Urban Development Grant has become the main government scheme for providing financial assistance in urban development projects, which have been jointly proposed by local authorities and the private sector. The Urban Development Grant is intended to create opportunities for private development companies to carry out redevelopment in the inner city, which would not otherwise go ahead without active public participation. The high cost of assembling the site, demolishing the existing buildings and constructing the new structure constitutes a powerful obstacle to redevelopment schemes, especially in a period of continuing high interest rates. The local authority partner is able to reduce some of these development costs, particularly by use of the power of compulsory purchase and the provision of site services and infrastructure works.

Despite the existence of the Urban Development Grant, public funds remain restricted, as do the grant funds. Not all redevelopment schemes will qualify for grant assistance and, frequently, the amount of grant aid may not be sufficient to make the scheme financially attractive. Often, a large measure of uncertainty may surround the expected net annual returns from the new alternative use and this will serve to lower the capital value of the cleared site. Until this value exceeds the value of the buildings in existing use, redevelopment will not take place.

Questions

1. Explain the nature of acquiring real property interests.
2. Discuss the claim that all property markets are characterised by imperfect information.
3. What is the evidence to demonstrate that institutional investors have favoured real property investments in recent years?
4. Identify the main ways in which investment in property can be said to be unique.
5. Explain the inverse relationship between the investment yield on property and its capital value.

6. Comment on the stability of the property market in the UK in the period since 1970.
7. Outline the main phases of the development process.
8. Demonstrate how, in a typical developer's budget, the price of the land can be regarded as a residual item of cost.
9. Identify the main costs involved in the acquisition of the development site and comment on the uncertainty attaching to the rate of interest and the period of time taken to complete the project.
10. Indicate some sources of information which are needed to prepare an estimate of the costs of producing a new building.
11. Discuss the sensitivity of the estimated developer's profit to changes in the level of rent obtainable on the building and the assumed market rate of investment yield.
12. Use the data in Tables 7.2 and 7.3 to analyse the impact of
a) a 10% rise in interest rates
b) a 20% increase in the length of the construction period on both the developer's yield and the developer's profit ratios.
13. Explain what you understand by the statement that redevelopment will occur when the present value of the site in current use falls below the capital value of the cleared site.
14. Identify the main obstacles to redevelopment in UK cities in recent years.

Further Reading

AMBROSE, P. and COLENUTT, B., *The Property Machine*, Penguin, 1975
BALCHIN, P. N. and KIEVE, J. L., *Urban Land Economics*, Chapters 4, 5 and 8, Macmillan, 1985
CADMAN, D. and AUSTIN-CROWE, L., *Property Development*, E. and F. N. Spon, 1983
FRASER, W. D., *Principles of Property Investment and Pricing*, Part 2, Macmillan, 1984
HALLETT, G., *Urban Land Economics*, Chapters 3 and 4, Macmillan, 1979
HARVEY, J., *The Economics of Real Property*, Chapters 5, 6 and 7, Macmillan, 1986
ROUGVIE, A., *Project Evaluation and Development*, Chapter 2, Mitchell, 1987
WINFIELD, R. G. and CURRY, S. J. *Success in Investment*, Chapters 1, 2 and 13, John Murray, 1981

8 Economic Aspects of Urban Land

In the previous chapter, the price paid for the site was an important parameter in the development decision. It was assumed that the price paid for the land could be regarded as a residual value to be finally determined, once the provisional budget had been analysed. However, in practice, the price required to secure the individual land site is set by the forces of supply and demand for land.

In this chapter, the nature of land as a factor of production is examined and the unique character of land is investigated. The supply of urban land is part of the general problem caused by the fixity of total land area. Within the urban area, various users compete to own the land and the potential user exhibiting the strongest demand, by way of bidding the highest price, will obtain use of the land. The intensity of this demand varies significantly between different urban centres, and also between individual sites within a single city. In consequence, land prices exhibit strong diversity and land markets, like those of real property, of which land is an integral part, are typically imperfect.

The government has persistently sought to intervene in land markets, in an attempt to raise the level of aggregate social welfare. Some indication of the nature of this intervention has already been provided in Chapter 4, where the policy of distributing industrial activity more evenly throughout the regions of the UK was outlined. In this chapter, the case for intervention is presented and the wider modes of intervention are briefly examined. The main form of intervention in land markets in use today is town and country planning control and regulation. The strengths and weaknesses of this approach are evaluated in this chapter.

1. The unique nature of land

Land means all free gifts of nature which can be used to yield an income. This definition includes minerals, water resources and

forests, and structures, such as buildings and dwellings, which have
been erected on the land are more properly regarded as capital. In
practice, this distinction is often difficult to achieve and, as in
Chapter 7, land and buildings may be counted together as real
property. Land is a unique factor of production, which is combined
with other factors and earns a revenue return—its economic rent.
Such an economic rent accrues to land which is in fixed supply, and
the amount of rent is determined wholly by demand factors.

Fixed supply of land

In Fig. 8.1, land is shown as being totally fixed in supply, so that rent
is determined wholly by the existing level of demand for this land.
When the level of demand is D1, the earnings from the land are
represented by the rectangle OR1DS and all of these earnings
constitute its economic rent. No matter how small the revenue
return to the land, its supply remains unaffected, so that its
opportunity or transfer cost is zero. When demand increases to D2,
the rent level is increased from OR1 to OR2 and the extra increase
in revenue is its additional economic rent. It is important to
appreciate that where rent is wholly determined by demand, as in
the present case, it is of no consequence to supply, whatever the
rental price actually charged. Attempts to tax away economic rent

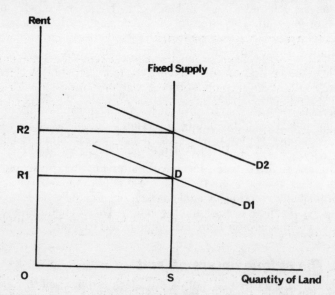

Fig. 8.1 *The economic rent of land in general*

will have no disincentive impact on the supply of land in general. This result does not hold for the supply of land for a particular use and that case, which is represented in Fig. 8.2, is dealt with in the next section.

The supply of urban land is relatively fixed in the short term. Over time, however, productive land can be either increased, through reclamation, or decreased, by abandonment, although such processes take time and in general, land cannot be created. In comparison to the other main factors of production—capital and labour—land is fixed in supply and its fixity will give rise to diminishing returns. Land can be used more or less intensively and can be extended by building higher storeys onto buildings, but usually this extra space can only be achieved at the price of increasing unit costs. Eventually, this fixity of urban land will serve to raise the costs of production, where further output is required from the same area of land.

Where land is taken to be strictly fixed, as in Fig. 8.1, it is the demand for land which determines its rental price; this means that it is the marginal revenue of the product produced on the land which sets the level of the rent. High rents on agricultural land are a consequence of high market prices obtainable for agricultural commodities. It is not the high land rents which cause the high farm prices, as is sometimes supposed.

2. Competing uses of land

While the supply of land in general may be taken as fixed, the supply of land for a particular use is likely to be more variable. Within the urban area, there is competition between the various users of land for the limited available area. In general terms, commercial and industrial organisations compete with housing developers and public authorities for use of the urban land. At the edges of the city, these same groups compete with agricultural interests for use of the land.

Variable supply of land for a specific use

In Fig. 8.2, typical supply and demand schedules are shown for land required for a specific use. The supply curve exhibits some rent elasticity, indicating that where the users are prepared to bid a high enough price, they can secure increasing quantities of land for their use. The rent which is paid is no longer purely an economic rent, but rather a commercial rent consisting of two components. Transfer earnings are an opportunity cost to be paid to prevent the land switching to an alternative use. The economic component of the rent is a payment reflecting the scarcity value of the land over and above its transfer cost. The proportions of commercial rent, which are 'transfer' and 'economic', vary according to the elasticity of the supply of land.

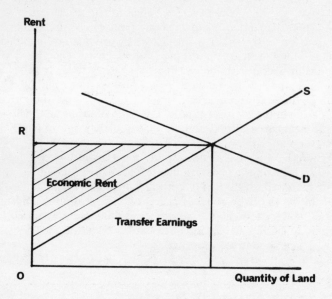

Fig. 8.2 *Commercial rent of land in a particular use*

Urban locational models

The strength of demand for urban land for a particular area is governed by the profit requirements. If a commercial organisation can generate most revenue from locating on a city centre site, it will bid the highest rental price for that site. Similarly, if a housing developer sees the potential to make significant profits on available land at the periphery of the city, the developer will bid a higher price than other potential users, such as farmers or transport organisations searching for warehouse locations.

The recognition that urban location is a key determinant of user's profitability has led to the development of a number of models to explain competing land uses in the city centre. In Fig. 8.3 the simple *Alonso model* is presented, where different users bid individual rent gradients, dependent on distance from the city centre. The use with the highest gradient prevails and the outer envelope of the respective curves indicates this gradient. In this particular representation, commercial interests occupy sites at the heart of the city, industrial users dominate the transitional zone just outside the centre and housing takes over the suburban locations. Agriculture, for which a centre location is least critical, occupies the land at the edge of the urban areas. The model illustrates the concept of urban land being moveable between uses, as the profitability of the various sectors changes and the process of gradual invasion of sectoral use proceeds.

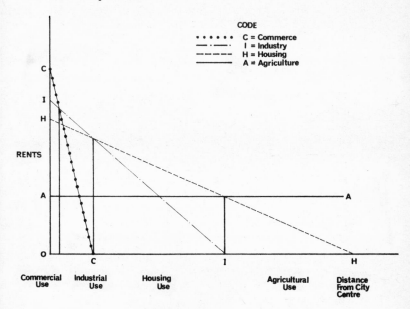

Fig. 8.3 *Urban location and land-use*

In practice, the land market, which is represented by this model and similar derivative forms, does not work so simply and land-use patterns cannot be easily classified. Balchin and Kieve[1] present a critique of various models of urban location, structure and growth, but no model can adequately account for the wide differences in land-use patterns found in different urban areas. Most models, including the Alonso scheme represented in Fig. 8.3, tend to assume perfect transmission of information between users, with land being allocated according to its relative value in production. Yet, as Keogh[2] has pointed out, the land market does not work in the smooth and efficient way suggested by models. Information is costly and imperfect inertia results from high transaction costs and the structure of property rights, while the uniqueness of each parcel of land introduces an element of monopoly power.

3. Specific use locations

Retailing

In practice, most urban centres exhibit similar locational patterns with regard to the siting of particular types of activity. Retailing efficiency is highly sensitive to specific location and, critically, most specialist shops and larger department stores will seek to locate in the heart of the city centre. Such retailers are concerned to maximise their accessibility to the largest catchment area and so create the highest possible turnover. In the central shopping area, the relationship between retail revenue and rental cost is very finely balanced and key sites continually change hands, as product demand fluctuates and intensive bidding occurs to secure prime locations.

Retailers selling convenience goods and services—grocers, bakers, and newsagents, for example, from whom purchases are made regularly but in relatively small amounts—tend to locate outside the central area. Such retailers have lower turnovers than the larger specialist shops, and they therefore bid lower rents to secure outlying sites, nearer the main residential centres. Many service shops, whose products are only purchased irregularly and who often have smaller sales turnovers, also seek suburban sites, where rents will be much lower.

In recent years, increasing congestion in city centres, along with reduced accessibility, especially for the private car, has rendered retailing less profitable in key central sites. In particular, food supermarkets have sought suburban locations, which convey better accessibility and initially low rents. Giant supermarkets, selling food, household goods, furniture, DIY services and electrical appliances, bid for locations on the edge of the urban area. While turnover per unit of floor area is much lower than in a city centre location, the very large floor area in total produces an acceptable level of revenue, which, when set against low rentals, yields satisfactory profits. High levels of car ownership hold the key to the success of these retailing ventures, and easier accessibility and lower prices, resulting from internal economies of scale, are the spur to the consumer. The quest for de-centralised sites brings retailers into competition with developers producing industrial and domestic buildings, and so may cause rents to be pushed up to higher levels than those which have prevailed historically.

Offices

Offices, like retailing organisations, are of many different kinds and the locational requirement varies according to the nature of the business. Where offices are attached to factories and workshops, it will be the siting of the production unit which determines the office location. Most independent offices will seek sites which provide good accessibility to customers and clients, yet at the same time provide close proximity to complementary businesses. Central locations for offices are obviously important, although the exact siting is usually less critical than in the case of specialist retailers. Frequently, offices will occupy sites in the upper storeys of buildings, leaving the ground floors for retailing displays.

In the 1980s, the UK economy has increasingly expanded its service sector activities, while its manufacturing sector has declined. In particular, financial and professional services have grown significantly and there has been a corresponding upsurge in the demand for prime office space, especially in central London. The so-called 'Big Bang' in financial services at the end of 1986 intensified demand for office accommodation in the City area of London. Such service organisations, by earning high revenues, are able to afford high rents and so they out-bid other potential users—most notably retailers, hoteliers and other entertainment services. In the high streets of most provincial cities, many traditional retailers have been forced out of key sites by banks, building societies and similar financial organisations, who are able to pay higher rents. Where it has proved practicable to develop multi-storey offices, these sites have become the most intensively developed in the urban area, and hence the most valuable sites of all.

Entertainment

Apart from retailing and offices, one other main activity which competes for central city locations is the entertainment industry. Hotels and catering outlets clearly require sites of maximum accessibility in order to generate high revenues. Where hoteliers can successfully charge high prices, without any detrimental impact on demand for rooms and meals, they will be able to bid high rents to secure key central sites. Hotels in Central London provide a good example of this competitive bidding for prime locations.

Government organisations

Government, both central and local, generates a high demand for office space in city centre locations. Public sector offices, which provide general services, need to be highly accessible and this usually requires a central site. It is also desirable to locate government offices in close proximity to each other, to achieve maximum efficiency. In consequence, the government sector competes with the various private sector activities for the valuable space in the heart of the urban area. During the 1970s, many government agencies successfully bid for key central sites and thereby the general level of rents was forced up. In the 1980s, public sector financial constraints have limited the ability of these agencies to compete in this way. The increasing use of computers to improve communication between offices has served to make the need for central location less important, but the city centre remains the most desirable site for the employees.

Factories and warehouses

Historically, manufacturing industry sought to locate as close to the city centre as possible, when accessibility was a major constraint. Many factories and warehouses still remain on sites adjacent to the central area in a large number of UK towns and cities. However, the development of road transport and competition from other activities, which push up rental prices on central sites, has encouraged industry to seek suburban locations on the periphery of the city. Here, factory and warehouse space can be secured at much lower unit rentals and the industrialist finds the competition for the land to be much less intensive. Inertia means that some firms remain on their historical central site, which is frequently cramped, possibly multistorey, and, typically, in poor physical condition, with out-dated services.

Manufacturing firms are strongly influenced in their locational decisions by government policy. On the one hand, regional policy may inhibit further development on the existing site and provide incentive to relocate elsewhere; on the other, local planning decisions may restrict the number of urban sites available to the firm. In the post-war period, manufacturing industries have been directed towards sites in planned industrial estates and parks. Usually, such estates are located on the outskirts of a city, where the planning authorities have designated land for industrial use alone, so that industry can be separately located from other activities. Rental prices in industrial estates are generally lower than those prevailing in scarcer sites nearer to the city centre. Firms may also experience external economies of scale by locating alongside similar companies.

Housing

Housing constitutes the largest form of urban land-use and in some cities it accounts for more than 50% of the total land area. As cities have grown and competition for central sites has served to raise rents, housing locations have spread outwards, pushing the urban limits out into the 'green belt' of surrounding agricultural land. With road transport improving over the present century, higher income house owners have moved away from central locations, seeking more spacious sites with lower land rents. Sites on the fringe of the city centre have come to be occupied by lower income families, who try to minimise travelling costs by living close to their work in the inner area of the city. Usually, housing densities on these sites are relatively high and the land is most commonly owned by the local authority, which regulates the rents of such dwellings. Private house-buyers, seeking spacious accomodation, cannot normally compete with retailing and office interests in bidding for prime central sites.

In many cities in the UK today, cheaper housing occupies the sites closest to the city centre and as distance from the centre increases, so too does the value of the dwellings. However, patterns of residential location are far from uniform, and frequently proximity to major roads and other transport routeways may lead to some modification in the basic pattern. (A fuller exploration of this has been undertaken by Evans.[3]) Most housebuilders are concerned to develop land at the periphery of the urban area. Here, the housebuilder will be able to bid the land away from agricultural use, yet still obtain the plot at a sufficiently low unit rental to facilitate construction which yields a good profit.

4. Government intervention in land markets

The previous section described how various potential users of land may compete in a free market to resolve the pattern of land-use. It is clear that each activity bids for the urban site in accordance with private profit motives. There is little guarantee under such a system that the limited land resources of the community will necessarily be put to the best possible use. The general case for government intervention rests on the state being able to raise the aggregate social welfare of the community by changing the pattern of the distribution of the land.

Specific arguments favouring intervention

Land markets are inherently imperfect and history has shown how rich individuals and institutions can accumulate very extensive interests in land and property. Such ownership of land conveys political power and it gives the owner economic control over leaseholders and tenants. The government may wish to intervene to ensure a more equitable distribution of land and so reduce the concentration of ownership of land resources. Where the ownership of land passes into the hands of the state, the government is able to control its distribution and use directly. The state can ensure easier access to land for everyone in society and it can guarantee security of tenure to the users of land.

Frequently, private individuals and institutions acquire and hold land for its potential future development value. Land may come to be hoarded and a scarcity of urban land may develop, where present demand outstrips supply. Intervention may be desirable in such circumstances, to restore an adequate supply and to prevent the price of this scarce resource being pushed to unacceptably high levels. More generally, the government may wish to control and regulate the specific use to which land is put. The state's perception of the best use of land for the whole community may differ significantly from the private individual's proposed use. The government is able to form a longer-term view of land development and it can ensure that the development of a specific site is compatible with land-use on adjacent sites.

Many owners of land grow rich when the value of their land increases, not through any improvement to the site, but simply through government granting planning permission. This increase in value is termed 'betterment' and a strong case can be argued for betterment gains to accrue to the state. Ratcliffe[4] has put the argument for betterment gains passing to the whole community, rather than to the individual landowner who stands to benefit from government planning decisions. The converse of betterment is 'worsenment' which may also sometimes occur, as a consequence of a planning change. Here, the state can compensate the individual for his or her loss.

Modes of intervention

The government has a wide range of measures which it can implement to effectively intervene in land markets. Such measures range from the simple provision of fuller information, through to the sweeping nationalisation of all urban land. In practice, government does not rely on a single measure, but it operates a number of different instruments which are frequently modified over time.

In the post-war UK, local planning permission over broad land allocations and general policy, contained in a set of development plans, is the principal mode of intervention. Planning regulations set the guidelines, within which market forces are allowed to work to allocate land between uses. A fuller consideration of planning control and regulation is provided in the following section.

Fiscal measures

In addition to planning controls, the UK operates a system of taxes on land and property. The most direct tax is the local authority rate levy, but there also exist taxes on the income from land, taxes on transactions in land and property, and taxes on capital gains upon the sale of land. In practice, such taxes do not attempt to re-allocate land resources between uses, nor are they used to adjust private costs, associated with land-use, to reflect full social costs. Rather these taxes are part of the government's revenue-raising exercise described in Chapter 2 (pp. 35–9). However, the local authority rate levy does distort the effective market price of property and land, especially since rates discriminate between agricultural, domestic, industrial and commercial land-users. (A theoretical exploration of how taxes and subsidies can be applied to produce a better allocation of land resources is provided by Harrison.[5]) Changes to the system of local rates were put into effect for Scotland in 1987 and changes for England and Wales are in prospect for the 1990s.

Public goods and services

Government intervenes directly in land markets to ensure that public goods and services are adequately provided for. Specifically, government needs to secure land to establish roads and other types of transport infrastructure. In addition, government will have to cater for walkways, playgrounds, parks and recreation space, which private developers, in the absence of public intervention, will seek to reduce to a minimum. Indeed, many basic services such as public utilities, education and medical care are traditionally provided mainly by the state, and land will be secured for these types of buildings and structures. Government will intervene in land markets to set aside suitable sites for military and policing needs, as well as for offices to be used by its civil servants. Many areas of the economy are supplied by the public sector and government intervenes directly, rather than allowing this type of development to be left to the uncertain dictates of the land market.

Land nationalisation

In the post-war period, there have been three major attempts to nationalise all urban land: the Town and Country Planning Act

(1947), the Land Commission Act (1967) and the Community Land Act (1975). Each of these initiatives failed and the legislation was subsequently dismantled by succeeding governments. In each case, the proposal for the public authority to progressively purchase development land was accompanied by a betterment tax. The Development Land Tax, which was established as part of the 1967 legislation, continued in existence, although at a lower value, until 1985. Today, gains from land transactions are subject to capital gains taxation, but there is no special charge, as previously. In practice, the attempts to nationalise urban land have foundered on insufficient public funds to carry out the purchase, coupled with a reluctance on the part of the owners of development land to offer such sites for sale. (Fuller details of the attempts at land national-isation are given in Lichfield and Darin-Drabkin.[6])

5. Planning controls and regulation

In Great Britain today, local planning control and regulation is the principal type of intervention used by government to modify the workings of both land and real property markets. Historically, town planning has its origins in the movement for social and sanitation reforms in the second half of the nineteenth century. The first Town Planning Act dates back to 1909, and other pieces of legislation dealing with aspects of planning were passed in the inter-war period. It is generally recognised that present-day planning began with the 1947 Town and County Planning Act, which instituted a new era in comprehensive land planning. This act required local authorities to prepare development plans for their areas and so define patterns of future land-use. Government approval was required for these plans and most forms of development required permission from the local planning authority before construction or implementation could be undertaken.

During the 1950s and 1960s, further pieces of town planning legis-lation were enacted; most of these were consolidated by the 1971 Town and County Planning Act. (A full account of this act is provided in Ratcliffe.[7]) This 1971 act introduced a two-tier level of planning involving the *structure plan*, the broad policy statement of how the area should be developed, and the *local plan*, the detailed proposal for development and the framework for planning control. Further changes and additions to town planning followed during the 1970s and some significant modifications were made in the 1980 Local Govern-ment Planning and Land Act. A comprehensive appraisal of planning legislation is beyond the scope of this book; anyone wanting fuller information is referred to the extensive literature on planning.

Impact of planning on development

It is necessary to obtain specific planning consent for every development, except for some minor modifications to land and property which are covered by General Development Orders. Development by government institutions is not strictly subject to this statutory planning process, but in practice such institutions do consult with the local planning authority. Each planning application is examined on a case-by-case basis and decisions are taken in conformity with laid-down plans and overall guidelines.

Structure plans are prepared by the higher tier of local government, usually the shire county or, between 1974 and 1986, the metropolitan county. The structural plans determine the broad guidelines for growth in population, employment, shopping, housing and transport, across the county area. Such plans integrate national, regional, economic, social and environmental policies and relate these policies to the pattern of land-use in the area. The county planning authority consults with the lower-tier district authorities in drawing up the overall framework. The district authority is responsible for preparing local plans that are consistent with the structure plan and, therefore, all development control resides with the district planning officers.

Anyone wishing to carry out a development for which planning consent is required must apply to the local planning authority for the necessary approval. In some instances, a developer may wish to seek outline planning approval before providing full details of the proposal. The local planning authority must give a formal decision on a detailed submission within eight weeks. When considering the application, the local planning authority will normally take account of the provisions of any approved development plan, although its decision need not be inexorably bound by such a scheme. Any proposed departure from plan must be widely advertised and the Secretary of State for the Environment, who is the ultimate planning authority, may issue countervailing directions. Where the district authority rejects a planning application, there is a right of appeal to the higher authority of the Secretary of State.

Planning permission may be granted subject to restrictive conditions. Generally, time limits are imposed, such that planning permission lapses unless the development is commenced within five years—or three years in the case of outline permission. In other instances, permission may be given for temporary buildings and works which, at the end of a stipulated period, must be removed and the site restored to its original condition. Planning permission may be granted with conditions limiting occupation to a particular class of occupier, defined by trade or vocation. Authorities are able to impose such conditions on the granting of planning permission as they think fit, providing the conditions are not unreasonable and that they have a planning context. In this way, where an industrial development locates adjacent to domestic dwellings, conditions on the time when machinery may be operated, or deliveries received, can be imposed to protect residents from potential noise.

Planning authorities normally consult with other interested authorities before granting planning permission. Such interested parties include the Highway Authority, the Environmental Health Office, the Health and Safety Executive and, possibly, the Water Authority. Developers may be required to provide new roadways, public open space, or amenity land, as a condition of planning permission. Land and property development is effectively constrained by planning regulation and control.

Advantages of planning controls

Town planning can be used to impose land-uses in the wider public interest, and so ensure that similar activities are located in close proximity and potentially conflicting activities separately developed. In this way residential estates can be located away from heavy industry or from major infrastructural investments such as motorways. Where it is recognised that the design of buildings and the use to which they are put may have an external effect on members of a community, planning can regulate the degree of this effect. The development of industrial estates on the one hand, and the creation of science parks on the other, provide further examples of such planning advantages.

Where local and structural plans are published, a large measure of uncertainty in the development process is removed. Potential developers gain information on present and likely future land-use. The possibility of the market becoming over-supplied with the same type of venture is greatly reduced. The planning process can help to create more balanced development, and the planning authority is in a unique position to phase simultaneous development of housing, industry, shops, offices and social infrastructure. The unfettered private market often suffers from time lags in supply and demand, which can result in expensive imbalances. The building of Britain's new towns in the post-war period provides a good example of how town planning can produce phased development.

Private developers will be concerned with the immediate profitability of the proposed investment and they are unlikely to take sufficient account of the community's future land-use needs. Planners are frequently concerned to preserve the 'green belt' zones around the towns and cities, and to prevent developers encroaching upon this agricultural land. Certainly, in the absence of strict planning controls in the immediate post-war period, much of the existing 'green belt' would have been destroyed, in the face of developers pressing to secure virgin sites at the edge of the urban area. In a less obvious way, planning authorities seek to protect listed buildings of special architectural or historic interest. Here, too, planning preserves for the future, counteracting the development proposals of the present.

The planning authorities are in a position to enter into agreements and partnerships with private developers to produce comprehensive redevelopment, where this is deemed appropriate. The government has the power to make compulsory purchase where this is an obstacle to development. Equally, the local planning authority may bargain with private developers to produce new infrastructure investment, as a condition of planning permission. Only a central planning authority is in a position to produce such gains for the benefit of the whole community. However, in recent years, this role of the planning authority in the process of comprehensive redevelopment has been much inhibited by a shortage of public funds.

Limitations of planning controls

Perhaps the most powerful argument against planning controls is the essentially negative character of the planning process. The planning authorities prepare the policies and plans to establish a development framework, but implementation depends primarily on private developers. In some instances, the local authorities themselves undertake housing, transport and education investment initiatives, but the planning authority remains restricted in its ability to positively encourage development. As Cadman and Austin-Crowe[8] observe, the planning system controls the development within the plan framework, by refusing the unacceptable and only rarely, investing in the acceptable.

The planning process frequently fails to take account of the wider cost implications of its imposed controls. Where planning restraint prevents firms from expanding in their preferred location, such firms may undertake no new investment and so potential jobs may be lost. Equally, where planners insist on minimum standards in buildings, too few dwellings or other structures will be created. The cost to society of the failure to carry out more development may well be very high, especially where unemployment is significant. In other situations, where for example a firm, thwarted in its plans to expand in a given location, chooses to rent a site elsewhere that already has planning permission, increased congestion costs may be created in the alternative location. In a similar way, planning decisions to make low cost public sector housing schemes into high density developments may result in a marked increase in social stress and a corresponding increase in social costs.

In comparison to taxation, planning as a mode of intervention sometimes appears inflexible and rigid. With taxation, the firm that is willing to pay a higher price for a specific location is able to do so, but frequently structure and local plans will eliminate this possibility. Equally, the case-by-case approach inherent in the making of planning decisions can lead to long delays when refusals and modifications are taken to appeal. Where the developer is incurring interest charges as the site is assembled, such delays may seriously increase the cost, and hence the profitability, of the project.

Land-use planning as a regulatory activity can create economic and social problems in a society through its unintended distributive impact. The separation of home from workplace can produce problems in the journey to work. The building of high-rise flats can lead to vandalism and produce social ghettos. The location of heavy industry away from its smaller suppliers and supporting service firms may raise production costs unnecessarily. All of these problems are largely unanticipated side effects of planning controls, which are intended to produce a better land-use than that which would prevail in a free market.

Questions

1. Explain your understanding of the concept of economic rent.
2. Discuss the claim that whilst the supply of land in total is more or less fixed, its supply for any specific urban use is variable.
3. Indicate which of the following two statements is correct and give your reasons:
   a) 'High land rents are a consequence of the high price of the product produced on the land.'
   b) 'Product prices are high because of the high price of land used in the production.'
4. Outline a model of urban location in which distance from the city centre is the key determinant.
5. What are the key locational requirements for:
   a) shops;
   b) offices?
6. Why are factories and warehouses, today, located mainly in suburban sites?
7. Explain why in most British cities cheaper housing occupies sites closest to the city centre and more expensive housing is located on the outskirts of the city.

8. What are the main arguments in favour of government intervention in land markets?
9. How can the state increase the aggregate social welfare of the community by changing the pattern of land distribution?
10. Analyse the main alternative modes of intervention available to governments seeking to regulate land markets.
11. Comment on the claim that government ought to nationalise all urban land in order to ensure the most efficient use of land.
12. Outline the main impact of planning regulation and control on development.
13. Explain the principal advantages of planning controls as a measure of intervention in land markets.
14. How far do you agree with the argument that all planning control is essentially negative in character?

Further Reading

BALCHIN, P. N. and KIEVE, J. L., *Urban Land Economics*, Chapters 2, 3 and 6, Macmillan, 1985

BARLOWE, R., *Land Resource Economics: The Economics of Real Estate*, Prentice-Hall, 1986

BARRETT, S. and HEALEY, P., *Land Policy: Problems and Alternatives*, Gower Press, 1985

BRUTON, M. J., *The Spirit and Purpose of Planning*, Hutchinson, 1984

HALLETT, G., *Urban Land Economics*, Macmillan, 1979

HARRISON, A. J., *Economics and Land-use Planning*, Part 2, Croom Helm, 1977

LICHFIELD, N. and DARIN-DRABKIN, H., *Land Policy in Planning*, George Allen and Unwin, 1980

RATCLIFFE, J., *An Introduction to Town and Country Planning*, Hutchinson, 1981

RYDIN, Y., *Housing Land Policy*, Gower Publishing, 1986

9 Cost-Benefit Analysis for Public Investment Decisions

1. Why cost-benefit analysis?

Earlier chapters have demonstrated the important role of the public sector in creating new investment. Chapters 1 and 2 emphasised the key role of government and its various agencies in maintaining demand for construction output. Data presented in Chapter 4 indicated that in the early 1980s the public sector typically accounted for just over 40% of contractors' new non-housing work. Indeed, the statistics for fixed investment in new buildings and works underline this key contribution of the public sector. Although in the 1980s the share of the public sector in fixed investment has tended to fall, especially when account is taken of new dwellings, government investment spending remains of vital significance for the fortunes of the construction industry.

The investment decision for the private sector firm was closely examined in Chapter 6 and wider aspects of property development were analysed in Chapter 7. Where organisations in the public sector operate under similar market conditions to their private sector counterparts, the investment decision will be taken in the same way. For example, many investments carried out by nationalised industries, such as British Steel and British Rail, will follow standard investment criteria of the kind described in Chapter 6. Routine plant, and smaller-scale building and works, decisions will be evaluated using discounted cash flow appraisals, based on information about market costs and prices. However, frequently the scale of the investment to be undertaken by the public sector organisation is far larger than that for any comparable private sector investment. The decision to build a new steel works, a new airport, or a new motorway is a vastly more complex undertaking than most private firms' plant and building investment choices.

The public sector investment decision

A central difficulty with many types of public sector investment decision is that information on both costs and benefits is difficult to establish with any degree of accuracy. Larger projects, such as new motorways, take many years to construct and estimates for the cost of the project are likely to be revised many times before completion. Some of the cost elements are very difficult to estimate—especially those associated with disruption and inconvenience to people living near the proposed motorway. Usually the major difficulty with a large public investment project lies in the inability to establish clearly the benefits or returns from the investment. A commercial investment leads to a product or service output which can be sold at an estimated market price over a number of years, and so statistics of net income can be used to guide the investment choice. A social investment, such as a new motorway, provides obvious benefits to the community, but it is not easy to quantify such benefits and produce a set of income returns which can be compared to the cost estimates.

It is not only central government, considering large social investments, who face the problems of evaluating costs and benefits. The same issues arise on a smaller scale for local authorities, pondering investment options in the area of public housing provision. The costs associated with new building are quite distinct from those involved in modernisation and rehabilitation, but the benefits arising from each option are also likely to be different. New housing which costs significantly more, will normally last longer, require less maintenance and, in theory, should be capable of commanding a higher annual rent. Once again, not all the costs and benefits arising from local authority housing investment are readily identifiable and capable of being measured. Standard commercial investment criteria cannot be easily applied to this area of local social investment, any more than they can to larger-scale central government projects. Cost-benefit analysis has evolved as a broadly based set of techniques to provide quantitative guidance for the public investment decision. The construction sector is the principle beneficiary, or otherwise, of such decisions.

Origins of cost-benefit analysis (CBA)

The idea that large-scale projects involving significant amounts of public funds should be assessed by evaluating all the identifiable costs and benefits, arising over a long future time-span, has been in existence since early in the twentieth century. The first systematic use of CBA was probably in US investment decisions concerning the North American water resources programmes of the 1930s.

Massive public expenditure was being undertaken to develop selected river valleys and the public benefit from such schemes was perceived to be uncertain. The early users of CBA were concerned to bring quantitative appraisal into the process of the allocation of public resources, in an attempt to realise greater economic efficiency. This objective has continued to lie at the heart of cost-benefit analysis, as the range of applications has increased.

It was not until the early 1960s that the first serious attempts were made to apply CBA in the UK. The Plowden Report on government expenditure decisions stressed the need to make improvements in the methods for measuring and handling public expenditure problems and, specifically, the report required government departments to make more widespread use of quantitative methods of appraisal. The pioneering attempt to apply CBA in the UK was in the economic assessment of the first stage of the M1 motorway between London and Birmingham. This exercise, carried out after the motorway had already been constructed, set up the basic methodology for CBA appraisal of major transport undertakings. After the M1 motorway study of 1960, there followed an important appraisal of the construction of the Victoria underground railway in 1963–5 and the comprehensive investigation into the third London airport, carried out by the Roskill Commission in 1969–70, which marked the coming of age of CBA in this country. (Fuller accounts of these early studies are provided by Newton.[1])

In recent years, CBA has been widely applied in this country and elsewhere to assist government decision-making on social investments. Frequently, the nature of the decision has not simply been whether to proceed with a single scheme or not, but rather to evaluate which of several options conveys the best net rate of return, after considering all the identifiable costs and benefits. (Some simplified examples of recent cost-benefit studies, most with construction implications, are provided in Mishan.[2]) Larger-scale applications include investment decisions on motorways, underground railways, airports, reservoirs and flood relief schemes, as well as power stations and, most recently, the Channel tunnel scheme. Smaller-scale uses of CBA include the evaluation of local authority housing investments, and the local provision of car parks and recreational facilities.

The basic CBA model

The basic approach follows the *discounted cash flow* concept used in private investment decision making, as described in Chapter 6 (pp. 173–6). In particular, use is made of the *net present value* model, but with cost-benefit analysis it is most common to measure costs and benefits separately, rather than to use a net income return. So, if C_t represents costs in year t, B_t represents benefits (implied income) in year t and i is the pre-determined annual discount rate:

$$NPV_C = \sum_{t=0}^{n} \frac{C_t}{(1+i)^t}$$

$$NPV_B = \sum_{t=1}^{n} \frac{B_t}{(1+i)^t}$$

The decision on which scheme is the best investment is made by using either the net present value, $NPV_B - NPV_C$, or the net benefit to cost ratio, NPV_B/NPV_C, whichever is deemed the more appropriate. In practice, there are often difficulties in obtaining full information to enable all costs and benefits to be incorporated into the equations. In some instances, competing investment schemes may be deemed to yield equivalent benefits, in which case only the discounted costs will be applicable. In other situations, costs may be treated as negative benefits and the two equations can be compressed into the more familiar single expression for net present value. When costs and benefits are brought together in one equation, it will be possible to estimate an internal rate of return for the project, where this approach is preferred to the use of an external rate of interest.

Discounting issues

Social investments invariably convey benefits over a much longer time-span than do most private firm investments. While plant and machinery is assumed to have a useful life of 5–10 years and commercial buildings are often taken to have an effective life of 30 years or less, an investment such as a motorway or an airport is likely to endure for many decades. Obviously, it is virtually impossible to predict with any degree of significance what the level of quantitative benefit will be 50 years or more into the future; it is not always an easy matter to forecast benefit for 10 years ahead. Future consumers of a social investment may come to value quite different benefits from those which are perceived today. In addition, relative prices may change (as oil prices changed in the 1970s) and so the valuation of future benefits will come to be distorted. For these reasons, the timespan over which benefit is assessed is often restricted to only a few decades, even when it is acknowledged that the real benefit from a social investment will continue long into the future.

A related issue is the choice of an appropriate external discount rate. When market rates of discount, appropriate for commercial investments, are applied, they serve to reduce the value of benefits receivable several years into the future. High discount rates mean that benefits receivable in the near future are much the most important component of net present value benefits. If benefit receivable in the more distant future is to have any significant influence on the investment decision, then a relatively low market rate of discount must be used. Some analysts have advocated a lower social rate of discount to ensure that current investment decisions take full account of the social value of future benefits. Other arguments suggest that to use a rate of discount lower than the market rate will lead to a misallocation of resources between the public and the private sectors. As Balchin and Kieve[3] make clear, there is no simple answer to the choice of discount rate, and in practice a variety of different rates are applied.

2. Large project applications

The key issue in cost-benefit analysis is the identification and measurement of all relevant costs and benefits associated with the proposed project. Whilst some cost and benefit items are specific to particular investments, many are common and the problems associated with measurement are shared by several social investment programmes. In Table 9.1 a list is provided of some of the typical cost and benefit items arising on a major transport undertaking such as a new motorway or underground railway link.

9.1   *Typical costs and benefits associated with a larger social investment,*
such as a major transportation undertaking

Cost components	Benefit components
(a) Acquisition of site and land	(j) Time savings to users
(b) Clearance and preparation of site	(k) Vehicle operating savings
(c) Construction costs	(l) Savings for non-users
(d) Capital equipment	(m) Reductions in accidents
(e) Interest costs	(n) Indirect spill-over benefits
(f) Maintenance costs	(p) Intangible benefits: less strain and more comfortable travel
(g) Dislocation costs	
(h) Intangible costs: noise and lack of amenity	

Cost estimates

In general, most cost components are easier to identify and evaluate than are the benefits; the major elements of cost arise early in the project, whereas the benefits accumulate over the long life of the investment. Before a major transport link can be constructed, land will need to be acquired; usually, there will be a significant cost involved in this. The cost of the land should reflect its *opportunity cost* which measures its worth in some alternative use. While some land may be derelict and have a very low opportunity cost, other land in the developed urban area, or in prime agricultural areas, may command a high opportunity cost. The market price at which the land or site may be purchased will not always accurately reflect its true social valuation.

The costs of preparing the site and the actual costs of construction are deemed relatively easy to estimate, but, as Chapter 7 makes clear, some of these costs are subject to high variability. Construction of a motorway takes several years to complete and in the UK, most major social investments turn out to cost a lot more, after allowing for inflation, than was envisaged at the estimation stage. The Thames Barrier provides an excellent recent example of the final cost exceeding the original estimate by a very large amount. In some instances, if the true final construction cost were known at the outset, it is doubtful whether the project could have been justified in cost-benefit terms.

Beyond the direct costs of construction, there remain the costs of equipping the completed project. In the case of motorways, this involves setting up directional signs, hazard warnings and lighting systems, whereas for an underground railway it includes the purchase of trains and the associated plant and equipment. Another important cost of a project is the accumulation of interest costs incurred on the capital borrowings. These costs relate to the amounts of borrowed capital employed and the period over which the loan funds are repaid. For many large social investments, funds are borrowed on a very long-term basis and the interest charges are incurred over the effective life of the project. In the same way, maintenance costs are likely to arise throughout the working life of the investments and estimates of expected repair and maintenance expenditure must be incorporated into the cost equation.

Items (a) to (f) in Table 9.1 are found in most types of investment; it is only the scale and accuracy of estimating these cost items which distinguishes the public from the private investment project. However, large social investments incur social costs which fall on many in society, both firms and private individuals. Some private investments which involve large factory locations may have a similar impact, but the firm making such an investment will not usually take such costs into account. Frequently a project—such as a motorway, an underground railway, an airport or even a reservoir—will involve a significant amount of dislocation of people and premises. Often people will need to be relocated on a permanent basis and they may be faced with continuing higher operating costs as a result. In a less obvious sense, a major transport undertaking will incur much higher noise levels for many households in the immediate vicinity, and almost certainly the quality of their visual environment will be impaired. In cases where power stations and major industrial works are constructed, leisure pursuits in the countryside may be destroyed. How can these largely intangible costs be assessed, and indeed is it worth bothering to try to make quantitative measurements of such costs? In an ideal cost-benefit exercise, the intangible costs ought to be included, but, as the Roskill investigation into the third London Airport demonstrated, a great deal of effort is required to estimate this type of cost item and, at the end of the day, such costs tend to prove relatively insignificant in the final decision-making for the investment project.

Benefit estimates

The measurement of benefit arising from a social investment is invariably much more difficult than the cost estimate. With a transport undertaking, the major area of benefit which is generated is in the time savings of travellers. But how can travel time be valued? Unlike commercial goods and services, there is no simple market price to afford a ready evaluation of a person's time. Nevertheless, if benefit is to be compared to cost, in a CBA exercise, it is necessary to assign some monetary value to the realised time savings. Where time is saved within working hours, an evaluation of this time can be made by using the average hourly rate of pay, but many journeys are made for leisure purposes and it is not obvious what value to attach to this time. In practice, leisure time has to be valued arbitrarily, as a proportion of the earnings rate; most studies adopt a figure of between 25% and 50% as the value of leisure time saved.

This price of time will need to be applied to estimates of the number of journeys made on the new transport undertaking, journeys both in working hours and in leisure time. Department of Transport records provide crude estimates of the number of journeys made by existing modes of transport, but it is no easy matter to forecast accurately the number of extra journeys people will make when a new transport facility comes into existence. The motorway programme in the UK has led to many more journeys being undertaken by car than was originally envisaged. In 1986 economic analyses produced widely varying estimates of the numbers of journeys likely to be made when the Channel Tunnel comes into existence.

Beyond time savings, the next most significant benefit arising is in the costs of operating the vehicle. With a motorway, distances may be reduced and higher average speeds may be maintained—both factors leading to reduced fuel consumption and less wear and tear on the vehicle. When an underground railway is constructed, it will offer commuters the opportunity to switch from road to rail and so produce vehicle cost savings. When a new airport is built, it may reduce vehicle distances for many users, and at the same time it may lead commercial operators to reduce the size of their vehicle fleets, in recognition of the improved access. All these vehicle cost savings are important sources of consumer benefit.

Benefit also accrues to other travellers who continue to use the original mode of transport, as others switch to the new facility and so reduce congestion costs and improve the speed of travel. In the case of the Victoria underground line, it was estimated that the savings for traffic which did not divert were greater than the benefits for that traffic which did switch. Indeed, without inclusion of the savings for non-users, the Victoria line investment could not have been justified in cost-benefit terms. Clearly, large projects convey gains to many people and one of the problems in measuring such benefit is to determine who exactly should be included in the benefit assessment. The operators of the Victoria line derive no revenue from non-users, yet it was this group of travellers which made the greatest gains. The issue of where to set the cut-off point in evaluating social benefit is common to most large scale public investments.

Another important area of benefit in transportation projects is the expected reduction in accidents, and the related saving of life. New motorways, in theory, allow motorists to travel more safely than on the existing roads, which are probably more congested. What monetary benefit should be attached to these savings in human life? As Harvey[4] points out, many alternative methods of evaluation have been devised, but each is beset by practical difficulties. Use is made of historical records of accidents to reach some quantitative assessment.

Large-scale public investments may also create spillover and intangible benefits for many not directly associated with the project. While construction of a motorway may well involve dislocation costs for some, for others it will serve to improve access and thereby increase property valuations. Many homes and business properties will experience increasing values as a result of transportation projects, and in rural areas the value of surrounding land may be enhanced by better communications. In a similar way, intangible benefits may arise: where traffic is diverted from urban areas residents may enjoy lower noise levels and less pollution as a result. It is no easy matter to place values on such gains as no market prices exist, but a full cost-benefit appraisal requires that some account should be taken of these benefits.

A final area of benefit is that of the intangible gains accruing to the users of the new facility. Those travellers using a new motorway can expect to make their journey in greater comfort, while drivers will experience less strain and fatigue. Similar types of consideration apply to those using a new underground railway or an airport. Where a new reservoir or river project is completed, better recreational facilities may be created. All these types of benefit defy easy quantification, yet they remain real factors in social investment decision-making.

Distributional effects

It is clear from studying the nature of the various costs and benefits arising from public investment that one result is likely to be a redistribution or transfer of wealth between various firms and individuals. The investment changes prices—not only of property and land, but also of the wages of operatives employed on the project—and in this way, income is redistributed within society. Generally, these redistributive effects are not taken into account in assessing the investment, although sometimes the government may wish to compensate various parties on the grounds of equitable treatment. It is difficult enough to measure the real spillover effects of a social investment and to determine meaningful cut-off boundaries, without attempting to allow for the transfer effects.

3. Small project applications

A large number of relatively smaller-scale investment decisions need to be made by local authorities and similar agencies. The concern to get the best value from limited public funds has led to the use of CBA techniques for evaluating investment alternatives. Probably the most common local application is in the provision of housing. Donnison and Ungerson[5] have observed how, as declining public resources have come to concentrate on the improvement of housing rather than on new build, work has focused on selected towns and areas of special need, and the choice of these areas has come to depend as much on social as physical criteria. It has become important to measure the social benefits against the related costs to ensure that the best use is made of public funds.

Housing renewal schemes

In 1978 the Department of the Environment[6] issued a research memorandum to the local authorities, in which it laid out a methodology for cost-benefit evaluation of housing renewal schemes. Table 9.2 presents a summary of the main costs and benefits which the DOE suggest should be evaluated for a range of different alternative schemes. The various options will include comprehensive clearance and redevelopment at the one extreme and a programme of minimal repair, at lowest possible cost, at the other. In between, various schemes involving different levels of demolition, repair, improvement, conversion and new build may be considered. All the respective costs and benefits are discounted to their present values and the scheme yielding the highest net present value benefit is identified as the best investment option.

9.2   Cost-benefit evaluation for various local housing renewal schemes

Costs	Benefits
(a) Acquisition of site and buildings	(j) Occupancy of unaltered dwellings
(b) Demolition and construction	(k) Occupancy of improved dwellings
(c) Infrastructure and environment costs	(l) Occupancy of converted dwellings
(d) Improvement costs	(m) Occupancy of new dwellings
(e) Conversion costs	(n) Intangible benefits
(f) Housing moving costs	
(g) Administration costs and fees	
(h) Intangible costs	

Costs of housing renewal

Only resource costs which incur an opportunity cost foregone by society enter into the list of cost components in Table 9.2. Where the local authority chooses to use derelict land in its investment programme, this is deemed to have zero cost, since it has no effective alternative use. In the same way, transfer costs, such as loan interest charges, which are very important in private investment decisions, are not usually considered as part of the social costs. Both costs and benefits are evaluated in terms of current prices and so it is assumed that future costs and benefits will remain constant in real terms.

Actual costs and their distribution over time will differ, depending on the specific investment option. The major cost component will be the acquisition of the existing site and its buildings; this cost will usually be common to all the renewal schemes under consideration. The acquisition cost will reflect the present market rentals of the property on the site which is to be improved. Schemes involving redevelopment will incur costs of demolition and costs of new construction. These new build costs will be spread over a number of future years. Most renewal schemes will involve some element of infrastructural and environmental investment. New roads, sewers and services may be installed to varying standards. The major alternative to new construction is improvement and conversion; this type of renewal work can be carried out to different standard levels and the expected costs will reflect the desired standards.

In most local authority housing schemes, some households will need to be decanted while construction takes place. These house-moving costs may be quite a significant component of the social cost, depending on the temporary arrangements which are made. Additionally, the local authority will incur administrative costs with any scheme, and fees may be payable to outside agencies. The nature of these costs is likely to vary with the particular investment option.

Beyond these directly measurable costs, there remain the intangible costs. Residents are likely to suffer a significant amount of disturbance, from contractors' noise to the inconvenience of dislocation. Any redevelopment may result in a loss of open space, the destruction of an historic building or the removal of some valued social amenity. Where higher density developments result, there may be an increase in social stress in the renewed area and the consequences of such stress may spread into surrounding neighbourhoods. The problems resulting from local authority tower blocks in the 1960s and 1970s, in some urban centres, are relatively well documented. It is virtually impossible to attach monetary values to such social costs, yet some account ought to be taken of these intangible factors in the final cost-benefit appraisal.

Benefits of housing renewal

The principal benefits which arise from a renewal scheme are contained in the occupancy of the dwellings, once renewal is complete. The market values of the dwellings are increased, and in most cases the effective life-span of the properties is extended. The benefit on any unaltered dwellings will simply be the existing market valuation, but the benefit on improved and converted dwellings will incorporate the increased market valuation. This rise in market value will often exceed the costs of carrying out the renovation, as the valuation of property is independent of the capital costs. The market demand for improved houses and flats may cause their value to increase by more than the amounts actually spent on improving their condition. Where the renewed properties are to be rented by the local authorities, the set rentals may not be a reliable guide to the true market values; these can be more readily established from comparable properties, which are privately owned.

New houses and flats are likely to have a significantly higher market valuation than improved properties and their expected life is greater. Against this, the costs of demolition and new build are appreciably higher than the costs of improved property. The higher benefits of new dwellings accrue over future years, whereas the higher costs must be met in the short-term. The cost-benefit analysis carried out by Needleman[7] has shown how the investment decision between new build and modernisation critically hinges on the expected life-span of the improved dwellings and the discount rate which is adopted. Where the modernised properties have a relatively long life-span after improvement and where higher interest rates, approaching market rates, are used to discount, the modernisation option emerges as the preferred investment in a high proportion of cost-benefit evaluations.

Any renewal scheme will also produce many intangible benefits—some to those directly involved in the project and others of a more indirect nature. The residents may enjoy social benefits: more open space, better leisure facilities or improved parking and road access. As a result of less overcrowding in a new housing scheme, residents may experience better health; also, possibly, less crime may result from better housing. Many of these gains will also be enjoyed by residents in neighbouring areas. Indeed, as a result of housing renewal, property values in adjacent areas, not directly involved in the renewal scheme, may also rise. Gains may accrue to commercial ventures in the vicinity of the renewal scheme. Frequently, much of the benefit that is created will not accrue to the local authority which is incurring the cost. Nevertheless, all these social benefits should be taken into account if the best investment decision is to be made.

Limitations of CBA

It is clear that where a local authority, or some other local decision-making branch of government, tries to adopt the CBA approach a great deal of detailed information will need to be collated. It is no easy matter to determine all the relevant costs and benefits associated with investment options. In particular, benefits must often be quantified without the aid of well-defined market prices and values. Valuation of property is a hazardous enough exercise, but how can the benefits from a sports complex or a local water facility be measured? Frequently, the prices which a local authority may charge will be subsidised and there is therefore no true market price to measure the value which consumers attach to the resulting benefit. The intangible costs and benefits may be every bit as important as their more obvious tangible counterparts, but measurement will remain impossible. Equally, costs and benefits may accrue outside the immediate area of the investment. Council car-parking decisions entail gains and losses to visitors from outside the town, but it is unlikely that these can be assessed as part of the cost-benefit analysis.

Sometimes, especially with housing renewal schemes, all the options under consideration produce negative net present value results. Does this mean that all schemes should be rejected, or that the scheme with the smallest negative NPV should be adopted? Perhaps changing some of the assumptions used to evaluate benefits, or use of a lower social discount rate, will produce positive NPVs. Either way, the vulnerability of the CBA to changes in underlying assumptions and parameters is emphasised. When higher rates of discount, in line with market interest rates, are adopted, this most commonly leads to schemes with the lowest levels of capital expenditure being favoured. In the housing context, this can lead to rejection of new build investments in favour of repair and improvement, and the average age of the local housing stock may increase—to the detriment of future generations.

Cost-benefit analysis concentrates on measuring economic benefit to the community. However, in many instances, financial feasibility may be more important to the local authority than economic gains. Where the authority is strictly restricted in its access to borrowed funds, there is little point in carrying out a full CBA if many of the investment options lie beyond its funding capacity. Indeed, even after CBA has been applied to identify the best economic scheme, there is no guarantee that this will be adopted. Many local authority schemes have floundered on financial restraints or political pressures. The Roskill Commission's identification of Cublington as the best site for a third London airport was never taken up—for these same reasons.

Questions

1. In what ways are the investment decisions undertaken by public sector agencies different from those taken by private sector firms?
2. Why should construction companies have an interest in cost-benefit exercises?
3. Describe the origins of cost-benefit appraisal in the UK and indicate its main areas of application.
4. Discuss the significance of:
   a) the length of the project life, and
   b) the chosen rate of discount
   to the CBA decision.
5. Identify the main cost elements associated with a large social transport undertaking and indicate any problems of measurement.
6. Describe how time savings benefits can be measured and indicate how these might be evaluated for the Channel Tunnel scheme.
7. Demonstrate your understanding of the following terms:
   a) 'the intangible benefits of a social investment'
   b) 'the distribution effects of a large public scheme'
   c) 'the opportunity cost of a public investment.'
8. Outline how a local authority could carry out a cost-benefit appraisal to determine the best scheme for housing renewal in a specific locality.
9. Comment on the main limitations of cost-benefit analysis and illustrate your answer with some practical examples.
10. It has been claimed that since we can rarely measure all the costs and benefits arising from a public investment undertaking with any accuracy, a cost-benefit appraisal is a worthless exercise. Discuss this claim and identify the value of cost-benefit analysis for the public investment decision-maker.

Further Reading

BARKER, P. J. and BUTTON, K. J., *Case Studies in Cost-Benefit Analysis*, Heinemann, 1975

LAYARD, R., *Cost-Benefit Analysis*, Parts 1 and 2, Penguin, 1972

MISHAN, E. J., *Cost-Benefit Analysis: An Informal Introduction*, George Allen and Unwin, 1982

NEWTON, T., *Cost-Benefit Analysis in Administration*, George Allen and Unwin, 1972

PEARCE, D. W., *Cost-Benefit Analysis*, Macmillan Press, 1981.

RUDDOCK, L., *Economics for the Construction and Property Industries*, Chapter 3, Polytech Publishers, 1983

SUGDEN, R. and WILLIAMS, A., *The Principles of Practical Cost-Benefit Analysis*, Part III, Oxford University Press, 1978

10 Sources of Company Finance

The willingness to invest in a project is often constrained in practice by the availability, or otherwise, of an adequate supply of funds. Whether it is an individual, a private sector firm or a public sector corporation planning an investment, the ability to proceed is determined by the finance available. Typically, the larger the organisation, the greater will be the sources of available finance, but even very large firms sometimes encounter limits to the amount of funds they can easily raise. Smaller firms have much less choice in their sources of finance, and frequently their investment plans are aborted or seriously delayed through shortages of suitable funds. While large public sector corporations are in theory in the best position for raising investment finance, in practice government contraints of the kind described in Chapter 2 will serve to limit their access to external funds.

It is usual to make distinctions between finance which is available to the firm in the short, the medium and the longer term. Most commonly, the short period is taken as up to one year ahead, whilst the medium term is between one to five years. The longer term by definition is anything over five years. Different analysts adopt different definitions, but all agree that the sources of long-term finance are substantially different from the sources of short- and medium-term finance. For investment purposes longer-term finance is by far the most important source, with most of the short-term funds being used to meet working capital requirements, rather than investment needs. The time period for which the capital is required is an important parameter influencing the sources available to the firm and the cost of the capital.

1. Main sources of longer-term finance

These sources are critical for the firm or institution investing in fixed assets with a relatively long life, such as buildings or property. In

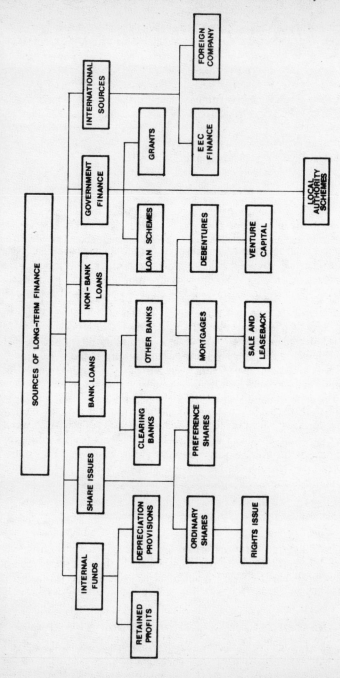

Fig. 10.1 Sources of longer-term finance

Fig. 10.1 a classification of the main longer-term sources is given. Initially, a firm will be dependent on share capital, supplemented by external sources such as bank loans, to provide the investment capital. Once the firm is established and trading successfully, the internally generated funds become the most important source of investment finance. Government statistics[1] for 1985 indicate that for industrial and commercial companies, internal sources accounted for some 71% of all funds. The other main sources of finance were: all share issues 10%, bank loans 15%, non-bank loans only 1% and international sources 3%.

Internal funds

When a firm retains profits rather than distributing them as dividend to the shareholders, it is creating a valuable source of funds for new investment. Such retained earnings represent an increased share in the firm by its owners and this will be reflected in the price of the firm's shares rising in excess of their nominal value. The firm has to decide each period what proportion of its profits it will retain for internal use and what proportion will be distributed as dividend. In a firm which is experiencing good profit growth, this distribution decision poses few problems, but, in other instances where earned profit is only small, the decision may be very difficult. Retained profit is an obvious source of capital for the established firm, and while the cost of such funds is certainly not minimal, it is usually less than with funds obtained from external sources[2].

Depreciation provision is another internal source of longer-term capital. Reserves are created by the process of depreciating fixed assets over their life and these funds are available for spending on new investments in the same way as profit reserves. Firms are permitted to write off depreciation charges against profits prior to the calculation of tax.

Share issues

It was explained in Chapter 3 how, when a firm wants to grow and acquire limited liability status, it will issue shares which convey an equity interest in the firm. When ordinary shares are offered for sale, the firm receives the par value or face value of each share and it will use these funds to buy investment assets, with which it hopes to make a profit for the shareowner. Shares may be fully paid-up or only partly paid-up, so that the shareholder may be required to contribute the difference at a later date. Normally, the value of the firm's share in the market will rise as the company increases its profit reserves, and the shareholders have an equity interest in these profits. The firm itself does not gain any direct capital from increases in its share price on the Stock Exchange. Equally, a firm that is badly managed may incur losses, in which case the value of shares may fall below their original par value. The directors of the firm are under no obligation to maintain the value of the shareholders' stake in the firm.

Shares can be of several different types and each conveys different rights of ownership. Ordinary shares, which normally entitle the holders to voting rights, are the most common type of share. In some companies, preference shares are issued to raise finance and these shares entitle the holder to a dividend up to a predetermined level, to be paid ahead of the ordinary shareholder. Preference shares are a safer form of investment, but the holders of such shares do not usually have voting rights, and the return on these shares tends to be lower over the longer period. There also exist cumulative and redeemable preference shares, but these are not particularly important classes of shares.

Issues of shares are a popular method of raising new investment funds for a public limited company. New shares may be offered for sale in a number of different ways, either directly by subscription, or by tender from prospective purchasers, or indirectly through a specialist intermediary, such as a merchant bank. Where a large profitable company is issuing new shares, it is likely to be able to sell all the shares without much difficulty, but where a smaller, perhaps less successful, company is attempting to raise new finance by this means, the result is much less certain. In this case, the firm may need the services of a merchant bank to ensure that the issue is fully taken up, or for the bank to underwrite the issue if share sales fall short of their target. Clearly, the services of the financial intermediary will be a significant cost to the firm issuing new shares. Firms with a poor record of profitability may find it difficult to attract prospective purchasers for its new shares and so this means of raising new finance will not be viable for all firms—especially very small firms.

A rights issue is where a firm offers its existing shareholders the opportunity of purchasing new shares in proportion to their existing shareholdings. Usually such shares will be offered at a price less than the prevailing market price of the company's shares, so an incentive is provided to ensure a high level of take-up. Any shares not bought by existing shareholders are sold direct on the Stock Exchange. The rights issue offers a relatively cheap way for the public limited company to raise new finance. Rights issues are probably the most popular method of issuing new shares. The rights issue should not be confused with the scrip issue, which is strictly an alternative method for the company to pay a profits dividend. With a scrip issue the firm does not raise any new capital, but rather it issues new shares instead of paying out dividends. In this way, it retains more profits within the company, but it does change the underlying capital structure of the company. Fuller details on the different types of shares and their methods of issue are given elsewhere[3].

Bank loans

Banks are important sources of finance for private sector firms, both in the long and the shorter time period. The UK clearing banks traditionally prefer shorter loans, although a small percentage of their loans are made for longer-term purposes. Most of the clearing banks do operate business loan schemes, whereby they are willing to lend relatively small sums for up to 20 years. Only the more profitable smaller firms are likely to be eligible for such loans. Firms requiring large amounts of investment capital, or firms looking to invest in inherently risky ventures, will be unlikely to qualify for clearing bank finance.

Apart from the clearing banks, there exist many other banks and financial institutions who will lend larger sums for higher-risk investment projects. Merchant and foreign banks are the most common source of such longer-term loans. Inevitably, such loans cost significantly more than do those from the clearing banks, and the interest charges will need to be met before any profits can be determined. Loans may be either of the fixed interest type, or their costs may vary with the basic rate of interest, in which case the cost becomes uncertain over future years. When the general level of interest is low, longer-term bank loans will appear a relatively attractive source of finance, but when rates are high, bank loans are not so favourable.

Non-bank loans

A debenture is a bond issued by a company in exchange for a long-term loan made by the public. Debentures carry a fixed rate of interest and the holders of debentures are creditors of the company, rather than owners. Debenture interest is a cost to the firm which will have to be deducted from gross profits, before taxable profit is determined. Usually, debenture finance is only used by larger companies which have relatively stable levels of profit. This form of fixed interest long-term loan is not widely used in the United Kingdom private sector, although local authorities and central government raise a large amount of their longer-term financial needs through bond issues of this type.

Companies, like individuals investing in dwellings, may raise loan finance through mortgages on their assets. Firms may obtain a mortage from a non-bank financial institution to purchase a particular building or similar existing development. The mortgage is usually repaid by annual instalments over the period of the loan, but the rate of interest is likely to vary with the general level of market rates. Often lenders are reluctant to give straight mortgages to industrial and commercial companies, because of the risks of default and the uncertain value of the property investment. An important variation on the straight mortgage is the mortgage debenture, where funds are advanced against the security of a particular property and in addition, the lender has a charge against the general assets of the firm. Usually, such mortgage debentures carry a fixed rate of interest and repayment is at the end of the loan period.

In recent years, the market for longer-term loan finance has expanded, as a large number of development and venture capital providers have emerged. Most of these loans are made to smaller companies in the high-technology manufacturing sector and few if any are made to firms in the construction sector. Many of these loans contain an equity component, where the lending institution takes an option to purchase shares in the borrowing firm, at some future date, at a fixed price. In other instances, the lenders demand both a fixed rate of interest on the loan and also an on-going share in the profits of the firm. A fuller account of some of these venture capital loan schemes is obtainable elsewhere.[4]

For property development companies who produce prime commercial buildings, such as shops and offices, an important source of long-term finance may be the 'sale and leaseback'. Under this system the completed development is sold to a financial institution, such as an insurance company, but the development is leased back to the property firm. This firm obtains the vital capital for use in new developments, while it is able to make a continuing profit from its renting operations, providing the rental income continues to exceed the lease costs. The financial institution is relieved of all management obligations, but it enjoys inflationary gains from the capital value of the development, as well as a guaranteed income from the leasing charges. Such arrangements have become increasingly important forms of long-term finance for construction companies engaged in property development.[5]

Government finance

There exists a very wide variety of schemes and incentives provided by central and local government and their various agencies to give financial assistance to firms in the private sector. Much of this financial aid works through the tax system and has already been described. Another significant area of government-aided investment finance is that associated with regional development; this has been outlined in Chapter 4. In addition to these sources, there are available a number of grants for investment projects in specific industries, such as textiles and steel. Apart from direct investment grants, government and its agencies may offer loan facilities to firms who are unable to raise finance for specific projects through the normal commercial channels. During the 1970s, the government used the National Enterprise Board to provide both loan and equity finance to a number of large companies who were experiencing difficulty in raising investment finance through the financial markets. In a similar way, the Industrial and Commercial Finance Corporation (ICFC) was originally set up by the government in 1945 to provide loans for smaller and medium-sized firms. Although ICFC is today operated by a consortium of clearing banks and the Bank of England, it continues to provide this key service to firms.

In the 1980s local authorities have become increasingly active in economic development initiatives, and many have sought to encourage firms to carry out local investments which create employment. In several areas, local authorities have established separate economic development corporations or enterprise boards; in others, they support local enterprise agencies or science parks. Local authorities are empowered to offer long-term loans to firms to purchase or lease land, carry out work on land, or erect buildings. Most local authorities do not have sufficient funds to provide investment grants to firms in the same way as central government. Inner urban area authorities have been the recipient of increasing amounts of government finance in the mid-1980s and some of these funds have been made available as grant incentives for firm investment.

International sources

A number of large companies operating in the UK are actually subsidiaries of foreign parent companies. Obvious examples are found in the motor car industry, with Ford, Vauxhall (General Motors) and Talbot (Peugeot). In this situation, longer-term finance can be obtained by capital transfers from the parent organisation. Frequently, government incentives are offered to foreign firms investing in the UK; many of these schemes are tied to regional policy. In the early 1980s, firms in the UK have tended to transfer more funds out of the country than have been received inwards. The net flow of international capital has been in an outward direction, but in the future, some of these investment funds might be persuaded back to the UK and this would constitute an important source of longer-term finance.

In recent years, the European Community has become a source of funds for project finance, as UK firms have taken advantage of EEC grants in the control of the European Regional Development Fund, the European Social Fund and various research programmes. In addition to such grants, the European Investment Bank (EIB) raises long-term finance on the world's capital markets, which it lends for industrial and social investment projects. (Fuller details of all the EEC sources of long-term finance are provided by Peat Marwick.[6])

2. Sources of short- and medium-term finance

There are many different sources available for shorter-term finance, which is required primarily to meet the firm's needs for working capital. The main sources of such finance are summarised in Fig. 10.2. Most firms make use of trade credit, which enables them to buy goods and services now, without having to pay until a later date. In a similar way, firms make use of funds set aside to pay both taxes and dividends, where they hold these funds until the date for payment falls due. Factoring is another important source of short-term funding and involves raising money on the security of the firm's debts, so that cash is received earlier than if the firm waited for its debtors to pay. Most firms make extensive use of shorter-term loans, both from banks and other sources. The most common form of such loans is the bank overdraft. For firms who are part of a larger company group, there is the possibility of obtaining short-term finance through intra-company transfers. Where one part of the group is generating high profits, some of this cash can be injected into associated firms to improve their liquidity.

Trade credit

As interest rates have increased in recent years, firms have sought to make greater use of trade credit, whereby firms take longer to pay their liabilities without incurring any interest charge. Almost all industries operate credit systems, but the terms of credit vary considerably between different industrial sectors. Often, credit conditions are determined by trade associations, or else by evolved custom and practice. Where the time-lag between the purchase of raw materials and the sale of the final output is relatively long, as with many construction products, the suppliers may well be

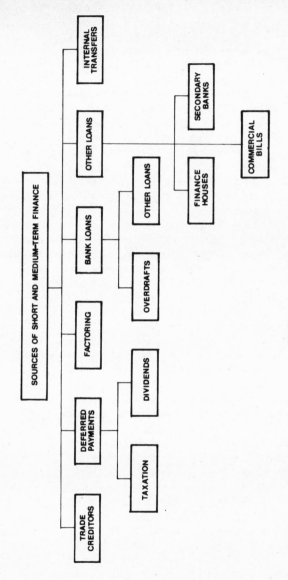

Fig. 10.2 *Sources of short- and medium-term finance*

prepared to give longer-term credit. If the financial position of the buyer is seen to be weak, the supplier may not be anxious to extend any credit facilities or, at best, only very restricted credit terms will be available. Conversely, the large established customer will usually enjoy the best credit terms, as the supplier will be anxious to retain the large volume of business. Large construction firms typically exhibit high amounts of outstanding trade credit on their balance sheets; this point is developed in the next chapter.

Often, the supplier providing the trade credit will also offer a discount to encourage early payment. In this situation, it is clear that the company who takes full advantage of the trade credit and fails to obtain the cash discount is incurring a significant cost for its trade credit facility. Samuels and Wilkes[7] make it clear that trade credit, in the face of discounts for early payment, is not a cheap source of finance and that if the buyer were fully aware of the real costs involved, alternative sources of finance might be used. However, for many small firms, such as those found in the construction sector, easily available alternatives are hard to find; trade credit therefore remains the single most important source of finance for such firms. In the construction sector, credit facilities are widely used between suppliers and sub-contractors, between sub-contractors and main contractors, and between main contractors and the client.

Deferred payments

A firm's liability for corporation tax becomes due for payment in the year following that in which the profit was actually earned. This means that the firm has use of these taxable funds for approximately one year before they must be paid. In a similar way, a firm that produces goods on which standard rate VAT is payable and only makes returns every three months will enjoy the use of these tax balances until they become payable. Another type of deferred payment arises where the firm has declared a dividend, and set funds aside, but delays actual payment until a later date. The firm will have short-term use of these funds to supplement its working capital. Similar deferred payments sometimes arise in respect of the firm's pension funds. For a large company, the total amount of all these deferred payments can be very significant, but for a smaller firm this source is likely to be much less important.

Factoring

Often a small, new company will encounter short-term liquidity problems, arising from its inability to collect payments due from its debtors. This is the opposite side of the coin to trade credit, where some larger firms systematically delay paying for goods they have received and thereby cause problems for the smaller supplier. A number of companies, dominated by specialist subsidiaries of the UK clearing banks, offer a factoring service to these smaller firms. This service consists of the administration of invoices, insurance against bad debts and, most important, the provision of finance by advancing the client firms up to 80% of the value of the debts to be collected. The factors charge significant fees for this specialist service, but it does help to ensure that the firm maintains an adequate source of working capital during a critical period of sales growth. Factors will only provide this service to a select few firms and many of the very small firms in the construction sector will not prove acceptable to the factoring companies.

Short-term loans

The most common form of shorter-term loan is the bank overdraft, which for most firms constitutes the most flexible form of borrowing. Overdrafts that are no longer required can be easily repaid and the interest costs on such loans remain a tax deductable expense. In theory, banks issue overdrafts with a right to call in the loan at short notice; in law, bank overdrafts are repayable on demand. In practice, banks usually assure the borrower that the overdraft will be extended for a specified minimum period. Banks cannot always be relied upon to grant an overdraft facility, nor can they be depended upon to extend the period of the overdraft or to increase its size. Much depends on the impact of prevailing monetary policy on the banking sector, as to whether the banks feel able to extend credit facilities, or whether they perceive the need to limit and squeeze advances. Inevitably, in the event of credit restraint, the least favoured customers are the smaller firms, such as those in the construction sector, and it is these firms who encounter the most binding limits on their important overdraft advances.

Banks much prefer self-liquidating loans, as opposed to open-ended overdrafts. A self-liquidating loan is one which will be repaid automatically in a specified time period. Banks may be willing to extend loans for specific contracts, where the details of the contract are known and the bank is assured that the loan will be repaid, once construction is completed. Small firms may need to provide information from their order books to convince the bank of their creditworthiness. It is not uncommon for banks to exercise a charge on the firm's assets, as security for any advance, or, in the case of the smaller private firm, a personal guarantee may be required from the firm's owners.

While borrowing from the commercial banks is generally accepted as being the cheapest form of loan for a company, frequently alternative sources may have to be used. When a firm wants to borrow a particularly large amount, or when it wants loan finance for a riskier type of venture, such as an overseas contract, it may well have to obtain its funding from other areas of the banking sector. Merchant banks have historically been identified with loans for higher-risk ventures, although their total amount of loan capital is relatively small and they usually prefer to make loans only to the larger established companies. Foreign and international consortia banks are another potential source of short-term loan finance, especially for the larger firm. The smaller company, denied access to commercial bank loans, may need to use finance houses to meet some of its capital needs. In particular, hire purchase facilities may be used to buy smaller items of plant and vehicles. Loans from secondary banks and finance houses will typically be much more expensive than those from commercial banks, and the lending institution will almost certainly make some sort of charge on the firm, or on the individual owner's assets.

A firm which is engaged in overseas trade may avoid bank loans as a means of generating working capital and instead may issue a commercial bill of exchange. This is similar to an individual using a post-dated cheque to obtain cash now. The buying company agrees to pay on demand at a fixed future date a stipulated sum, either to the supplier or to any financial institution who has discounted the bill for the original supplier. Obviously, the buying firm will have to pay for this extension of credit, but it may well prove to be a relatively cheaper means of raising working capital than a straightforward bank loan.

3. Capital structure decisions

A firm raises capital from several different sources. The composition of these sources is likely to vary significantly, both between firms and within a given firm over time. The underlying determinant of a firm's capital structure is the nature of its business. A manufacturing company will tend to have a relatively high proportion of fixed assets and so it will have a corresponding need for a larger amount of long-term capital. Within the construction sector, firms investing in property will also use more longer-term sources of funds. Most larger contracting firms maintain high stocks of materials and need to finance a great deal of work-in-progress. This type of business operation determines a need for extensive amounts of working capital and a large use of trade credit. Smaller building firms rarely carry any significant stocks of materials, but they frequently need to finance work-in-progress and they require short-term finance to bridge the period between completing the contract and receiving the final payment.

Firms operating within the same industrial sector often exhibit similar general capital structures, particularly in the balance between long- and short-term financing. However, the exact composition of a firm's sources of finance is a function of its costs of capital and this tends to be unique to the individual firm and also highly variable over time. Most fundamentally, the managerial efficiencies of firms differ and this is reflected in profitability differentials, which not only govern the supply of the crucially important internal sources of funds, but also indirectly affect the terms and conditions on which the firm can borrow externally. The successful and profitable firm can raise loans more cheaply than its struggling counterpart.

Costs of capital

At first sight it may appear that there is no cost attaching to the firm's use of its own retained earnings; however, such funds do have an opportunity cost, as they constitute an increased stake in the firm by its shareholders. The costs of issuing new shares are easier to identify. In addition to the measured expenses of the new issue and the discount premium, which might have to be offered to ensure satisfactory take-up of the shares, there is the impact on the yield on the existing shares. The firm will need to pay enough dividends to meet the shareholders' required yield on their investment. It is generally agreed by most financial analysts that the costs of raising finance by equity share issues will normally be greater than those associated with fixed interest loan capital.[8]

The cost of fixed interest debt is significantly reduced in the first instance by a company's ability to offset this cost against profit for tax purposes. This tax saving reduces the costs of external borrowings for the profitable firm, but it does nothing for the firm which does not earn any profit which is subject to tax. The cost of loan capital may be further reduced when account is taken of inflation, for the impact of inflation is to reduce the real costs of borrowing still further. During the 1970s, many large, highly profitable firms, faced with inflation rates greater than fixed interest rates, found external borrowing an extremely advantageous and low-cost source of capital.

A firm which chooses to employ a high proportion of debt finance in its total capital is said to be highly 'geared'. This high gearing means that the firm must earn good profits, if it is to be able to pay its shareholders an acceptable dividend once all the fixed interest debts have been met. As a firm becomes more highly geared, so its proportion of debt finance increases and it becomes more risky from the shareholders' standpoint. Equally, the lending institutions will take note of a firm's gearing structure and where an already highly geared firm seeks further loan finance, it will only be provided at a relatively high cost. This increasing cost of capital serves to check the debt gearing of the company.

The issue of how a company can minimise its costs of capital is, in reality, a rather complex matter, dependent on a wide range of financial variables. The topic lies beyond the ambitions of the present text, but the interested reader is directed to some of the more specialised financial studies listed in the further reading for this chapter. Further aspects of finance in the firm are taken up in Chapter 11.

Questions

1. Outline the main sources of long-term finance available to a firm.
2. Discuss the value of new share issues as a means of raising long-term capital.
3. Distinguish the main agencies who provide longer-term loan finance to the corporate sector.
4. Demonstrate your understanding of the following terms:
   a) 'debentures'
   b) 'sale and leaseback'
   c) 'bill of exchange'
   d) 'capital gearing'
5. How do short- and medium-term sources of finance differ from their longer-term counterparts?
6. Explain why trade credit is such an important source of finance for the smaller construction firm.
7. How might
   a) factoring, and
   b) deferred payments
   be used by a company to increase its working capital base?
8. What are the main determinants of a company's capital structure?

Further Reading

DAVIS, E. and POINTON, J., *Finance and the Firm*, Part IV, Oxford University Press, 1984

FELLOWS, R., LANGFORD, D., NEWCOMBE, R. and URRY, S., *Construction Management in Practice*, Chapter 8, Longman, 1983

HARRIS, F. and MCCAFFER, R., *Modern Construction Management*, Chapter 12, Granada, 1983

MIDGLEY, K. and BURNS, R. G., *Business Finance and the Capital Market*, Parts 1 and 2, Macmillan, 1979

PEAT MARWICK, *Finance for New Projects in the UK*, Peat, Marwick, Mitchell and Co., 1985

ROCKLEY, L. E., *Finance for the Non-accountant*, Chapter 14, Hutchinson, 1984

SAMUELS, J. M. and WILKES, F. M., *Management of Company Finance*, Nelson, 1980

WOODCOCK, C., *Raising Finance: The Guardian Guide for the Small Business*, Guardian Newspapers, 1986

11 Financial Control of a Building Firm

The construction firm is in business to achieve profitability, as demonstrated in Chapter 3 (pp. 90–7). In practice, firms will not always seek to maximise short-run profits, but they will attempt to produce the highest returns for their shareholders over the longer period. At times, firms will be concerned with survival, which involves staying solvent and avoiding bankruptcy. At other times, firms will seek to grow as a means to generating higher profits. Here too, the firm will be concerned with ensuring liquidity in its quest for greater profitability. As the construction firm pursues these central objectives, it will need to maintain a strong measure of financial control and it will need to understand the nature of its underlying cost relationships.

In this chapter the main categories of cost arising in the construction firm are examined. Particular attention is drawn to the categories of cost used for control purposes. As Sizer[1] explains, cost has many meanings in different situations and the costs necessary for control tend to be different from those used for decision-making. The accountant in the construction firm works in terms of direct and indirect costs, in contrast to the economist who formulates the theory of the firm in terms of fixed, variable, average and marginal costs.

The control of cost is a critical consideration both to the client/developer of a project and to the construction company carrying out the work. This chapter examines some of the methods available for the construction firm to control its costs of a project. Consideration of the client's approach to cost control lies beyond the scope of this book, but the topic is fully treated elsewhere.[2]

A particularly important area of financial control for the construction firm is cash flow forecasting and the need to ensure that the firm does not run out of cash resources before the completion of its projects. The relatively high number of bankruptcies recorded in the construction sector testifies to the importance of cash flow to the building firm. Cash is a critical component of working capital, but it is the *timing* of the cash flow which is of paramount importance in an activity with so many potential cash inflows and outflows.

The final section of this chapter looks at the principles of financial control for the complete building firm. The financial information contained in the balance sheet and profit and loss account, which the firm is legally required to produce, provides a rich source of data for control purposes. Use of financial ratios to analyse these basic accounts enables the firm's performance to be regularly monitored and an assessment to be made as to how well the firm is realising its basic objectives.

1. Basic cost relationships

In construction, the terms 'cost' and 'price' are often used inter-changeably. 'Cost' refers to what the firm has to pay to complete the project; 'price' refers to the amount the construction firm charges the client for carrying out the project. Most simply, the difference between price and total cost is a measure of the firm's profit (or loss) on the contract. The uncertain nature of much construction activity means that cost estimates, which are used to determine a tender price, usually differ significantly from the actual costs incurred. Within a firm's total costs on a contract, a number of different cost classifications can be identified. The essential difference is between direct costs, which are directly attributable to the specific contract, and indirect costs which cannot be associated with any individual contract yet have been apportioned to it.

Direct costs of a contract

Table 11.1 details the direct costs that can be allocated to a specific contract. Clearly, all site labour, whether direct or sub-contracted, is a direct cost, as is the cost of materials used and the charges for plant used specifically on the contract. Owned plant may also incur an associated depreciation charge which is unrelated to actual usage, and this component of plant cost is an indirect expense. On any contract, costs will arise which cannot easily be attributed to any one factor of production. These include the site overhead charges, some of which are fixed in nature and remain unchanged regardless of the amount of work done and others of which are variable with the level of output achieved. Preliminary site items, such as the cost of site offices and the provision of temporary services, are examples of fixed overheads, while operative travelling expenses and general insurances are representative variable overheads. From the perspective of the firm, these site overheads constitute a direct contract cost, quite distinct from the indirect overhead costs arising in respect of the firm's head office costs. For the purposes of cost control on the individual contract, the site overheads may need to be apportioned to other direct cost factors.

11.1   The direct and indirect costs of the construction firm

Direct cost items for allocation to contract		
1. Labour	:	Contractor's direct labour – site management.
2. Sub-contractors	:	Nominations – domestic.
3. Materials	:	Nominated supplies – general purchase.
4. Plant	:	External hire or lease – internal use charges.
5. Site overheads	:	Fixed preliminaries – variable charges.
Indirect cost items to be absorbed by contracts		
6. Head office services to site	:	Quantity surveying – design – engineering – purchase.
7. Head office administration costs	:	Estimating – accounts – marketing – legal – research– secretarial – management.
8. Head office building charges	:	Rents – maintenance – vehicle hire – office equipment.
9. General depreciation charges.		
10. General finance charges.		

Within the direct cost classification, it is common to distinguish the prime cost (PC) sum of the particular contract. In the construction sector, this means those items which are specifically nominated in the bill of quantities. They include all nominated sub-contractors and any specifically nominated materials and services. Outside the construction sector the term 'prime cost' is more widely applied to describe all material, labour and plant costs which can be directly allocated to a specific project or production unit.

Indirect costs of a firm

These costs arise from the expenses associated with operating a head office and maintaining centralised services, utilising these across a wide range of contracts. Table 11.1 details the principal categories of such indirect costs. Many construction firms operate centralised quantity surveying, design, engineering and purchasing services and the salary bill which accrues in respect of these central staff is an indirect overhead item. Similar costs are incurred through the employment of the firm's managerial, administrative and technical staff, whose services are spread over the whole of the firm's activities, and this cost cannot thereby be directly apportioned to any one contract or cost centre.

Apart from employees, head office costs arise from the operation of buildings, vehicles, and plant and equipment, which are not specifically allocated. Fixed rental and leasing charges have to be met and depreciation arises through the passage of time, even when plant remains idle. In addition, the construction firm may take on general loans, as described in the previous chapter. The finance charges on these loans are a significant item of expense, which must be recovered from a range of contracts.

The indirect costs of the construction firm cannot be directly allocated to any single contract or production cost unit. Rather, such costs have to be apportioned to the individual contracts, in such a way that all this indirect cost is absorbed by the total number of contracts being carried out. Where the firm fails to absorb indirect cost in this way, these costs will have to be set against the total operating profits and, if the profits are insufficient to cover the costs, losses will accrue and the firm's long-run survival is threatened. There is no simple or universal basis for apportioning indirect costs across contracts, and different firms are likely to adopt different solutions.

Bases for apportioning indirect costs

In a manufacturing-type operation, the bases for apportionment tend to be more clear-cut than in the case of construction activity. Typically, the manufacturing firm uses either the relative sales volumes of its respective products and services, or the indirect costs of production. If a firm manufactures only two products, whose expected annual sales ratio is 3:1, the first product might be expected to carry 75% of the firm's indirect costs and the second product only 25%. Alternatively, if the ratio of the two products' direct production costs were 2:1, then indirect overhead might be apportioned on a basis of two-thirds to one-third. Other bases of absorption are possible, such as the relative direct labour costs of the different products. The firm will choose a basis which is simple to apply and which will ensure that the total indirect costs are well covered by the revenue proceeds from the different products.

The apportionment basis for the construction firm is frequently more difficult to resolve. An example is provided in Table 11.2, where a highly simplified breakdown of some representative direct costs are given. Since it is the contractor's own direct work which absorbs most of the head-office services, it might be deemed most appropriate to use cost category (1) as the basis for absorbing indirect costs. Alternatively, the contracts manager will want to preserve options between own direct work and use of domestic sub-contractors. Where indirect overheads are apportioned on the basis of costs (1), this may prove to be unacceptably narrow, when extensive use is to be made of sub-contracting. A more appropriate basis will be all contractor's direct costs, category (3). This provides a much wider base for apportionment and leaves contract management free to choose how production will be fulfilled, without potentially restraining overhead implications. The firm's financial management may prefer to spread indirect cost recovery over a still wider base, such as total direct cost of the contract, category (5). This basis ignores the breakdown between contractor work and nominated work and allows the firm to recover indirect costs in proportion to overall contract values.

11.2 *Alternative bases for apportioning indirect costs to a contract*

(a) *Composition of direct contract costs*

		£000
(1)	Contractor's own direct cost	500
(2)	Domestic sub-contractors	500
(3)	Contractor's work	1,000
(4)	Nominations	1,000
(5)	Total direct (prime) costs	2,000

(b) *Bases for apportioning indirect overhead*
   A 15% on contractor's direct cost (1)
   B 10% on contractor's work   (3)
   C 8% on total direct costs   (5)

(c) *Total absorption costs*

	Basis A	Basis B	Basis C
Total direct cost	2,000	2,000	2,000
Indirect cost	75	100	160
Absorption cost[1]	*2,075*	*2,100*	*2,160*

[1] The absorption cost forms the basis of the tender-bid price.

In Table 11.2, it is assumed that the construction firm examines each of these three alternative apportionment bases and, from past experience, chooses suitable overhead recovery rates to apply to the various contracts. Hence, higher rates are applied to the more narrowly defined own direct cost base, the lower rates to the wider, total direct cost base. The objective of the exercise remains the same, namely to ensure that the chosen rates, when applied across all contracts, will permit recovery of all the firm's indirect costs.

In the present example, it can be seen how by using cost base (1) and applying overhead at 15%, some £75,000 or 3.75% is added to the total direct cost. Similarly, use of cost base (3) applied at 10% adds £100,000 or 5%, and cost base (5) applied at 8% adds £160,000 or 8%. The implications for the total absorption cost of the contract are quite different and, given that it is this absorption cost which is normally used as the cost base for formulating tender price, the competitive pricing implications are also different. If, for instance, it was supposed that three different contractors A, B and C, each bidding for this same contract and all working from a common direct cost breakdown, adopted different approaches to indirect cost absorption, significant differences in their bid prices could result. Firm A would produce an absorption cost basis which was lower than that of its competitors before profit margins were applied. (Details are taken from Table 11.2)

The apportionment of indirect cost not only affects the total costs of the contract, but also the tender price, and by definition the firm's ability to win the contract in a competitive bidding situation. Of course, where contracts are lost, the firm fails to secure any recovery towards indirect cost and so those contracts which the firm does win must carry a correspondingly higher burden. In situations where tendering is particularly competitive, firms may choose to vary their procedures for apportionment and to base the tender price only on direct cost. Such an approach can be described as 'marginal' rather than 'full-cost' pricing; the difference between the price obtained and the direct marginal cost constitutes a contribution towards indirect cost and profit. Where prices are cut to a level below full absorption cost, the firm is failing to cover its indirect costs. This situation may be acceptable in a short-run survival situation, or where other contracts fulfilled by the firm can be made to yield high contributions and so effect a cross-subsidy. (A fuller account of marginal costing can be found in Batty.[3])

2. Budgeting principles

At the outset of each contract, estimates of direct costs and apportioned indirect costs will be established. Table 11.1 (p. 254) indicates the principal direct cost categories, and each of these is capable of disaggregation to a finer level of detail. It is usual on construction contracts to estimate costs according to the various activities or elements which constitute the total job. Hence, cost estimates are established for foundations, superstructure, services, internal finishes and external works, with sub-divisions within each of these broad categories. Cost estimates are often prepared for individual tasks, so that within the cost of foundations, separate estimates for the costs of excavating drains and the bases will be drawn up. These various sets of cost estimates provide the basis for establishing a standard budget, which can be used for comparison with the actual cost out-turns.

Cost control systems

A cost control system should enable management to take corrective action, where it is found that incurred cost is deviating significantly from the standard budget. In order to be effective the budget system should be as detailed as possible, so that the precise source of any variance can be isolated. In the manufacturing sector, many companies producing a range of basic products have adopted the so-called 'standard costing system'. With appropriate records it is possible to analyse categories of cost into broad 'labour', 'material' and 'general overhead' variances and to produce further sub-variances for each of these cost factors. For example, it is usual in the standard costing system to break the labour cost variance into one sub-variance arising from differences between the actual wage rate and its budgeted standard, and another sub-variance measuring the deviation between actual hours worked and budgeted hours. In this way, management is able to separately control the rates of pay for its workforce, and also the working efficiency, as recorded by hours worked, in order to produce a standard output. (A fuller account of how such a system operates is provided in Robson[4] and is discussed in many similar basic accounting textbooks.)

In the construction sector, it is not usually possible to operate this detailed standard costing system without significant modification. The construction product is usually a one-off project for which standard budgets may be difficult to specify in all areas of activity. Labour is frequently casually recruited for an individual contract and the terms on which such operatives are employed will vary enormously, dependent on the local intensity of demand for skilled labour. National wage rates and rates prevailing in earlier time periods may not, in such circumstances, be appropriate for establishing the standard rate on a particular contract. Equally, the productivity of labour varies significantly from site to site and it is influenced by factors such as climate and material delivery. Again, a detailed standard costing approach will not always prove to be suitable for highlighting discrepancies in site working efficiency.

Cost control for materials

In the case of materials it is extremely difficult to control variances on site with any degree of accuracy. In particular, quantity discrepancies arise through wastage, theft and incorrect deliveries, as well as through imprecise measurement of work done. Price variation in materials is attributable not only to inflation, but also to frequent changes in purchasing conditions since the original budgets were prepared. Changes in material qualities, and modifications in available discount and rebate structures, may lead to significant price discrepancies. During the comparatively long period of time taken to complete a contract, material budgets will rapidly become out-of-date, and the problem of control is compounded where client variations become significant. In practice, the expense of attempting to control material variances to any degree of detail could hardly be justified in terms of potential savings. A rough control of materials can be maintained by comparing the value of materials in measured work against the cost of materials used. (Some detailed suggestions for controlling materials on site are provided in Harris and McCaffer.[5])

A simplified example

Generally, a contractor will adopt a simplified form of the standard costing system, and costs will be allocated for different activities or elements of the total contract. Table 11.3 represents a simplified cost control budget for a small warehouse and it has been adapted from information provided by the Building Cost Information Service.[6] The costs have been broken down according to the main elements in the bill of quantities. It is assumed that sufficient information is available to permit the costs in each main element to be subdivided into direct materials, labour and plant components, or to estimate a budgeted cost for where the work is to be sub-contracted. Site overhead costs have been allocated across each of the elements of the job, to facilitate more accurate control of this item of cost.

As the job proceeds and actual costs are incurred, these cost outturns can be compared to the budgeted values in the table, and variances can be identified. In practice, it may be possible to produce a finer breakdown of cost than that given in the table. For example, within the substructure element, the separate activities of producing the stanchion bases, putting down the strip foundations and laying the floor slab may be costed individually. It should be possible to separate out the cost of reinforced concrete and related materials from the cost of the labour and plant required to complete each operation. Cost control will involve a careful recording of the

11.3 Simplified cost control budget for a small warehouse contract

Elements	Cost components (£)					
	(1) Materials	(2) Labour	(3) Plant	(4) Sub-contract	(5) Site o/h	(6) Total[1]
A. Substructure	90,000	27,000	33,000	—	18,000	168,000
B. Superstructure						
(i) Frame	—	—	—	87,000	10,000	97,000
(ii) Roof	—	—	—	83,000	10,000	93,000
(iii) External enclosures	25,000	18,000	2,000	—	5,000	50,000
(iv) Internal partitions	2,000	1,000	—	—	500	3,500
C. Internal finishes	12,000	17,000	—	—	3,500	32,500
D. Fittings and furnishings	18,000	8,000	—	—	3,000	29,000
E. Services	—	—	—	17,000	2,000	19,000
F. External works	78,000	26,000	30,000	—	24,000	158,000
Total budget	225,000	97,000	65,000	187,000	76,000	650,000

[1] Total excludes any allotted component of firm indirect cost or any profit margin, which will be incorporated in the tender price.

actual costs as the work is carried out, and a continuous monitoring of this cost against the expected budget. Where significant differences are revealed, management will need to intervene to discover the cause of this variance.

The more sophisticated the cost control system in use, the more expensive it is to operate. Where the cost headings are very detailed, a large number of staff must be used, both to prepare the budget and, particularly, to maintain accurate daily records of on-going costs. Clearly, the cost of operating the control system must be assessed against the benefits it yields in terms of information for managerial action. (A fuller appraisal of cost control in the construction sector can be obtained from specialist texts, such as Gobourne.[7])

3. Cash flow analysis

As well as controlling the various cost elements of a contract, the building firm must also pay attention to its cash budget. There may be large flows of cash in and out of a company over the duration of a contract. A firm may be winning a lot of new business, which promises eventual profit, but often, before this profit can be realised, the firm may need to finance additional work-in-progress and investment in material stocks and plant. Particular attention must be paid to short-term fluctuations in a firm's cash position and the firm must ensure that sufficient working capital is available to finance its contracts. Failure to monitor cash flow can result in a firm 'overtrading' and, unless short-term credit facilities can be secured, the firm may become illiquid and be forced out of business—despite the existence of potentially profitable contracts and orders.

The working capital cycle

The management of cash flow is bound up with the working capital cycle represented in Fig. 11.1. As this figure shows, some cash is required to finance the purchase of materials and labour so that construction work may commence. As far as possible, the construction firm will attempt to minimise this cash requirement by utilising trade credit and delaying payments to its sub-contractors for as long as possible. Much of the completed work-in-progress will be paid for by interim payments from the client and it may also be possible for the client to reimburse the cost of materials, once these appear on site. When the contract is complete, there may follow a significant delay before the contractor receives the full and final payment. It is usual to provide a period of credit to clients, just as the building firm expects to be given credit by its materials suppliers, builders merchants and plant hirers. Where difficulties arise over claims against variations, the delay in the client making the final payment may be significantly long. This frequently occurs when the client is a public sector agent.

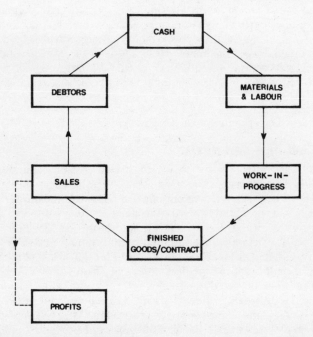

Fig. 11.1 *The working capital cycle*

As Fig. 11.1 shows, cash is only released once debts have been collected. It is clear that the timing of receipts and payments is critical to the amount of cash which the firm will need to maintain to service the working capital cycle. Chapter 10 presented the wider issues of financing the firm's working capital needs, from which it is clear that the firm will obviously want to minimise its cash injection in order to keep down its costs. Where the complete working capital cycle is relatively rapid, the firm will only need to maintain relatively small balances to finance the cycle. Receipts from sales will be utilised to pay for purchase of materials and labour services and, providing the firm is not adversely affected by rising factor prices or by attempts to expand too rapidly, existing cash resources should ensure the firm's liquidity.

Cash flow difficulties in building firms

In the manufacturing sector, the working capital cycle is usually well-determined, and shorter than that obtaining in the construction sector. Building projects frequently last for several years and the exact durations are usually uncertain. Over the course of such contracts, the prices of raw materials, labour and plant can increase significantly. During 1974, UK raw material costs rose by 26%, while basic weekly wage rates increased by 28% in the same period. Existing cash balances will prove inadequate in such circumstances and in the absence of careful cash flow forecasting, liquidity crises may easily arise.

Building firms usually run a number of different projects in parallel and each of these will have a unique cash flow pattern associated with it. The firm must take steps to ensure that the periods of maximum net cash outflow (see Fig. 11.3, p. 265) do not coincide. Particular problems may arise where the firm is building speculatively, as in most private housing developments. Here the firm must finance all its work-in-progress and it cannot rely on interim payments from the client. The contractor will only receive the cash when the sale is completed and payment is received from the financing institution. In this case, the cycle can be quite long and failure to sell the completed building rapidly may produce acute cash flow problems for the contractor. Certainly, it may mean that the firm will have to delay or curtail new building starts, unless it is willing and able to take on short-term bank loans to boost its cash flow.

The building firm uses an extensive network of trade credit with its material and plant suppliers, as well as with its sub-contractors. It also receives credit from the tax authorities and sometimes, from its shareholders in respect of dividend payment. Should anything happen to disturb these arrangements, there will be implications for the working capital cycle—and so for cash flow. Faced with rising interest rates, suppliers will frequently seek to reduce the effective period of credit, and in general they may be expected to take measures to limit the amount and duration of trade credit. If the contractor is obliged to use alternative sources of supply, the terms of credit may not prove so favourable and changes in the timing of payments will be transmitted into the cash flow.

Contractors are particularly vulnerable to delays in receiving payments from the client. Where the client is suffering liquidity problems, the contractor is put under pressure and it is quite common to find situations where a developer goes into liquidation; this has a 'domino impact' on the contractor and on any sub-contractors awaiting payment. A chain of bankruptcy and liquidation may well ensue. Where retention conditions are changed during the course of a contract, cash flow will be affected and it will also suffer when variations on a contract produce claims which result in a delay in the final settlement. Where late payment or non-payment difficulties arise on a major contract, it can have spill-over implications for the company's overall cash flow.

Forecasting cash flow on an individual contract

If construction companies are to achieve control over their cash flows, they will need to forecast the flows on each individual contract and aggregate across all projects to obtain the overall cash flow. Inevitably, a considerable amount of data is required to set up a detailed cash flow projection. The basic information consists of a valuation of the work to be done, drawn up over time. Such a valuation incorporates the cost estimate and the firm's margin to cover both indirect overheads and profits. This valuation forms the basis for the payments the contractor will eventually receive for carrying out the work. The actual rate at which payments are made is set by the agreed retention conditions and the systems for measurement; allowances must be made for time intervals between measurement, certification and actual receipt of cash.

Against the profile of expected receipts must be set the contractor's costs, distributed over time. This necessitates estimating cost liabilities arising from labour, plant, materials and subcontractors, as they are incurred over the duration of the project. Allowance for cost overheads must also be built into these estimates. The actual point at which these cost liabilities are met depends upon the credit arrangements which the firm has negotiated. In practice, different firms will approach this cost and value breakdown in a variety of ways, some favouring a very detailed appraisal, while others may only attempt an outlined assessment.

Fig. 11.2 presents a highly simplified model for bringing the receipts and payments statements together. In this figure, all the information is entered cumulatively against time. It can be seen how the cumulative contract value describes an S-shaped profile; this general result can be used as a predictive basis for the nature of revenue and cost receipts over time. Receipts of cash, in respect of the value of work done, will occur at monthly intervals against certification. These receipts appear as a step-like schedule in the graph. Payments of cash by the contractor are made continuously as the work progresses. The cumulative sum of these incurred costs is also shown.

When the actual receipts of cash-in are taken together with the actual payments of cash-out, the result is the net cash position,

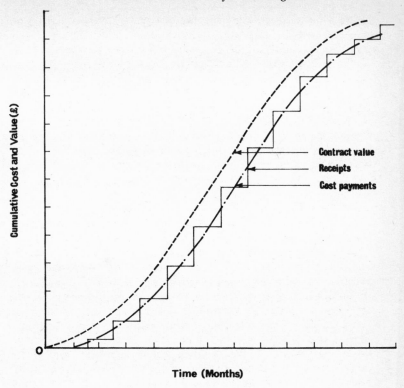

Fig. 11.2 *Net cash flow analysis*

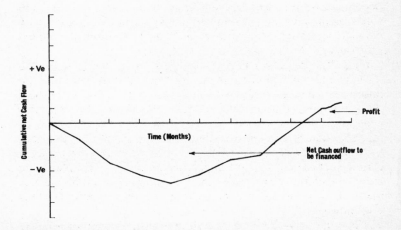

Fig. 11.3 *Cash flow over time*

shown in Fig. 11.6. This clearly shows how, in the first few months of
the contract, the net cash outflow reaches a maximum and
thereafter diminishes. Later in the project, cash inflow begins to
exceed outflow, so indicating the margin of hoped-for profit. This
type of analysis indicates to the firm the amount of cash it will need
to have available at different times to finance the work. Where the
information is put on a computer, a fuller analysis, testing the
sensitivity of the net cash requirement to changes in the underlying
credit and payment arrangements, can be attempted. (A fuller
account of cash flow forecasting is given in Fellows.[8])

4. Ratio analysis

While the control of cost budgets and the determination of the cash
flow are primarily exercised at the level of the individual contract,
overall control of the firm's financial position is achieved through
analysis of the corporate financial statements. Information is
contained in the balance sheet, which describes the firm's stock
position at the end of the accounting period, and in the profit and
loss account, which records the flow of income and expenditure
during the annual accounting period. Although other financial
statements, such as the flow of funds, may also provide useful
information, it is the balance sheet and profit and loss account which
provide the basic data necessary for financial control. This data is
most conveniently analysed by use of accounting ratios that shed
light on the firm's overall liquidity position, its profitability and
capital return, as well as several supplementary aspects of its
operation.

In the Appendix (p. 291) a simplified set of basic accounts is given
for a typical large PLC building firm in the 1980s. The actual data is
adapted from a leading contractor's annual report. In the analysis
which follows, accounting ratios are computed, using this basic data
for firm ABC. Ratios are most useful when their values are
examined over time. For this reason the ratios in this section are
given for both the present and the previous year, so that a
comparative basis exists. In practice, it would be useful to compare
the present ratios against their values for a number of preceding
years. Additionally, the ratios for any one firm need to be viewed
against those achieved by other firms in the same industry. A
number of organisations publish inter-company business ratios; one
of the better-known publications for the construction sector is that
produced by ICC.[9]

Liquidity ratios

A firm needs to closely monitor changes in its overall working capital, and for this purpose a number of inter-linked ratios are of value. In Table 11.4, some of these ratios are presented. The *current ratio* (A) provides a measure of the cover available against short-term demands from creditors for repayment. Generally, this ratio will have a value in the range between 2 and 1.5, as in the present case. The higher the value of this ratio, the more liquid the firm. A more searching test of liquidity is the 'acid test' or *quick ratio* (B), which indicates the firm's ability to meet its immediate liabilities in the worst possible circumstances. While most firms normally require this ratio to be close to unity, in the case of construction firms the ratio is usually much lower, reflecting the relatively large amount of working capital tied up in work-in-progress and stocks. There is some cause for concern in the case of firm ABC in the example in the Appendix, as the quick ratio is deteriorating as the firm increases its existing work-load, and the sums available to cover all current liabilities are decreasing. In a case such as this, the management may need to take steps to improve this aspect of the firm's liquidity.

11.4 Liquidity ratio analysis: example for ABC firm

Name of ratio	Basis	Present year	Previous year
A. Current ratio	$\dfrac{\text{Current assets}}{\text{Current liabilities}}$	1.76	1.68
B. 'Acid test' or quick ratio	$\dfrac{\text{Cash + debtors}}{\text{Current liabilities}}$	0.34	0.52
C. Working capital ratio	$\dfrac{\text{Sales turnover}}{\text{Net current assets}^{1}}$	6.09	7.01
D. Fixed asset turnover ratio	$\dfrac{\text{Sales turnover}}{\text{Fixed assets}}$	9.75	11.18

[1] Net current assets = Current assets − Current liabilities

Another ratio which sheds light on the short-term liquidity of the firm is the so-called *working capital ratio* (C). This ratio compares sales turnover to net current assets, and, while the value of such a ratio will vary between different firms, stability in the ratio is the key requirement. Similarly, the *fixed asset turnover ratio* (D) indicates how well the firm is using its fixed assets. Any decrease in this ratio, as in the present case, will give cause for concern. Generally, construction firms, when compared to manufacturing organisations, have a low investment in fixed assets and so this ratio will always be quite high. In this context, the ratio achieved by any given building firm needs to be compared to the same ratio for other building firms, to check the efficiency with which the fixed assets are used.

Profitability and operating ratios

The primary objective of any firm is to be profitable. A number of ratios can be formulated to facilitate an analysis of a firm's profitability; these ratios are given in Table 11.5. The main *profitability ratio* (E) measures gross profit, before tax, as a percentage of sales turnover. This ratio is used to assess annual trading performance and it is also valuable in inter-firm comparisons. While there is no absolute criterion on which to judge successful profitability, it is usual for firms to aim to achieve more than 10% gross profits on sales. In the construction sector, however, lower profit mark-ups tend to be commonplace, as is seen for firm ABC in the Appendix. It should be noted that profit on sales is not the same as the profit return on capital employed and, since capital employed is typically much lower in a construction firm relative to a manufacturing firm, profitability, in terms of return on capital, may be viewed as a more meaningful indicator of performance. The *primary ratio* (F) measures gross profit as a percentage of all capital employed and it can be seen that firm ABC exhibits acceptable profitability according to this measure. When the profitability ratio is multiplied by the inverted primary ratio the result is the *turnover ratio* (G), which gives turnover as a proportion of capital employed. For the construction firm, this turnover ratio is usually quite high—to compensate for the low profitability ratio.

Firms exist to make profit for their owners, the shareholders. The profit which is attributable to these shareholders is gross profit, with taxation and loan interest charges deducted. The *return to shareholders ratio* (H) is attributable profit, as a percentage of shareholder capital—both ordinary shares and the reserves. In the formulation of this ratio, any component of loan capital is removed from the capital-employed base. Table 11.5 shows how for firm ABC this ratio (as well as the profitability and primary ratios) is increasing. From an investor's standpoint, a key measure of profitability is the amount of attributable profit, averaged out over the total number of issued shares in the firm. This is the *earnings per share ratio* (J), and it is a standardised measure which investors apply when considering whether or not to buy a firm's shares at the prevailing share price quoted on the Stock Exchange.

The profitability and operating ratios reported in Table 11.5 are

11.5 Profitability and operating ratio analysis

Name of ratio	Basis	Present year	Previous year
E. Profitability ratio	$\dfrac{\text{Gross profit}}{\text{Sales turnover}}$	5.13%	3.68%
F. Primary ratio	$\dfrac{\text{Gross profit}}{\text{Capital employed}^1}$	17.54%	14.29%
G. Turnover ratio	$\dfrac{\text{Sales turnover}}{\text{Capital employed}}$	3.42	3.87
H. Return to shareholders ratio	$\dfrac{\text{Attributable profit}}{\text{Share capital + reserves}}$	12.77%	11.63%
J. Earnings per share	$\dfrac{\text{Attributable profit}}{\text{Number of equity shares}^2}$	30p	25p

[1] Capital employed = Share capital + Revenue and general reserves + Long-term loans.
[2] Number of shares = 20 million.

the more common accounting measures in use. It is also possible to produce ratios which show profits as a percentage of net current assets, fixed assets and total operating assets, as well as profits to various items of capital employed, especially loan capital. No strong reliance should be placed on any individual ratio but, rather, several ratios should be taken together to ensure a full analysis.

Supplementary ratios

It is possible to use other information from the firm's general accounts to compute further ratios, which are potentially valuable for exercising financial control. A sample of such ratios is given in Table 11.6. When the firm's debtors are taken together with sales turnover and the result is converted to a monthly measurement by multiplying by 12, the resulting *debtor time ratio* (K) provides an indication of the average number of months' credit the firm is extending to its customers. This ratio needs to be assessed in conjunction with the *creditor time ratio* (L), which shows the average number of months of credit which the firm is receiving from its suppliers. Clearly, good management requires that the creditor time ratio should be greater than the debtor time ratio, as is the case for firm ABC. However, the calculations in Table 11.6 indicate that while the average period of credit being given is increasing, the average period of credit being received is falling. The ratio analysis

11.6 Supplementary ratio analysis

Name of ratio	Basis		Present year	Previous year
K. Debtor time ratio	$\dfrac{\text{Debtors}}{\text{Sales turnover}}$	× 12	1.05 months	0.95 months
L. Creditor time ratio	$\dfrac{\text{Creditors}[1]}{\text{Sales turnover}}$	× 12	1.85 months	2.08 months
M. Productivity employee ratio	$\dfrac{\text{Sales turnover}}{\text{No. of employees}}$		£102,632	£95,000
N. Productivity wage ratio	$\dfrac{\text{Sales turnover}}{\text{Wage cost}}$		92.86	95.00
P. Gearing ratio	$\dfrac{\text{Long-term loans}}{\text{Capital employed}}$		17.54%	12.24%

[1] Creditors = Trade credits + Dividend payable + other creditors

suggests that some managerial action may be necessary to avoid future working capital difficulties.

Another important area for managerial control is that of labour productivity. One possible measure is afforded by the *productivity employee ratio* (M), which yields the sales turnover per direct employee. According to this ratio, productivity in firm ABC is seen to be improving, but a second ratio, the 'productivity wage ratio' (N) suggests otherwise. This second ratio indicates that sales, deflated by the annual direct wage bill, are actually falling. Although the firm has reduced its number of employees, the total wages paid have increased over the last year. The wider aspects of labour productivity in the construction sector are examined in the next chapter.

Many firms are concerned to control the contributions of different sources of finance to the total capital employed. Specifically, firms and their owners will want to avoid the proportion of loan capital becoming excessively high. To this end,use is made of the *gearing ratio* (P). The data in Table 11.6 indicates that firm ABC's dependence on external loans is increasing, although the present proportion remains within the bounds of acceptability. This gearing ratio is a representative sample of a range of possible ratios to monitor the components of the firm's total capital employment.

Questions

1. What are the most important areas over which a building firm must maintain financial control?

2. Distinguish the difference between the direct and indirect costs of a building firm.
3. Explain why a firm's indirect costs have to be absorbed by a number of different contracts.
4. Describe the different bases which can be used for apportioning indirect costs to a contract.
5. Examine the data presented in Table 11.2 and re-work the absorption cost estimates, if the composition of direct costs was as follows:

	£000
(1) Contractor's own direct cost	1300
(2) Domestic sub-contractors	400
(3) Contractor's work	1700
(4) Nominations	300
(5) Total direct costs	2000

Assume that the bases for apportioning indirect overhead remain those given in Table 11.2. Comment on your result and draw the implications for tender-bid pricing.
6. Outline the difference between full absorption cost pricing and marginal cost pricing.
7. Discuss the desirability of implementing cost control systems and identify why such systems may be difficult to establish for the construction firm.
8. Why is a detailed cost control system for materials not usually deemed practical in a construction company?
9. Outline the information you would require to set up a cost control system for a firm building a small warehouse.
10. Explain your understanding of a firm's working capital cycle.
11. Discuss the importance of the timing of a firm's receipts and payments for its cash flow budget.
12. What are the peculiar cash flow difficulties facing building firms?
13. Describe the steps involved in setting up a detailed cash-flow projection for a building contract.
14. How can an analysis of accounting ratios help a firm to achieve better control of its finances?
15. A firm has the following simplified accounts:

(a) *Balance sheet (£000)*			(b) *Profit and loss A/C (£000)*		
	1987	*1986*		*1987*	*1986*
Fixed assets	45	35	Turnover	225	210
Investments	5	5	Trading profit	14	15
Cash	10	18	Interest received	1	1
Debtors	20	12	Gross profit	15	16
Stocks	5	4	Tax	−4	−4
Work-in-Progress	30	20	Interest paid	−2	−1
Bank overdraft	8	4	Attributable profit	9	11
Creditors	32	26	Dividend	6	6
Net assets	75	64	Transfer to reserve	3	5
Share capital	25	25			
Reserves	40	35			
Long loans	10	4			
Total capital	75	64			

Compute a set of accounting ratios to analyse the firm's liquidity position in 1987. Comment on the results you obtain.

16. From the data in question 15, calculate the profitability ratio, primary ratio and turnover ratio for both 1987 and 1986. Advise the firm's management in the light of these ratios.

17. Discuss why no strong reliance should be placed on any individual accounting ratio, but rather several ratios should be considered jointly.

18. Using data for the firm in Question 15, calculate and comment on changes in:
    a) the debtor time ratio
    b) the creditor time ratio
    c) the gearing ratio

Further Reading

BIRD, P., *Understanding Company Accounts*, Pitman, 1983

COOKE, B. and JEPSON, W. B., *Cost and Financial Control for Construction Firms*, Macmillan, 1979

FANNING, D. and PENDLEBURY, M., *Company Accounts—A Guide*, George Allen and Unwin, 1984

HUGHES, D. A., *Basic Accounting for Builders*, Longman, 1983

KNOTT, G., *Practical Cost and Management Accounting*, Pan Books, 1983

LEE, T., *Cash Flow Accounting*, Van Nostrand Reinhold, 1984

SIZER, J., *An Insight into Management Accounting*, Penguin, 1982

12 Productivity of the Building Firm

Productivity is usually taken to mean some measure of output per unit of labour input; in its most simple form this can be called output per man. Most building firms are concerned to achieve high levels of productivity, as this is normally associated with high profitability. However, productivity is frequently difficult to quantify and, as Hillebrandt[1] has observed, its measurement is fraught with difficulties, such that in recent years there have been few attempts to assess it. The various approaches to measuring productivity in the construction sector are considered in this chapter. A number of studies have made comparison of the British construction industry with foreign construction sectors. A fair comment on these comparative exercises was made by Peter Trench[2] in 1976, who concluded that Britain has a low productivity economy, and in construction we take the booby prize for speed of erection compared with other industrial countries. Although there have been some improvements and changes since 1976, these comments remain valid for many parts of the industry.

This chapter also investigates the causes of low productivity, which are many and complex. Again, comparison of the British construction sector with the industry overseas, and the contrast between the construction and the manufacturing sectors here, serve to highlight the key factors. Finally, the implications are drawn for management in the building firm, concerned to raise the level of productivity. The key areas within management control are identified, although a full appreciation of how to improve productivity within the firm lies outside the scope of this book.

1. Measures of productivity in the construction industry

There is no simple unambiguous measure of productivity, whether on an individual contract, for a particular firm, or for the construction industry as a whole. Most of the published measures of productivity are given for the total construction sector in Great Britain, but different statistical measures do no necessarily describe a consistent pattern. Several government agencies, such as the Business Statistics Office of the Department of Industry, the Department of Employment and the Department of the Environment collect data, which can be used to measure productivity trends in construction. However, the sample of firms constituting the construction industry differs between the respective government departments and the measures, of both output in the numerator and labour input in the denominator vary.

Construction sector productivity

In Table 12.1 two published measures of the recent trend in construction productivity are listed. The first series is based on data collected from the annual census of production in the construction industry. Output is measured as gross value-added. The number of persons employed is measured by those workers on the books of the construction firms in the census survey. The resulting measure is a monetary value per head and the series is unadjusted for inflation, so that productivity appears to increase every year. The second series is derived from Central Statistical Office constant price output data, together with Department of Employment industry employment estimates, which include direct employees and the self-employed for all firms in the industry. The resulting series is published as an index number and the trend it describes is quite

12.1   *Measures of productivity for the GB construction sector*

Year	Gross value added[1] per person employed (£ current prices)	Output per[2] person employed (1980 = 100)
1977	4.289	102.9
1978	5.365	108.5
1979	6.325	107.3
1980	7.764	100.0
1981	7.946	95.1
1982	8.879	100.2
1983	9.384	104.1
1984	10.171	104.9
1985	—	105.9
1986	—	107.9

Sources: [1] *Census of Production*, Business Statistics Office.
        [2] *DE Gazette*

different from that given by the BSO series. All that can be safely concluded from such measures is that construction sector productivity has grown significantly since 1980, although the DE series suggests that productivity in 1986 remained at a lower level than that achieved in 1978.

Consideration of these two measures alone highlights some of the problems involved in measuring productivity. Initially, there is the problem of how to define the construction sector—a difficulty which was outlined in Chapter 1. If the industry is defined so as to exclude many of its small firms, average productivity is likely to turn out appreciably higher than when such firms are included. This problem becomes significant when productivity in construction is compared to that in other sectors of the economy, as below, or when British construction is viewed alongside foreign construction industries.

The concept of industry output is not as simple as it first appears. Physical work done must be valued at an appropriate set of market prices to determine recorded output. While private sector firms include their profit margin in the valuation, public sector organisations commonly do not and their valuation is often at cost. It is quite likely that some part of the work done by construction firms is not fully recorded, as some small firms and self-employed workers do not make accurate statistical returns. Output is measured for the calendar year, but this does not necessarily correspond with the accounting year for many construction firms, so there is a further element of error in estimating the timing of output. When output valued in current prices has to be converted into constant price measures, difficulties may arise over the appropriate price indices to apply. Government statisticians frequently revise their published constant price output series when new price deflators become available.

The usual denominator in the standard measure of productivity is the number of persons employed. This figure is usually an annual average estimate for the whole construction sector and it will take no account of whether the worker is employed over the whole year, or just a part of it. Where the number of workers is used to measure labour input, no recognition is given to the number of hours actually worked. Over time, the average number of hours worked each week varies, and when man-hours are used as the productivity denominator, different results are achieved than when number of men alone is used. Similarly, the crude measure of number of persons employed fails to distinguish between the various qualities of the labour input. Under this measure, the input of a part-time clerical assistant is treated as equally important as that of a full-time senior manager. Given their relative rates of pay, their respective contributions to the production process are seen to be markedly different. Sometimes, the total wage bill for the construction sector is used as an alternative measure of labour input and this approach will weight the various workers' contribution to output according to their rates of pay. Again, different measures of productivity result from using the wage bill, rather than numbers employed, as the labour input denominator.

Where the construction sector adopts more capital intensive methods of production, as, for instance, when industrialised building is substituted for traditional methods, the output per man will be expected to rise. This result comes about through the substitution of capital for labour and the reduction in the number of workers employed. If account were taken of the increasing capital input into the production process, such that the measure of productivity embraced a combined labour and capital input in the denominator, the observed increase might not be so marked. This idea of measuring total factor productivity, rather than simply labour productivity, is sound in theory, but in practice it involves another set of daunting measurement problems with respect to the capital input.

Construction relative to other industrial sectors

While Table 12.1 presents measures of construction sector productivity over time, Table 12.2 examines the absolute level of output per person employed, in the context of construction, relative to other GB industrial sectors. This data for 1984 is based on census of production information and it shows how construction is a comparatively low productivity sector. Certainly, when set against the manufacturing sector, construction is seen to achieve signific-

12.2   *Absolute productivity levels in selected UK industries in 1984*
Gross value added per person employed

Industry	£
Construction	10,171
All industry	13,545
All manufacturing	14,052
Chemicals	25,491
Metal manufacture	15,688
Car manufacture	13,218
Mechanical engineering	13,642
Textiles	9,177

Source: *Annual Abstract of Statistics*, CSO/HMSO, 1987

antly lower output per head; construction productivity is only 72% of that for manufacturing. Historical data for earlier years confirms this finding and while the size of the differential varies to some small degree, construction is a consistently low productivity industry.

The results of Table 12.2 indicate how, compared to a capital-intensive industry such as chemicals, construction achieves a very low level of absolute productivity. Perhaps a fairer comparison is with mechanical engineering, but even here the differential is quite marked. Construction does have a higher output per person employed than the textile sector, which is known to be very labour-intensive. Some reasons for this low productivity are explored below (pp. 282–6). Low productivity in a sector such as construction will mean that the industry is not able to pay its workforce such high wages as those paid in the industries experiencing higher productivity.

Productivity differences between construction firms

It is possible to achieve a crude comparison of productivity between individual firms by utilising the productivity ratios described in the previous chapter. Here, company turnover is expressed as a ratio of the number of employees, yielding the value of sales per worker. While such a measure may be useful to assess one firm's progress over time, there are some severe difficulties in using this measure to compare firms' productivities at a given point in time. The major objection to this type of measure concerns the validity of applying the number of employees as a meaningful indicator of the firm's labour input. Most contracting firms use sub-contracting quite extensively and so their gross sales turnover may bear little relationship to the number of direct employees. Two large contractors with roughly comparable turnovers might show markedly different sales per employee if one firm sub-contracts a high proportion of its workload whereas the other prefers to use direct labour.

A more useful approach to observing productivity differences between construction firms arises from the annual census of production, which provides measures of gross value-added per employee, analysed across firms of different size. This analysis for 1984 indicates how small firms (those employing less than 20 employees) achieved only 76% of the productivity of large firms (those employing more than 100 employees). Medium-sized firms (those employing between 20 and 100 employees) achieved productivity levels only slightly lower than those of the larger firms.

Productivity in the private and public sectors

It is frequently argued that productivity levels in the private sector of the construction industry are significantly higher than those achieved by the Direct Labour Organisations (DLOs) of the public sector. Indeed, a crude attempt at measurement, using DOE output and total manpower statistics for 1985, suggests that private sector output per man was then about 33% higher. However, DLOs employ a larger number of APTC staff who are not directly engaged in construction output, and when these staff are removed from the labour input statistics, the resulting productivity differential is quite small. Problems of accurate and consistent valuation of output, together with difficulties in measuring the appropriate labour input, tend to make these comparative exercises of rather limited value. In general, given the DLOs' concentration on repair and maintenance work, and the private sector's greater proportion of new work, higher productivity levels ought to be achieved in the private sector. (A fuller discussion of the difficulties of achieving higher productivity in the DLOs is provided in Langford.[3])

Direct measures of productivity for the individual firm or project

Within an individual firm, it is often possible to measure productivity on a particular contract, or on a key operation which forms part of the contract. Such a direct approach involves the collation of a large amount of detailed input and output data. For example, it might, on a large industrial contract, be useful to measure the amount of pipework installed, in length or weight units, and to express this as a ratio to the number of recorded man-hours paid for in the installation work. Equally, for a standard type of housing unit it might be useful for the firm to record the total number of man-hours used in its construction; such man-hours could be usefully analysed according to specific labour skills. In this way, productivity indices for particular construction tasks can be compiled.

Measuring productivity directly for the individual firm or project in isolation is not always very helpful, and, certainly, the results obtained for one firm cannot be taken to be representative of the industry as a whole. Researchers have been able to collate wider samples of direct productivity measures, taken from several firms and projects. Lemessany and Clapp, in a BRE study,[4] examined productivity in house-building by analysing contract records for several private contractors and also for local authority projects. Their results indicate productivity differences between traditionally-built dwellings and non-traditional dwellings, commissioned mainly by the local authorities. However, many measurement difficulties were encountered in the execution of this study and it remains extremely doubtful whether productivity results based on a few sample firms—or on a particular type of construction—have any general validity for other parts of the construction industry.

2. UK productivity versus overseas productivity

While changes in productivity over time are an important standard of achievement, comparison of productivity achieved in the UK with that realised in other developed countries is often taken to be more significant. Countries with higher absolute levels of productivity will enjoy higher standards of living and higher rates of economic growth. Over time, such countries will experience relatively lower rates of price inflation, which will yield more favourable terms of trade. The low productivity nation will frequently face balance of payments deficits and there will be continuing downward pressure on that nation's foreign exchange rate. Those sectors of the nation's economy which are characterised by particularly low productivity will experience significant import penetration, resulting in structural unemployment in these industries.

Statistical evidence

Over the post-war period, productivity growth in the UK has generally been lower than that achieved in other developed countries, especially other EEC members, USA and Japan. It can be seen in Table 12.3 how by 1980 income per head for the whole economy was lower in real terms than for most of these comparable nations. Since 1980, there has been some improvement in UK

12.3   *International comparison of income per head in real terms (GDP per capita at purchasing power parities; UK = 100)*

	1980	1986
United Kingdom	100	100
Germany	133	114
France	136	103
Belgium	124	98
Netherlands	108	103
Italy	86	86
USA	170	151
Japan	112	108

Source: Central Statistical Office

productivity and this is reflected in a narrowing of the differentials shown in Table 12.3. Relative to the USA, UK income per head was more than 30% lower in 1986; it was also significantly lower than in Germany and Japan. A recent study by Ray,[5] analysing output per man-hour for the manufacturing sector alone, found Great Britain to have much lower productivity than any of the other countries in Table 12.3. Again, there had been some improvement between 1980 and 1986, but manufacturing output per man-hour remained lowest in GB and this resulted in higher unit labour costs compared to the other countries.

Comparing absolute levels of productivity between nations is a very difficult exercise, partly because of differences in national price systems and partly because of differences in the relative exchange rates. When differentials are drawn between the construction sectors of the various countries, these problems are compounded by differing definitions of the industry and the use of inconsistent measures of output and labour input. However, an earlier exercise by Ray[6] compared absolute output per worker per year for the construction sectors of several leading industrial nations, using statistics for 1980. This analysis indicated that UK construction productivity was the lowest of all the major EEC nations, including Italy. While output per worker was also lower in the UK than in the USA, it did appear to be significantly higher than that achieved in Japan. The construction sector in Japan, on this evidence, would appear to lag behind that country's highly productive manufacturing sector.

Further evidence of the UK construction industry's comparatively low international productivity status is provided in another statistical study by Smith, Hitchens and Davies.[7] Here, productivity is measured both as output per employee and output per man-hour, and the UK construction sector is compared with, first, its German counterpart, and then with the USA construction industry. Measurements were made for the years 1968 and 1977. In each year, and by the two methods of measurement, UK productivity turns out to be significantly inferior to that of both Germany and the USA. On average, both these countries appear to enjoy construction outputs per man-hour of about twice those of the UK.

Direct measurement studies

The analyses of Ray and Smith, Hitchens and Davies make use of published government statistics and inevitably their conclusions are conditioned by the underlying measurement problems. A very different approach to the comparison of international productivity is afforded by studies which examine strictly comparable construction projects, carried out in a number of different countries. Specific measurements of the time taken to complete the standardised building are compared, and other aspects of productivity, such as the average unit output per site operative and the cost of building per square metre of floor-space, are recorded. While it is difficult to generalise from such particular comparisons, the cumulative evidence supports the conclusion of the statistical analyses—that UK construction suffers from comparatively low productivity.

An early NEDO study[8] compared the time taken in constructing major engineering structures (power stations, oil refineries and chemical plants) in the UK with similar projects in Europe and the USA. A very detailed interview-and-questionnaire approach was adopted and, wherever practical, physical measurements were taken to provide objective comparability. The overall results indicated that, generally speaking, foreign construction times were shorter, and that over-run times (actual time minus planned time) were less on the foreign projects. Most critically, the ratio of total work content to recorded man-hours of labour input was higher on the foreign projects and, where attempts were made to measure productivity on specific tasks, this too was higher abroad than in the UK. It was found that the UK sites usually operated with many more operatives than did their foreign counterparts, yet this did not result in higher levels of output.

A study of comparable international factory developments, carried out by Slough Estates,[9] also found that, in general, the time taken to complete a building was greater in the UK than elsewhere. In this study, similar factories in the UK, Canada, Australia, Belgium, France, Germany and the USA were analysed; where discrepancies between the UK and elsewhere were identified, the reasons for inferior performances were also analysed. UK factory construction was put at a disadvantage by both inferior pre-construction practices (slower planning approvals, for example) and lower site productivity. Again, it is dangerous to generalise on the basis of a single example about the whole UK construction sector, but the Slough Estates study must be taken as a piece in a jigsaw which presents a consistent overall picture.

One of the more recent studies undertaken comparing the UK and overseas construction sectors is the BEC[10] comparison of the UK and USA building industries. Such a study is one in a long line of opinion-based comparisons, which look at a number of similar projects in each of the countries. The general conclusion of this exercise was that US construction times appear to be about 10% faster than those in the UK. The extra productivity is primarily attributable to the methods of construction and the modes of organisation used in the USA. This finding suggests that the British construction industry has improved very considerably compared to the US over the last few years. Earlier comparative exercises suggested a larger differential in favour of the USA.

3. Causes of low productivity in construction

There is no simple, single factor which can be held responsible for low productivity in building firms when compared to companies in other sectors. Clearly, the nature of the construction product relative to the manufactured product means that high output per man is much more difficult to achieve, in the absence of long, continuous, standard production runs. The difficulties of achieving economies of scale in the construction firm have already been examined and the same factors which lead to high unit costs of production also contribute to low productivity. Nevertheless, it is apparent that some building firms achieve much greater productive efficiency than others, and that some countries manage to realise higher productivity than others. There would seem to be a wide range of common factors which bring about the low level of construction output per man.

Low and discontinuous demand

Most building firms retain a fixed number of employees, and many employ direct labour on a semi-fixed basis. When demand is low and falling, the firm may find it difficult to fully utilise their workforce. Some workers will not be active for all the hours for which they are paid, and, while the firm will attempt to adjust its labour requirements to suit lower levels of output, this adjustment process will take time. Consequently, as the denominator in the productivity ratio is slow to change, while the output numerator is falling, the resulting productivity will be low and declining.

When demand increases, firms will often prove equally slow in hiring new direct labour. Many firms will attempt to meet their labour needs through the use of sub-contractors. Frequently, this leads to problems in achieving the required quality of labour. It will often take some time for the new labour force to adapt to the requirements of the new contract, and productivity may therefore be quite low initially. Continuity of work will assist 'learning-by-doing' and productivity will increase—providing there is sufficient demand to keep the labour force working on similar tasks. High and sustained demand for the product is a central factor contributing to high labour productivity.

Many building firms have a very diverse work-load at any one time; the types of building activity may be varied and the physical locations may be quite widespread. Where the firm is attempting to switch its direct labour resources between different sites, performance is likely to suffer from undue fragmentation. Many paid-for hours will be absorbed in travel and administration, and output levels will not be as high as they might be. This is a major obstacle to improved productivity. Where larger firms are able to specialise and concentrate resources on one type of construction activity, higher productivity is likely to result.

Frequent changes in specification

It is common in the UK for the client or the design team to make significant changes in building specifications after construction has already commenced. Such variation orders, which prove a lucrative source of profit for the contractor, inevitably slow up the production process—and thereby contribute to low productivity. Variations are frequently used as a justification for slow building. In particular, there is a very high propensity to issue variation orders on larger contracts commissioned by public sector clients. Such clients often specify complex engineering designs which need considerable modification at the production stage. Equally, unique design specifications, which involve non-standard building solutions and the use of specialist materials and components, will lead to lower levels of output per man at the construction stage.

In the USA it is much more common to give the responsibility for producing the detailed design to the specialist sub-contractor who will actually carry out the installation. Such a sub-contractor is likely to seek better and faster ways of carrying out the task and so raise productivity. In the UK, this responsibility remains predominantly with the architect and the design team. Frequently, communications difficulties arise between the designers, the contractors and the sub-contractors. These difficulties often lead to delays in the production process—and so productivity is reduced.

Another aspect of specification difficulties arises where planning consent is required for a particular development. As explained in Chapter 8 (pp. 216–20), the local planning decision may take up to eight weeks to be made, and permission may only be granted subject to restrictive conditions. If changes in specification are called for, this will lead to delays; if appeals are made to higher planning authorities, further time lapses will occur. The various comparative productivity studies described earlier in this chapter indicate that planning rules and regulations are more rigorously enforced in this country. As a consequence, the role of the planning authorities in agreeing the specification of a building, and monitoring its construction, may often be a factor contributing to lower productivity.

Inefficient methods of building

In many countries, much wider use is made of industrialised building methods than in the UK, where in many areas of the construction sector, especially house-building, there remains a preference for traditional methods. Stone[11] has described the economic conditions under which industrialised systems will be preferred to traditional building methods, and it is clear that industrialisation will lead to greater site productivity. With industrialisation, more components, like timber-frame, are manufactured off-site under factory conditions—and then simply assembled on site. Inevitably, this system leads to a substitution of capital plant for skilled labour, and many of the labour intensive skills, such as bricklaying and similar wet trades, become less in demand. Industrialisation is well established in the construction of large buildings in the UK, but in house-building unfavourable experiences with, first, systems of concrete cladding and, later, timber-frame, have led to a move back towards traditional methods.

Industrialisation leads to the use of factory-made materials and components that can be easily assembled on site. Pre-cast concrete sections are widely used, as are timber sections, plastic components and large areas of glass panelling. Dry construction methods replace wet trades, with little use of screeds or plaster. Emphasis is placed on standardised components and there is little opportunity to specify non-standard items, which need to be specially designed and made for a specific building. In theory, industrialised materials and components should be easier to obtain as a result of this standardisation, and delays caused by stock shortages of non-standard materials should not arise. Certainly, in countries where industrialised methods are better established than in the UK, construction productivity is higher.

Whatever the method of construction, greater use of capital plant and mechanical aids will help to raise labour productivity. While most large firms in the UK enjoy good plant availability, this is not always the case with small firms. Often, smaller firms will use labour intensive methods rather than incur the cost of acquiring capital plant; thus, their productivity is effectively reduced.

Over-manning on site

Whenever contractors want to increase output, their first action is to increase the labour input, by increasing the hours of overtime worked, or possibly by recruiting more operatives on a casual basis. However, the law of diminishing returns suggests that unless the other factor inputs, such as the available plant and the management team, are simultaneously increased in the same proportion, the marginal product of this labour will decline. In other words, output will increase but at a diminishing rate, so that labour productivity falls, and, as the firm continues to increase the labour input, the overall output per man continues to decline. This law does not operate at low levels of output, so on small sites with relatively few operatives the problem rarely arises. It is on larger sites that the law asserts itself, and on the largest sites in the UK, relative to comparable projects in other countries, over-manning is a common occurrence.

Not only do large UK contractors often have too many men working on one site, but frequently the composition of this workforce is not conducive to good productivity. The ratio of skilled operatives to labourers is often comparatively low on UK sites, and shortages of workers with key skills can lead to production delays. Equally, the ratio of management and supervisory staff to operatives is also low, suggesting that there is insufficient management expertise to ensure the best performance from the workforce. In many smaller firms, operatives do not always have appropriate training for the skilled functions they are expected to discharge and this may lead to production inefficiencies.

One indirect result of over-manning may be poor industrial relations, which lead to stoppages and slow-working on site. During the 1960s and 1970s, many large UK construction sites became well-known for their poor industrial relations—and associated low productivity. Often, several trade unions were represented on site, and different operatives were paid at varying rates, according to the particular working rules agreement by which they were bound. Other workers on site were self-employed and their rates of pay were governed by sub-contract prices. Inevitably, some dissatisfaction arose in the light of these earning differentials, and, where this took the form of stoppages, productivity fell on these sites. In the 1980s, significant unemployment amongst construction operatives, coupled with less large-site activity, has served to soften this problem, but large sites employing a high number of operatives continue to suffer from problems of low morale; where this manifests itself in the form of absenteeism, productivity again falls. Comparative studies of large sites in the UK and in other countries reveal that absenteeism tends to be significantly higher in the UK.

Poor management

When all the preceding factors have been discounted, there remains the observation that some firms achieve much higher productivity than others, and that even within the same firm some projects produce higher output per man than others. The quality of construction management is an important residual factor which helps to explain low productivity. It operates at the director and senior manager level within the firm's core, and also at the project manager and site agent level on the individual site.

Senior managers are responsible for determining the organisation of a firm, the pattern of its overall work-load and the type of contract under which the firm is prepared to work. Historically, the majority of UK building firms exhibit a preference for contracts which allow inflationary cost increases to be reimbursed. In contrast, many foreign firms work under a fixed price discipline and management contracting is far more commonplace in the US than in the UK. Where contractors are working for fixed fees, with only very limited reimbursable costs, they will have a greater incentive to raise productivity to secure better profit margins. Indeed, where a firm's central management team is concerned with improving the firm's productivity, they are likely to organise the firm's structure and to implement systems with incentives which lead to higher output per man.

Managers at site level are responsible for co-ordinating the various inputs to the construction process and for liaising with the design team to ensure that the project is built according to specification. Good management will ensure that materials are promptly delivered to site; that sub-contractors are scheduled to do their tasks, with their performance being closely monitored; that the direct labour force is suitably motivated, with good pay incentives related to performance; and that the necessary plant is readily available when required. Frequently, the quality of site management is highly variable and, where failures occur in the co-ordinating function, low site productivity results.

4. Managing for higher productivity

It is clear from the previous section that a firm's management has a key role to play in raising productivity levels. In 1983 the National Economic Development Office[12] published a research study to investigate the key factors affecting construction times for new industrial and commercial buildings. The study was particularly concerned with finding out why the process in the UK tends to take longer than overseas, and with making recommendations for better

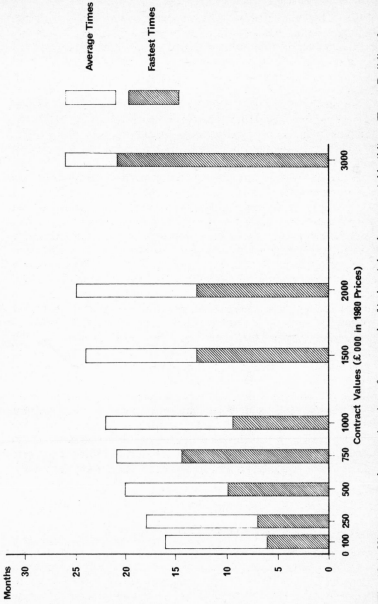

Fig. 12.1 *Histogram to show project times for a sample of industrial and commercial buildings (Faster Building for Industry, NEDO/HMSO, 1983)*

practice in the future. This research examined a large number of project case studies collated by the BRE, and employed management consultants to carry out follow-up interviews to gather fuller information. The NEDO results are particularly relevant to the present concern.

Analysis of project times

According to the NEDO study, construction times generally increased with contract value, although not in direct proportion to it. While the average time for projects of £100,000 value (1980 prices) was 5 months, for projects of £3 million value, the average building time was only 15 months. However, there was considerable variation about these averages, with the fastest projects taking only 30% of the average time, and the slowest projects taking twice as long as the average. Similar patterns of variation were found in the distribution of pre-construction times. When pre-construction is taken together with construction, to yield total project times, the resulting distribution is shown as in Fig. 12.1. This histogram shows that project time does not increase in proportion to contract values' rise, and that the fastest times attainable are often only about half of the average time. It would appear that it is possible to increase the speed of many projects, and that there is much room for improvement in building productivity.

Key areas for management action

Where a client is experienced in the building process, and prepared to insist on accurately specified dates and deadlines, a contractor is put under an obligation to build to the client's timetable. Contracts may be drawn up with financial penalties for late completion, so reinforcing the need to maintain a tight schedule. Where the client, through managing agents, maintains an on-going close interest in the progress of the project, better results tend to be achieved. Equally, it may be necessary for the client to minimise the number of variation orders, as these are a major area of project delay, according to NEDO. Where the contractor provides the client with fuller information on project details, a better and more productive working relationship is likely to yield faster completion.

The NEDO research indicates that non-traditional forms of contract organisation, such as management contracting and design-and-build, tend to produce faster projects. Many larger UK builders have branched out into management contracting in the 1980s, and, certainly, private-sector clients appear to increasingly favour this more disciplined form of organisation. Under this

system, the managing agent has tighter control over the participating sub-contractors and there is a greater likelihood of the
project being completed within the planned time. Where the
designer's function is combined with production, so as to take
account of 'buildability', more rapid completion is possible.

A lot of time is often lost on a project before the construction
process actually gets under way. Wherever it is possible to institute
overlapping pre-construction activities, valuable time will be saved.
Obviously, some non-traditional forms of organisation will accommodate this overlap better than the traditional system, where
design work needs to be largely completed before the contractor is
engaged. Early planning for procurement of plant and materials, as
well as forward preparation for construction, will produce more
rapid completion. In the 1980s, greater use is being made of
computerised planning schedules, which can be analysed to identify
impediments to faster construction.

On site, the central consideration is the efficient management of
production resources. The key areas are (a) the performance of
sub-contractors, and (b) the deliveries of materials. These aspects
have been analysed in some depth in Chapter 5. Management must
operate control systems which highlight the important areas for
intervention, to prevent cumulative delays occurring. Site
managers must be effective in communicating with all the partici-
pants in the building process, including the client's representatives,
the designers, the planning authorities, the sub-contractors and the
direct employees. It is the site management team's job to motivate
the workforce to obtain higher levels of productivity. Consideration
will need to be given to the systems of pay incentives applied to
stimulate higher output.

Further consideration of the manager's role in increasing
productivity lies outside the scope of this book. The interested
reader is referred to the growing literature in the area of construction management.

Questions

1. Discuss the difficulties which arise in trying to measure
   productivity for a sector such as the construction industry.
2. a) What have been the main trends in construction sector
   productivity over the last decade?
   b) How does the construction industry in the UK compare, in
   terms of absolute productivity, with the manufacturing sector?
3. Examine the statistical evidence in support of the claims that
   (a) Britain has a low productivity economy, and (b) the

construction sector is especially slow, when compared to other industrial countries.

4. Explain why it is difficult to use published statistics (a) to compare the productivity of different construction firms, and (b) to establish differences between the productivity of the private contractor and that of the DLO.

5. Comment on why a country and an industrial sector should be concerned about low productivity.

6. To what extent does the evidence from direct measurement studies support the statistical conclusion that the construction sector in the UK is less productive than that of comparable nations?

7. Analyse the main causes of low productivity in the construction industry.

8. Discuss the claim that the principal cause of low productivity in the construction sector is its failure to implement industrialised building methods on a large scale.

9. In what main ways should construction management seek to improve productivity in the industry?

10. What is the evidence for concluding that project times on industrial and commercial buildings in the UK could be significantly reduced?

Further Reading

ARDITI, D., 'Construction Productivity Improvement', *ASCE Journal of Construction Engineering and Management*, March 1985

BECKERMAN, W., *Slow Growth in Britain*, Clarendon Press, 1979

BENNETT, J., *Construction Project Management*, Chapter 2, Butterworths, 1985

DREWIN, F. J., *Construction Productivity*, Chapters 1 and 2, Elsevier, 1982

FREEMAN, I. L. 'Comparative Studies of the Construction Industries in Great Britain and North America: a Review', *Building Research Establishment: CP5*, 1981

HARRIS, F. and McCAFFER, R., *Modern Construction Management*, Chapters 3, 4 and 5, Granada, 1983

STONE, P. A., *Building Economy—Design, Production and Organisation: A Synoptic View*, Part II, Pergamon, 1983

TURIN, D. A., *Aspects of the Economics of Construction*, Chapter 3, George Godwin, 1974

Appendix

The financial accounts of company ABC

The balance sheet at 31 December (£ million)

Item	Present year	Previous year
Long-term assets		
1. Fixed assets	20	17
2. Investments	5	5
Total	*25*	*22*
Current assets		
3. Cash	8	20
4. Debtors	17	15
5. Work-in-progress	46	30
6. Stocks	3	2
Total	*74*	*67*
Current liabilities		
7. Bank loans	12	7
8. Trade credits	20	25
9. Dividend payable	2	2
10. Other creditors	8	6
Total	*42*	*40*
All assets (1–6) minus current liabilities (7–10)	57	49
Capital employed		
11. Ordinary share capital	5	5
12. Revenue reserves	34	30
13. Special reserves	8	8
14. Long-term loans	10	6
Total capital	*57*	*49*

The profit and loss account for the year

	(£ million)	
Item	Present year	Previous year
15. Sales turnover	195	190
16. Trading profit	10	7
17. Interest received	1	1
18. Gross profit (before tax and loan interest)	11	8
19. Taxation	−3	−2
20. Loan interest	−2	−1
21. Attributable profit	6	5
22. Proposed dividend	2	1
23. Transfer to reserve	4	4

Other information

24. Earnings per share	30p	25p
25. Number of employees	1,900	2,000
26. Annual wage cost	£2.1m	£2m

Notes to the Accounts

In the accounts for Firm ABC the main items can be briefly explained:

1. *Fixed assets*: These are the current values, after allowing for depreciation, of the land, buildings, plant, machinery and vehicles, owned by the firm and used in its operations.

2. *Investments*: A firm may also invest in associated companies or in property, which is not directly used in its own business. Such investments are made to generate an income, which appears as item 17 in the profit and loss account.

3. *Cash*: This constitutes money in the till, current bank deposits and near cash equivalents, such as commercial bills.

4. *Debtors*: These are normal trade debtors, for whom work has been carried out and from whom payment is due within the next trading year. Also included under this heading are the value of any prepaid bills, or any tax which the firm has recovered, but not yet received.

5. *Work-in-progress*: This is the valuation of work completed, but not yet actually sold or due to be paid for. Once terms of payment are agreed, work-in-progress passes into the debtor

category, until payment is received. For construction firms, this item is usually a comparatively large component of assets.

6. *Stocks*: These are bought-in inventories, or sometimes finished products awaiting sale.

7. *Bank loans*: These are short-term overdrafts or loans, which are theoretically subject to be repaid over the next year.

8. *Trade credits*: These are the sums owing to material suppliers, builders' merchants, plant hirers and sub-contractors. They constitute normal on-going credit arrangements and the sums will fall due for payment in the next year.

9. *Dividends payable*: The public company will from time to time declare a dividend to be paid to its shareholders out of its earned profits. Often, there is a delay between establishing the scale of the dividend and actually paying it out.

10. *Other creditors*: These may include taxes which have been incurred, but not yet paid, and items such as rentals which are due to be paid within the next year.

11. *Ordinary share capital*: This is the capital raised by selling ordinary shares which convey ownership in the firm. Sometimes, a distinction is made between the basic share capital and any extra capital raised by selling additional shares at a premium, above their par value. A separate share premium account may be created.

12. *Revenue reserves*: These are the accumulated profits retained by the firm and, in theory, available for eventual distribution to its shareholders. Annual retained profits (item 23) are usually transferred into these reserves.

13. *Special reserves*: The company may choose to set aside part of its accumulated revenue (or capital) for a special purpose, and thereby render these sums unavailable for distribution. Revenue arising from the revaluation of fixed assets, such as land and property, is often treated in this way.

14. *Long-term loans*: These are loans which are not required to be repaid within the next year. Unlike item 7, they constitute part of the long-term investment capital of the firm. The source of such loans is various and they may take the form of bank loans, mortgage loans, debentures and preference shares.

15. *Sales turnover*: This is the measure of the value of the firm's sales, or trading activity, over the most recent year.

16. *Trading profit*: When the cost of producing and distributing

these sales is deducted from the value of the turnover, a measure of the firm's profit from its trading activities is achieved. While the firm's accounts will show the cost of some selected items (e.g. directors' remuneration), the overall cost of production can only be estimated, on the basis of the trading profit on the sales turnover.

17. *Interest received*: As a result of its investments (item 2) the firm will usually be in receipt of interest and dividends. Such receipts increase the firm's profits.

18. *Gross profit*: This is the overall measure of profit, before taxes and any interest charges are deducted.

19. *Taxation*: A firm will usually pay corporation tax on its profits. The exact amount in any year depends on allowances, adjustments from previous years and the basic rate of the tax.

20. *Loan interest*: These are the charges which accrue in respect of loans obtained, as items 7 and 14.

21. *Attributable profit*: When tax charges and loan interest is deducted from gross profit, the amount remaining is attributed to the owners of the firm. This item may be more simply referred to as 'net profit'.

22. *Proposed dividend*: The attributable profit can either be retained for use in the firm (item 23) or passed directly back to the ordinary shareholders in the form of dividend.

23. *Transfer to reserve*: This is the residual component of attributable profit, after the dividend has been deducted. It is transferred into the revenue reserves at item 12.

A fuller description of these key items can be obtained from the basic accounting texts, recommended in the further reading for chapter 11.

References

Chapter 1 (pp. 3–20)

1. R. H. Barnard, 'Survival or Success: Developing an appropriate response to a fluctuating demand for the building firm', *Chartered Institute of Building Occasional Paper No. 25*, 1979
2. P. H. Hillebrandt, *Economic Theory and the Construction Industry*, Chapter 2, Macmillan Press, 1985
3. Building and Civil Engineering EDC, *How Flexible is Construction?*, Chapter 7, NEDO/HMSO, 1978
4. M. C. Fleming, *Construction and the Related Professions, Reviews of UK Statistical Sources*, Volume XII, Pergamon Press, 1980

Chapter 2 (pp. 21–60)

1. H. Copeman, *The National Accounts: A Short Guide*, CSO/HMSO, 1981
2. D. Burningham, *Understanding Economics*, pp. 211–17, Hodder and Stoughton, 1984
3. F. S. Brooman, *Macroeconomics*, Chapter 9, Allen and Unwin, 1981
4. D. Gowland, *Controlling the Money Supply*, Chapter 2, Croom Helm, 1984
5. N. J. Gibson, in *The UK Economy*, Chapter 2, Section III, edited by A. R. Prest and D. J. Coppock, Weidenfeld and Nicolson, 1986
6. J. S. Metcalfe, in *The UK Economy*, Chapter 3, Section III, ibid
7. K. A. Chrystal, *Controversies in Macroeconomics*, Chapter 10, Philip Allan, 1983

Chapter 3 (pp. 61–99)

1. P. M. Hillebrandt, *Analysis of The British Construction Industry*, Chapter 7, Macmillan, 1984
2. D. A. Langford, *Direct Labour Organisations in the Construction Industry*, Gower Press, 1982
3. D. Burningham, *Understanding Economics*, Chapter 6, Hodder and Stoughton, 1984

4. R. G. Lipsey, *An Introduction to Positive Economics*, Part 4, Weidenfeld and Nicolson, 1983
5. P. M. Hillebrandt, *Economic Theory and the Construction Industry*, Chapter 8, Macmillan, 1985

Chapter 4 (pp. 100–139)

1. S. J. Prais, *The Evolution of Giant Firms in Britain*, Cambridge University Press, 1976
2. Office of Fair Trading, *Annual Reports of the Director General of Fair Trading*, HMSO, 1974 onwards
3. The Labour Party, *Building Britain's Future*, Transport House, 1977
4. P. N. Balchin and G. H. Bull, *Regional and Urban Economics*, Chapter 2, Harper and Row, 1987
5. Department of the Environment, *English House Condition Survey 1981*, Housing Survey Report No. 12, HMSO, 1981
6. Department of the Environment, *Housing Policy: A Consultative Document*, Cmnd 6851, HMSO, 1977
7. Building Societies Association, *Housing Finance into the 1990s*, BSA Bulletin No. 41, January 1985
8. R. N. Balchin, *Housing Policy and Housing Needs*, Macmillan, 1981
9. J. English, *The Future of Council Housing*, Chapter 2, Croom Helm, 1982
10. NEDO, *Construction to 1990*, Chapters 4 and 5, Building and Civil Engineering EDC/HMSO 1984
11. P. M. Hillebrandt, *Economic Theory and the Construction Industry*, Chapter 5, Macmillan, 1985
12. NEDO, *Construction to 1990*, Chapters 6 and 7, ibid
13. NEDO, *Investment in the Public Sector Built Infrastructure*, HMSO, 1985
14. NEDO, *The Public Client and the Construction Industries*, HMSO, 1975
15. Department of the Environment, *An Inquiry into the Condition of the Local Authority Housing Stock in England*, HMSO, 1985
16. Department of the Environment, *Home Improvement Grants*, Housing Booklet Number 14, HMSO, March 1984
17. Department of the Environment, *Home Improvement—A New Approach*, Cmnd 9513, HMSO, 1985
18. P. M. Hillebrandt, *Analysis of the British Construction Industry*, Chapter 5, Macmillan, 1984

Chapter 5 (pp. 140–163)

1. P. M. Hillebrandt, 'Small Firms in the Construction Industry', *Commitee of Inquiry on Small Firms: Research Report No. 10*, HMSO, 1971
2. National Housing Building Council, *Private House Building Statistics* (quarterly), 1986
3. Joint Forecasting Committee of the Building and Civil Engineering EDC, *Construction Forecasts*, NEDO/HMSO (bi-annual)

4. National Council of Building Material Producers, *BMP Forecasts*, NCBMP (tri-annual)
5. P. M. Hillebrandt, *Analysis of the British Construction Industry*, Chapter 6, Macmillan, 1984
6. NEDO, *Construction to 1990*, Building and Civil Engineering EDC, HMSO, 1984
7. Institute of Marketing Construction Industry Group, *The Construction Industry into the 90s*, Institute of Marketing, 1981
8. NEDO, *How Flexible is Construction?*, Chapter 7, Building and Civil Engineering EDC/HMSO, 1978
9. P. A. Stone, *Building Economy—Design, Production and Organisation: A Synoptic View*, Part III, Pergamon Press, 1983
10. The Labour Party, *Building Britain's Future*, Chapter 7, Transport House, 1977
11. National Joint Council for the Building Industry, *Working Rule Agreement*, NJCBI, 1985
12. S. MacVicar, 'Self-employed Labour: Pros and Cons', *Building*, 22 June 1984
13. The Aqua Group, *Tenders and Contracts for Building*, Granada, 1982
14. G. A. Hughes, *Building and Civil Engineering Claims in Perspective*, Construction Press, 1983
15. F. Harris and R. M. McCaffer, *Construction Plant: Management and Investment Decisions*, Granada, 1982

Chapter 6 (pp. 167–186)

1. P. M. Hillebrandt, *Economic Theory and the Construction Industry*, Chapter 5, Macmillan, 1985
2. NEDO, *Construction to 1990*, Chapter 4, Building and Civil Engineering EDC/HMSO, 1984
3. J. Murdoch and J. A. Barnes, *Statistical Tables*, Macmillan, 1970
4. P. N. Balchin and J. L. Kieve, *Urban Land Economics*, Chapter 7, Macmillan, 1985
5. R. Pilcher, *Principles of Construction Management*, Chapter 2, McGraw-Hill, 1976
6. F. Harris and R. McCaffer, *Modern Construction Management*, Chapter 11, Granada, 1983
7. F. Harris and R. McCaffer, *Construction Plant: Management and Investment Decisions*, Chapter 9, Granada, 1982
8. F. Harris and R. McCaffer, *Construction Plant: Management and Investment Decisions*, Chapter 6, ibid.
9. J. M. Samuels and F. M. Wilkes, *Management of Company Finance*, Chapter 11, Thomas Nelson, 1980
10. C. Dent, *Construction Cost Appraisal*, Chapter 4, George Godwin, 1974

Chapter 7 (pp. 187–204)

1. P. N. Balchin and J. L. Kieve, *Urban Land Economics*, Chapter 4, Macmillan, 1985

2. J. Rose, *The Dynamics of Urban Property Development*, Chapter 4, E. and F. N. Spon, 1985
3. J. Harvey, *The Economics of Real Property*, Chapter 5, Macmillan, 1981
4. P. N. Balchin and J. L. Kieve, op. cit. Chapter 4
5. W. D. Fraser, *Principles of Property Investment and Pricing*, Part II, Macmillan, 1984
6. Department of the Environment, *Structure and Activity of the Development Industry*, HMSO, 1980
7. National Economic Development Office, *Faster Building for Industry*, Building EDC/HMSO, 1983
8. P. Byrne and D. Cadman, *Risk, Uncertainty and Decision-Making in Property Development*, Chapter 4, E. and F. N. Spon, 1984
9. J. Harvey, op. cit. Chapter 7

Chapter 8 (pp. 205–221)

1. P. N. Balchin and J. L. Kieve, *Urban Land Economics*, Chapter 3, Macmillan, 1985
2. G. Keogh, 'The Economics of Planning Gain', in *Land Policy: Problems and Alternatives*, edited by S. Barrett and P. Healey, Gower Press, 1985
3. A. W. Evans, *The Economics of Residential Location*, Macmillan, 1973
4. J. Ratcliffe, *Land Policy*, Chapter 2, Hutchinson, 1976
5. A. J. Harrison, *Economics and Land-use Planning*, Chapter 7, Croom Helm, 1977
6. N. Lichfield and H. Darin-Drabkin, *Land Policy in Planning*, Chapter 5, George Allen and Unwin, 1980
7. J. Ratcliffe, *An Introduction to Town and Country Planning*, Chapter 25, Hutchinson, 1981
8. D. Cadman and L. Austin-Crowe, *Property Development*, Chapter 4, E. and F. N. Spon, 1983

Chapter 9 (pp. 222–236)

1. T. Newton, *Cost-Benefit Analysis in Administration*, Part II, George Allen and Unwin, 1972
2. E. J. Mishan, *Cost-Benefit Analysis,* Part I, George Allen and Unwin, 1982
3. P. N. Balchin and J. L. Kieve, *Urban Land Economics*, Chapter 7, Macmillan, 1985
4. J. Harvey, *The Economics of Real Property*, Chapter 10, Macmillan, 1981
5. D. Donnison and C. Ungerson, *Housing Policy*, Chapter 12, Penguin, 1982
6. Department of the Environment, 'The Economic Assessment of Housing Renewal Schemes', *Improvement Research Note 4–78*, DOE, 1978

7. L. Needleman, 'The Comparative Economics of Improvement and New Building', *Urban Studies*, June 1969

Chapter 10 (pp. 237–251)
1. Central Statistical Office, *Financial Statistics*, Table 8.2, HMSO, April 1986
2. J. M. Samuels and F. M. Wilkes, *Management of Company Finance*, Chapter 4, Thomas Nelson, 1980
3. F. W. Paish and R. J. Briston, *Business Finance*, Chapter 6, Pitman, 1978
4. Peat Marwick, *Finance for New Projects in the UK*, Appendix 4, Peat, Marwick, Mitchell and Co., 1985
5. P. N. Balchin and J. L. Kieve, *Urban Land Economics*, Chapter 5, Macmillan, 1985
6. Peat Marwick, *Finance for New Projects in the UK*, Chapter 15, ibid
7. J. M. Samuels and F. M. Wilkes, op. cit, Chapter 14.
8. E. Davis and J. Pointon, *Finance and the Firm*, Chapter 12, Oxford University Press, 1984.

Chapter 11 (pp. 252–272)
1. J. Sizer, *An Insight into Management Accounting*, Chapter 4, Penguin, 1982
2. I. H. Seeley, *Building Economics*, Chapter 1, Macmillan, 1983
3. J. Batty, *Cost and Management Accountancy for Students*, Chapters 10 and 11, Heinemann, 1980
4. A. P. Robson, *Essential Accounting for Managers*, Chapter 5, Cassell, 1979
5. F. Harris and R. McCaffer, *Modern Construction Management*, Chapter 6, Granada, 1983
6. Royal Institution of Chartered Surveyors, *Building Cost Information Service* (Section G2; CI/SfB 28), RICS, 1986
7. J. Gobourne, *Site Cost Control in the Construction Industry*, Butterworth 1982
8. R. Fellows, D. Langford, R. Newcombe and S. Urry, *Construction Management in Practice*, Chapter 9, Longman, 1983
9. ICC Business Ratios, *Building and Civil Engineering (Major)*, ICC Information Group, 1986

Chapter 12 (pp. 273–290)
1. P. M. Hillebrandt, *Analysis of the British Construction Industry*, Chapter 12, Macmillan, 1984
2. P. Trench, 'Low Productivity: High Time For A Re-think', *Building*, 10 September, 1976
3. D. A. Langford, *Direct Labour Organisations in the Construction Industry*, Chapter 7, Gower Press, 1982
4. J. Lemessany and M. A. Clapp, 'Resource Inputs To Construction:

The Labour Requirements of Housebuilding', *Building Research Establishment CP 76*, 1978
5. G. F. Ray, 'Labour Costs in Manufacturing', *National Institute Economic Review*, May 1987
6. G. F. Ray, 'Labour Productivity in 1980: An International Comparison', *National Institute Economic Review*, August 1982
7. A. D. Smith, D. M. Hitchens and S. W. Davies, 'International Industrial Productivity: A Comparison of Britain, America and Germany', *National Institute Economic Review*, August 1982
8. NEDO, *Engineering Construction Performance*, Mechanical and Electrical Engineering EDC/HMSO, 1976
9. Slough Estates, *Industrial Investment: A Case Study in Factory Building*, Slough Estates Ltd, 1979
10. BEC, *A Fresh Look at the UK and US Building Industries*, Building Employers Confederation, 1986
11. P. A. Stone, *Building Economy—Design, Production and Organisation: A Synoptic View*, Chapter 8, Pergamon, 1983
12. NEDO, *Faster Building for Industry*, Building EDC/HMSO, 1983

Index